ALMOST CHRISTIAN

ALMOST CHRISTIAN

*What the Faith of Our Teenagers Is Telling
the American Church*

KENDA CREASY DEAN

OXFORD
UNIVERSITY PRESS
2010

OXFORD

UNIVERSITY PRESS

Oxford University Press, Inc., publishes works that further
Oxford University's objective of excellence
in research, scholarship, and education.

Oxford   New York
Auckland   Cape Town   Dar es Salaam   Hong Kong   Karachi
Kuala Lumpur   Madrid   Melbourne   Mexico City   Nairobi
New Delhi   Shanghai   Taipei   Toronto

With offices in
Argentina   Austria   Brazil   Chile   Czech Republic   France   Greece
Guatemala   Hungary   Italy   Japan   Poland   Portugal   Singapore
South Korea   Switzerland   Thailand   Turkey   Ukraine   Vietnam

Published by Oxford University Press, Inc.
198 Madison Avenue, New York, NY 10016

www.oup.com

Oxford is a registered trademark of Oxford University Press

Library of Congress Cataloging-in-Publication Data
Dean, Kenda Creasy, 1959–
Almost Christian: what the faith of our teenagers is telling
the American church /Kenda Creasy Dean.
p. cm.
Includes bibliographical references and index.
ISBN 978-0-19-531484-7
1. Teenagers—Religious life—United States. I. Title.
BV4531.3.D43 2010
277.3′0830835—dc22
2009051989

9 8

Printed in the United States of America
on acid-free paper

for two American young people,
Brendan and Shannon:
Keep the faith.

An almost Christian . . . [chiefly] is one that . . . is fond of the form,
but never experiences the power of godliness in his heart.
—*George Whitefield, "The Almost Christian" (1739)*

The Church is full of almost Christians who have not gone
all the way with Christ.
—*John Wesley, "The Almost Christian" (1741)*

Contents

Acknowledgments   ix

PART I   Worshipping at the Church of Benign Whatever-ism

1. Becoming Christian-ish   3
2. The Triumph of the "Cult of Nice"   25

Part II   Claiming a Peculiar God-Story

3. Mormon Envy: Sociological Tools for Consequential Faith   45
4. Generative Faith: Faith That Bears Fruit   61
5. Missional Imaginations: We Are Not Here for Ourselves   85

Part III   Cultivating Consequential Faith

6. Parents Matter Most: The Art of Translation   109
7. Going Viral for Jesus: The Art of Testimony   131
8. Hanging Loose: The Art of Detachment   157
9. Make No Small Plans: A Case for Hope   185

Appendix A   199
Appendix B   201
Appendix C   207
Appendix D   211
Appendix E   215
Notes   217
Index   249

Acknowledgments

As a member of the research team for the first wave of the National Study of Youth and Religion, which focused on the religious lives of American thirteen- to seventeen-year-olds, my job was to wrestle to the ground some of the findings relevant for Christian churches and pin down some hope for ministry with young people. Like Jacob struggling with the angel at Jabbok (Gen. 32:22–32), this wrestling match left me limping but blessed. I am especially grateful to Christian Smith and Melinda Denton for sowing the seeds of this project. Chris showed me more about how to run a research project, and how to work with doctoral students, than all my years of graduate school and teaching combined. In the process, he became a glad friend and co-conspirator in trying to make things right in the world.

This book was finished thanks to the generosity of others. Cynthia Read and Joellyn Ausanka at Oxford University Press patiently waited out the manuscript's multiple personalities. I was honored by scores of teenagers who let me to eavesdrop on their lives; our conversations challenged and changed me, and to the person they seemed glad for the conversation. I am deeply indebted to David C. Dollahite, professor of Family Life, Brigham Young University, and to graduate students Emily Layton, Carma Martino, Laura Nelson, and Toshi Shichida, who generously read an early draft of this manuscript and provided gracious critiques, critical insight, and additional resources on young people, families, and the Church of Jesus Christ of Latter-day Saints as I ventured into the unknown territory of Mormon theology and practice. Friends and colleagues—Christian Andrews, Blair Bertrand, Marti Reed Hazelrigg, Andrew Root, Matthew Schultz, and David White, especially—served as beloved and honest critics, chastening each incarnation of the manuscript with much needed straight talk. My colleagues in Princeton Seminary's Tennent School of Christian Education and Institute for Youth Ministry—Leslie Dobbs-Allsopp, Margo Dudak, Pat Heran, Bo Karen Lee, Gordon Mikoski, Rick Osmer, Dayle Rounds, Amy Vaughn, and my dean, Darrell Guder—offered daily doses of humor and intellectual traction. Without them, I would have long ago quit and gone to the beach.

I am blessed to work with extraordinary youth pastors who come into my life by way of graduate school. I have benefited from the advice of scores of them, generously offered over coffee, email, lunch, and late-night conversations at continuing education events. A few gave these pages their professional attention. In the project's murky beginnings, Christina Beck Koppes's wise spirit and unflappable calm conquered the software necessary to pin down the data's loose edges. Jason Santos generously "go-fered" his way through his last year of seminary, downloading interviews and spelunking in the library before he wised up and wrote a lovely book of his own. Nathan Stucky's serendipitous scrutiny found errant endnotes. Abigail Visco's irrepressible spirit helped me "get my life back," and Ryan Timpte's cheerful determination ordered unruly footnotes and finally put the manuscript to bed. I owe Andrew Zirschky a special debt, for he made finishing this book possible. In addition to providing the technical wizardry that turned wishful thinking into footnotes, Andrew became a trusted critic and sounding board during a tormented year, and at several points served as healer to the manuscript's disjointed parts. Even as the project dragged out long past its due, Andrew gave his all to it, and to me, in ways that I can only call amazing grace.

My husband, Kevin, is the most generous person I know. You can thank him for this book and for everything else I do. During this book's gestation, our family entered a new chapter, and Kevin remains the one—always—who assures me that all is well. I will miss the high school antics of our witty filmmaker Brendan, who taught me to write with "band practice" screaming over my head, and who is packing for college as I write these words. Meanwhile, Shannon is buying school supplies for her first day of ninth grade. I look forward to these years together, for she is a hilarious, huge-hearted tour-de-force, an author in her own right, and my conscience: we have a long list of overdue "mother-daughter" projects to get started, and time is short. I adore our life together, the four of us. God must laugh at us all daily—but, oh God of grace: thank you.

Kenda Creasy Dean
Ocean Grove, New Jersey

PART 1

Worshipping at the Church of Benign Whatever-ism

A person will worship something, have no doubt about that. . . . That which dominates our imaginations and our thoughts will determine our lives, and our character. Therefore, it behooves us to be careful what we worship, for what we are worshipping we are becoming.
—*Ralph Waldo Emerson*

1

Becoming Christian-ish

We have come with some confidence to believe that a significant part
of Christianity in the United States is actually only tenuously Christian
in any sense that it is seriously connected to the actual historical
Christian tradition. . . . It is not so much that U.S. Christianity is
being secularized. Rather, more subtly, Christianity is either
degenerating into a pathetic version of itself or, more significantly,
Christianity is actively being colonized and displaced by quite a
different religious faith.
—*Christian Smith with Melinda Denton*

I am personally not very much worried about the reduction in
numbers where Christianity . . . [is] concerned. I am far more
concerned about the qualitative factor: what kind of
Christianity . . . are we talking about?
—*Douglas John Hall*

Let me save you some trouble. Here is the gist of what you are about to
read: American young people are, theoretically, fine with religious
faith—but it does not concern them very much, and it is not durable
enough to survive long after they graduate from high school.

One more thing: we're responsible.

If the American church responds, quickly and decisively, to issues
raised by studies like the National Study of Youth and Religion (NSYR)—
the massive 2003–05 study on adolescent spirituality in the United
States that served as the original impetus for this book—then tending
the faith of young people may just be the ticket to reclaiming our own.
As the following pages attest, the religiosity of American teenagers must
be read primarily as a reflection of their parents' religious devotion (or

lack thereof) and, by extension, that of their congregations. Teenagers themselves consistently demonstrate an openness to religion, but few of them are deeply committed to one. As sociologists like Robert Wuthnow blame young adults' absence from American religious life, not on congregational practices but on demographic patterns like the postponement of marriage, the chance of churches becoming places that young people call their own seems like a distant, maybe even delusional, hope.[1]

I want to suggest another way to read this research, including the NSYR and the spate of smaller studies that largely echo its findings: they are not just about youth. Youth, after all, "tell ourselves," which means that the significance of the NSYR does not lie in what it revealed about young people (very few of its findings surprise anyone working with teenagers). It is significant because it reframes the issues of youth ministry as issues facing the twenty-first-century church as a whole.[2] Since the religious and spiritual choices of American teenagers echo, with astonishing clarity, the religious and spiritual choices of the adults who love them, lackadaisical faith is not young people's issue, but ours.[3] Most teenagers are perfectly content with their religious worldviews; it is churches that are—rightly—concerned. So we must assume that the solution lies not in beefing up congregational youth programs or making worship more "cool" and attractive, but in modeling the kind of mature, passionate faith we say we want young people to have.

The National Study of Youth and Religion reveals a theological fault line running underneath American churches: an adherence to a do-good, feel-good spirituality that has little to do with the Triune God of Christian tradition and even less to do with loving Jesus Christ enough to follow him into the world. It is hard to read the data from the NSYR without the impression that many American congregations (not to mention teenagers themselves) are "almost Christian"—but perhaps not fully, at least not in terms of theology or practice. To be sure, this is hardly an original position. During the Great Awakening in England, both George Whitefield and John Wesley preached (different) sermons titled "The Almost Christian," based on King Agrippa's reaction to Paul in Acts 26:28: "Almost thou persuadest me to be a Christian" (KJV). Both sermons took aim at the half-hearted spirituality of the realm, especially the inclination of Christians to obey church commandments without loving God and neighbor "as Christ loved us." Wesley in particular identified with this arid approach to faith. "Suffer me to speak freely of myself," he confessed. "I did go thus far for many years, . . . doing good to all men; constantly and carefully using all the public and all the private means of grace . . . and, God is my record, before whom I stand, doing all this in sincerity. . . . Yet my own conscience beareth me witness in the Holy Ghost, that all this time I was but *almost a Christian*."[4] For Wesley, the difference between an "almost Christian" and an "altogether Christian" boiled down to love:

> The great question of all, then, still remains. Is the love of God shed abroad in your heart? Can you cry out, "My God, and my All"? Do you desire nothing but him? Are you happy in God? Is he your glory, your delight, your crown of rejoicing? And is this commandment written in your heart, "That he who loveth God love his brother also"? Do you then love your neighbour as yourself? Do you love every man, even your enemies, even the enemies of God, as your own soul? as Christ loved you?[5]

The tremors of loveless faith still rumble through American Christianity. The philosopher James K. A. Smith suggests that these rumblings haunt contemporary Christian education in particular: "Could it be the case that learning a Christian perspective doesn't actually touch my desire, and that while I might be able to *think* about the world from a Christian perspective, at the end of the day I love *not* the kingdom of God but rather the kingdom of the market?"[6] After two and a half centuries of shacking up with "the American dream," churches have perfected a dicey codependence between consumer-driven therapeutic individualism and religious pragmatism. These theological proxies gnaw, termite-like, at our identity as the Body of Christ, eroding our ability to recognize that Jesus' life of self-giving love directly challenges the American gospel of self-fulfillment and self-actualization. Young people in contemporary culture prosper by following the latter. Yet Christian identity, and the "crown of rejoicing" that Wesley believed accompanied consequential faith born out of a desire to love God and neighbor, requires the former.

The predicament described in this book—namely, that American young people are unwittingly being formed into an imposter faith that poses as Christianity, but that in fact lacks the holy desire and missional clarity necessary for Christian discipleship—will not be solved by youth ministry or by persuading teenagers to commit more wholeheartedly to lackluster faith. Most teenagers seem quite content with maintaining what the sociologist Tim Clydesdale calls a "semireligious" position after they graduate from high school, and most churches seem happy to leave it at that.[7] At issue is our ability, and our willingness, to remember our identity as the Body of Christ, and to heed Christ's call to love him and love others as his representatives in the world.

RELIGION IN AMERICA: A VERY NICE THING

Youth ministry is the de facto research and development branch of American Christianity, which is why attending to the faith of adolescents may help reclaim Christian identity for the rest of us as well. For that reason, this book focuses on Christian adults and congregations as well as on teenagers themselves. We are the ones charged with "handing on" the good news of Jesus Christ to the teenagers on our watch, but the reports from the front are not encouraging. We have successfully convinced teenagers that religious participation is important for moral formation and for making nice people, which may explain why American adolescents harbor no ill will toward religion. Many of them say they will bring their own children to church in the future (a dubious prediction statistically).[8] Yet these young people possess no real commitment to or excitement about religious faith. Teenagers tend to approach religious participation, like music and sports, as an extracurricular activity: a good, well-rounded thing to do, but unnecessary for an integrated life. Religion, the young people in the NSYR concurred, is a "Very Nice Thing."[9]

What we have been less able to convey to young people is *faith*. In Christian tradition, faith is a matter of desire, a desire for God and a desire to love others in Christ's name—which results in a church oriented toward bearing God's self-giving love to others, embodied in a gospel-shaped way of life. Love gives Christianity its purpose and its meaning. Religion functions as an organized expression of belief, but faith—to quote the theologian Douglas John Hall—is a "dialogue with doubt," a personal reckoning with God's involvement in the world, and investment in our own lives.[10] Hall reminds us that one of the great themes in twentieth-century theology was chronicling Christianity's fall from faith to religion.[11] Yet Christianity has always been more of a trust-walk than a belief system. In Christian tradition, faith depends on who we follow, and that depends on who we love. Believing in a person—having utter confidence in someone—creates a very different set of expectations than believing in "beliefs." For Christians, faith means cleaving to the person, the God-man, of Jesus Christ, joining a pilgrim journey with other lovers and following him into the world.

Christian formation invites young people into this motley band of pilgrims and prepares them to receive the Spirit who calls them, shapes them, and enlists them in God's plan to right a capsized world. Teenagers with consequential Christian faith share a profound and personal sense of God's love and forgiveness on this journey. They know that the family stories the church tells along the way include them. They are confident that Christ has a part for them to play in bringing about God's purposes, and that the journey they are on contributes to God's good direction for the world. But such consequential faith—faith that grows by confessing a creed, belonging to a community, and pursuing God's purpose and hope—is not the faith that most American teenagers seem to have. The faith most teenagers exhibit is a loveless version that the NSYR calls Christianity's "misbegotten stepcousin," Moralistic Therapeutic Deism, which is "supplanting Christianity as the dominant religion in American churches."[12] That is the issue the NSYR prods us to address.

But first: a story.

WHY TWENTY-ONE IS THE NEW SIXTEEN

You've heard this one: A hot, hungry, strapping young fellow, all sweat and hair and muscle, looms in a doorframe. He has been plowing fields and shearing goats and swatting off flies since dawn, and now he swoons at the smell of supper (Gen. 25–27). So Esau tells Jacob, his brother: "I'm dying of hunger. Give me some of that porridge."

Jacob, the wily one, tosses out a condition: "First sell me your birthright." Just like that. First, go wash your hands. First, pass me that pomegranate. First, sign over your future. Too exhausted for another one of his brother's mind games, Esau grunts the ancient equivalent of "Whatever" and seals his fate. Who knew Jacob was serious? Who knew that indifference before dinner could cost your inheritance? And really, who can blame Esau—a young man after a hard day—for thinking with his stomach?

Jacob may be the twin who gets the most press, but Esau is just as much like us. Like Esau, American Christians tend to think with our stomachs, devouring whatever smells good in order to keep our inner rumblings at bay, oblivious even to our own misgivings. Sociologists paint American Christians as restless people who come to church for the same reasons people once went to diners: for someone to serve us who knows our name, for a filling stew that reminds us of home and makes us feel loved, even while it does a number on our spiritual cholesterol.[13]

Ancient youth like Jacob and Esau grew up at a time when questions like "Who are my people? Why am I here? What gives my life meaning and coherence?" were answered, literally, by the faith of their fathers, not by theories of ego development. Yet these questions of belonging, purpose, and ideology remain at the core of human identity; while we have learned to think of them as psychological issues, such questions have historically fallen to religion to answer, ritualized in the traditions and practices of communities that seek to embody a particular story of identity. The developmental theorist Jeffrey Arnett reminds us that becoming adult requires coming to terms with questions that address our place and purpose in the cosmos, and that evoke a governing ideology that gives life meaning. Whether young people view themselves as "religious" or not, human beings "invariably address religious questions as part of our lives," writes Arnett. "Forming religious beliefs appears to be a universal part of identity development."[14]

Of course, identity development was not a problem for Jacob and Esau. Until the early twentieth century, you were either a child or an adult; there was no transitional period of "becoming" in between, unless you were among the privileged few who could afford the moratorium offered by travel or formal education. Adolescence is an invention of the

Industrial Revolution, a social pattern devised to keep young workers out of the factories so as not to displace older employees. By the twentieth century, thanks largely to access to public education, the "moratorium" associated with adolescence had become widespread. The resulting age-stratification of American society (which allowed advertisers to target youth as a "market") created the crucible in which the American "teenager"—a post–World War II youth with free time and disposable income—was born.

Today, adolescence continues to be a moving target. Puberty starts sooner and adulthood starts later; fertility and adolescence no longer go hand in hand. Scholars now posit emerging adulthood as a youthful life stage of its own, since the developmental tasks once associated with identity exploration (and therefore with adolescence) are increasingly postponed. Most young Americans eschew the title of "adult" until their late twenties or early thirties.[15] We have learned to accept twenty-one as the "new sixteen." Today, adolescence functions as a lifestyle as well as a life stage, a state of consciousness as well as a period of life that young people can and often do prolong, with the full cooperation of American culture.

DOES CHURCH STILL MATTER?

In the midst of these swirling currents, teenagers—like centuries of young people before them—find themselves in search of a faith, religious or otherwise, that they can call their own.[16] In fact, the faith teenagers develop during adolescence serves as a kind of barometer of the religious inclinations of the culture that surrounds them, giving parents, pastors, teachers, campus ministers, youth pastors, and anyone else who works closely with teenagers fifty-yard-line seats from which to watch America's religious future take shape. For most of the twentieth century, we studied the religious and spiritual lives of adolescents in order to answer the question, "How can we keep young people in church?" Today, our question is more pressing: "Does the church *matter*?" Religious stories are told for the sake of forming identity, and Christian communities, like all religious communities, seek to embody them. The account of Jesus Christ's life, death, and resurrection—the story that gives Christianity its life-and-death urgency and that insists on the Holy Spirit's living presence in the world today—goes to the heart of profoundly human questions about belonging, purpose, and meaning. So when the NSYR points to American churches' inability to meaningfully share the core content of Christian faith with young people, it points to a church that no longer addresses the issues of being human, and whose God is therefore unimportant.

Instead, churches seem to have offered teenagers a kind of "diner theology": a bargain religion, cheap but satisfying, whose gods require little in the way of fidelity or sacrifice. Never mind that centuries of Christians have read Jesus' call to lay down one's life for others as the signature feature of Christian love (John 15:13), or that God's self-giving enables us to share the grace of Christ when ours is pitifully insufficient. Diner theology is much easier to digest than all this—and it is far safer, especially for malleable youth. So who can blame churches, really, for earnestly ladling this stew into teenagers, filling them with an agreeable porridge about the importance of being nice, feeling good about yourself, and saving God for emergencies? We have convinced ourselves that this is the gospel, but in fact it is much closer to another mess of pottage, an unacknowledged but widely held religious outlook among American teenagers that is primarily dedicated, not to loving God, but to avoiding interpersonal friction.[17] There are inspiring exceptions, of course, but for the most part we have traded the kind of faith confessed and embodied in the church's most long-standing traditions for the savory stew of Moralistic Therapeutic Deism. And, for the most part, young people have followed suit.

A NEW GAME IN TOWN

Three out of four American teenagers claim to be Christians, and most are affiliated with a religious organization—but only about half consider it very important, and fewer than half actually practice their faith as a regular part of their lives.[18] Sociologists and church leaders tend to draw opposite conclusions from these findings. The sociologists involved in the NSYR hailed this as good news for American religion:

significant numbers of young people think faith is important. Church leaders, on the other hand, greet these statistics with enormous ambivalence. As a Christian pastor and seminary professor, I place myself in the latter group. The NSYR's blunt assessment that many churches are "failing rather badly in religiously engaging and educating youth" names what many pastors and parents already know: whatever the strengths of American congregations, we struggle mightily when it comes to handing on faith to young people.[19] Most professional church critics—myself included—have tended to blame teenagers' lukewarm religiosity on the church's warmed-over teaching of a life-giving gospel. But this is not the whole story. Youth ministers today are better educated, better resourced, better paid, and "longer lasting" in their positions than ever before.[20] Some young people we encounter in ministry come away with life-changing faith, but many (perhaps most) do not. Why?

The answer may simply be that most youth ministry is not accomplished by youth ministers. Neither young people nor youth ministry can be extracted from the church as a whole, any more than the musculature of the Body of Christ can be separated from its circulatory system. We have known for some time that youth groups do important things for teenagers, providing moral formation, learned competencies, and social and organizational ties.[21] But they seem less effective as catalysts for consequential faith, which is far more likely to take root in the rich relational soil of families, congregations, and mentor relationships where young people can see what faithful lives look like, and encounter the people who love them enacting a larger story of divine care and hope.

Overall, the challenge posed to the church by the teenagers in the National Study of Youth and Religion is as much *theological* as methodological: the hot lava core of Christianity—the story of God's courtship with us through Jesus Christ, of God's suffering love through salvation history and especially through Christ's death and resurrection, and of God's continued involvement in the world through the Holy Spirit—has been muted in many congregations, replaced by an ecclesial complacency that convinces youth and parents alike that not much is at stake.[22] In the view of American teenagers, God is more object than subject, an Idea but not a companion. The problem does not seem to be that churches are teaching young people badly, but that we are doing an exceedingly good job of teaching youth what we really believe: namely, that Christianity is not a big deal, that God requires little, and the church is a helpful social institution filled with nice people focused primarily on "folks like us"—which, of course, begs the question of whether we are really the church at all.

What if the blasé religiosity of most American teenagers is not the result of poor communication but the result of excellent communication of a watered-down gospel so devoid of God's self-giving love in Jesus Christ, so immune to the sending love of the Holy Spirit that it might not be Christianity at all? What if the *church* models a way of life that asks, not passionate surrender but ho-hum assent? What if we are preaching moral affirmation, a feel-better faith, and a hands-off God instead of the decisively involved, impossibly loving, radically sending God of Abraham and Mary, who desired us enough to enter creation in Jesus Christ and whose Spirit is active in the church and in the world today? If this is the case—if theological malpractice explains teenagers' half-hearted religious identities—then perhaps most young people practice Moralistic Therapeutic Deism not because they reject Christianity, but because this is the only "Christianity" they know.

CHRISTIAN PARASITOLOGY

Let me venture an analogy. By the time our son, Brendan, was eight, he had amassed an impressive array of Spiderman action figures, including a few of Spidey's over-appendaged adversaries, each of whom could imperil human existence but not find its way back to the toy box. I picked up a garish humanoid spray-painted with a black and white bodysuit, whose grin had all the charm of a T. rex. "I don't like this guy," I muttered.

"You're not s'posed to like him," said Brendan. "That's Venom. He sucks out all your life energy. I want to be him for Halloween."

It turns out that Venom (stay with me here) came from a *symbiote*, a parasitology term that Marvel Comics co-opted in 1984 for its newest Spiderman nemesis. In the comic books, the symbiote—an alien creature unable to survive on its own—struck a bargain with the devious Eddie Brock: the symbiote would give Brock its power in return for Brock's "life energy." But (newsflash!) symbiotes from outer space cannot be trusted. Once the symbiote inhabited Brock, it absorbed his "life energy" and morphed into the evil Venom.

It was Faust à la Marvel Comics, the oldest story in the book: a snake in a fruit tree, a pretty promise, a cataclysmic outcome. Beguiling and helpful, the symbiote did not appear dangerous. On the contrary, the symbiote seemed like a near-perfect copy of Spiderman himself, an accommodating "I'll-help-you, you-help-me" kind of guy. What could be more neighborly? What could be more American? Here was a villain who preyed on our deepest desires by helping us realize our fondest hopes—all the while sucking out our souls while we weren't looking.

Parasitologists define a symbiote as the weaker of two organisms inhabiting the same space, so that the weaker can draw life from the stronger. In the most dramatic cases, by the time the host notices, the symbiote has siphoned off its nutrients, guaranteeing the symbiote's survival but leaving the host seriously weakened. Venom's symbiote occupied its hapless victims while inhaling their souls so completely that they became hideous creatures themselves: human beings whose depleted souls left them too weak to resist the symbiote's beguiling allure. Once, the symbiote even inhabited Spiderman, leaving a trace of Venom behind, so it was often impossible to tell them apart. The result? When the imposter threatened to supplant the original, no one was the wiser.

Has a symbiote taken up residence in American Christianity without our knowledge? This is the view expressed by Christian Smith with Melinda Denton, the principle investigators for the NSYR, who see in the Moralistic Therapeutic Deism of American teenagers an "alternative faith that feeds on and gradually co-opts if not devours" established religious traditions. This alternative faith "generally does not and cannot stand on its own," so its adherents are affiliated with traditional faith communities, unaware that they are practicing a very different faith than historic orthodox Christianity. If teenagers wrote out this common religious outlook, it would look something like this:

GUIDING BELIEFS OF MORALISTIC THERAPEUTIC DEISM

1. A god exists who created and orders the world and watches over life on earth.
2. God wants people to be good, nice, and fair to each other, as taught in the Bible and by most world religions.
3. The central goal of life is to be happy and to feel good about oneself.
4. God is not involved in my life except when I need God to resolve a problem.
5. Good people go to heaven when they die.

Moralistic Therapeutic Deism, say Smith and Denton, seems to be "colonizing many historical religious traditions and, almost without anyone noticing, converting believers in the old faiths to its alternative religious vision of divinely underwritten personal happiness and interpersonal niceness."[23] For Smith and Denton, this is a moral indictment on American congregations, not teenagers, which leads them to draw an astonishing conclusion: Moralistic Therapeutic Deism is supplanting Christianity as the dominant religion in the United States. Smith and Denton feel confident enough about these conclusions to write:

> Moralistic Therapeutic Deism is, in the context of [teenagers'] own congregations and denominations, actively displacing the substantive traditional faiths of conservative, black, and mainline Protestantism, Catholicism, and Judaism in the United States. . . . It may be the new mainstream American religious faith for our culturally post-Christian, individualistic, mass-consumer capitalist society.[24]

While Smith and Denton refrain from describing how this "colonization" affects other religious traditions, they are forthright about asserting its influence on Christianity: "We have come with some confidence to believe that a significant part of Christianity in the United States is actually only tenuously Christian in any sense that it is seriously connected to the actual historical Christian tradition, but has rather substantially morphed into . . . Christian Moralistic Therapeutic Deism."[25]

In short, the National Study of Youth and Religion provides a window on how well American young people have learned a well-intentioned but ultimately banal version of Christianity offered up in American churches. Most youth seem to accept this bland view of faith as all there is—nice to have, like a bank account, something you want before you go to college in case you need to draw from it sometime. What we have not told them is that this account of Christianity is bankrupt. We have not invested in their accounts: we "teach" young people baseball, but we "expose" them to faith. We provide coaching and opportunities for youth to develop and improve their pitches and their SAT scores, but we blithely assume that religious identity will happen by osmosis, emerging "when youth are ready" (a confidence we generally lack when it comes to, say, algebra). We simply have not given teenagers the soul-strength necessary to recognize, wrestle, and resist the symbiotes in our midst—probably because we lack this soul-strength ourselves.

Fortunately, it is not all up to us. Because Christians believe that transformation belongs to God, Christian formation—the patterning of our lives and our communities after Christ's own self-giving love— requires grace, not determination. The church's job is to till the soil, prepare the heart, ready the mind, still the soul, and stay awake so we notice where God is on the move, and follow. It is in following Jesus that we learn to love him; it is in participating in the mission of God that God decisively changes us into disciples. Whenever ministry settles for less than this, the church becomes vulnerable to symbiotes, and risks "morphing" into a community that is almost Christian.

WAKE-UP CALL FOR THE CHURCH

In the course of conducting interviews for the NSYR, I spent hours talking to young people in malls, bookstores, and neighborhood pizza parlors as they told me about—well, about almost everything *but* faith, as it turned out. Remarkably articulate young people stammered and groped for words when the conversation turned to religion, as if no one had ever asked them these questions before, or as if we were asking questions in another language. Many youth said religion was important, though when pressed they generally could not say how; almost all of them thought religion was a good thing, though most could not describe the difference it made to them personally.

Correlation is not causality, and just because teenagers fail to recognize how religion shapes them does not mean it has no effect. Decades of research consistently links high levels of adolescent religiosity with prosocial behavior and success in both academics and social and familial relationships.[26] At the same time, it matters that American teenagers are largely immune to religion's existential claims and unaware of religion's effects on their daily lives. Most religious traditions set out to impress human beings at precisely these points: identity and practice. Time and time again in our interviews, we met young people who called themselves Christians, who grew up with Christian parents, who were regular participants in Christian congregations, yet who had no readily accessible faith vocabulary, few recognizable faith practices, and little ability to reflect on their lives religiously. There were exceptions, but not many. Not surprisingly, the script that emerged about teenage spirituality in the United States read like a B-movie: entertaining at points but ultimately forgettable. Exposing adolescents to faith, as it turns out, is no substitute for teaching it to them.

THE PROJECT'S CONTOURS

The National Study of Youth and Religion (conducted from 2002 to 2005) is the most ambitious study of American teenagers and religion to date, involving extensive interviews of more than 3,300 American teenagers between the ages of thirteen and seventeen (including telephone surveys of these teenagers' parents), followed by face-to-face follow-up interviews with 267 of these teenagers. The study also involves an ongoing longitudinal component that has so far revisited more than 2500 of these young people to understand how their religious lives are changing as they enter emerging adulthood.[27] My assignment as part of the research team was to help conduct the original round of face-to-face interviews with teenagers, and to interpret the study's findings for churches.

As a longtime youth minister, an ordained United Methodist pastor, and a professor who teaches youth ministry and Christian formation at a mainline Protestant seminary, I am hardly a disinterested bystander. My husband, Kevin, and I are the parents of two adolescents who make us ridiculously proud—but whose own faith sometimes dangles on the ropes despite almost twenty years of (what seems to them to be) excruciatingly intentional Christian education. This book is for people like us, people who care that the teenagers we love, love God—and who are in "youth ministry" by virtue of the fact that we are Christians who promise, with each and every baptism, to help raise each other's children as followers of Jesus.

The primary findings from the first wave of the National Study of Youth and Religion appear in Appendix A and B. For the sake of our current discussion, let me briefly outline five findings from the NSYR's first wave data that are most important for the book you are reading:

1. Most American teenagers have a positive view of religion but otherwise don't give it much thought

The good news is that teenagers are not hostile toward religion. That surprised some of the researchers in the study, who expected to find teenagers rebelling against religion—arguing with parents, looking for more "authentic" kinds of religious expression, trying to be "spiritual" but not "religious." None of these patterns showed up in the teenagers we studied. According to Smith and Denton, "The vast majority of U.S. teens view religion in a benignly positive light."[28] Teenagers tend to view God as either a butler or a therapist, someone who meets their needs when summoned ("a cosmic lifeguard," as one youth minister put it) or who listens nonjudgmentally and helps youth feel good about themselves ("kind of like my guidance counselor," a ninth grader told me).[29] Most young people (even nonreligious ones) believe that religion has much to offer, and those who attend church tend to feel positively about their congregations even when they are critical of religion in general. Almost all teenagers say that religion benefits individuals or society or both.

The bad news is the *reason* teenagers are not hostile toward religion: they just do not care about it very much. Religion is not a big deal to them. People fight over things that matter to them—but religion barely causes a ripple in the lives of most adolescents. Butlers and lifeguards watch from the sidelines until called upon; therapists and guidance counselors offer encouragement and advice. The NSYR defined spiritual "seeking" not as the developmental longing for meaning described by Jeffrey Arnett, but as an active cobbling together of spiritual beliefs and practices taken from multiple religious traditions. This kind of spiritual seeking was almost invisible among the thirteen- to seventeen-year-olds we interviewed. Teenagers gladly grant people the right to explore other religions, or to construct their own eclectic spiritualities, but they are not doing it themselves. So while religion is seldom a source of conflict for teenagers, it is also seldom a source of identity, as we will see in chapter 2.

2. Most U.S. teenagers mirror their parents' religious faith

Perhaps parents and teenagers do not argue much about religion because they seem to believe almost the same things. Contrary to popular opinion, teenagers conform to the religious beliefs and practices of their parents to a very high degree. The "breaking away" from authority figures associated with the teenage years comes later in adolescence, but the thirteen- to seventeen-year-olds in the NSYR were highly conventional, content to adopt their parents' religious inclinations.[30] By and large, Smith and Denton concluded, parents "get what they are" religiously.[31] This theme is taken up in detail in chapter 6, for overwhelming every other finding of the National Study is one recurrent theme: Parents matter most when it comes to the religious formation of their children. While grandparents, other relatives, mentors, and youth ministers are also influential, parents are by far the most important predictors of teenagers' religious lives.

3. Teenagers lack a theological language with which to express their faith or interpret their experience of the world

The vast majority of U.S. teenagers, to quote Smith and Denton, are *"incredibly inarticulate* about their faith, their religious beliefs and practices, and its meaning or place in their lives" (emphasis original).[32]

When asked to describe what they believed, many youth defaulted and just said they had no religious beliefs, or they unknowingly described beliefs that their own churches deem heretical (for a comparison of theological versus therapeutic terms used by teenagers in the interviews, see Appendix E). These patterns were consistent even in teenagers who regularly attend church, with mainline Protestant young people being "among the least religiously articulate of all teens," and Catholic youth following close behind.[33] It is easy to wonder whether this religious inarticulacy may have been a function of research methods that fail to plumb deeply held beliefs (more on that in chapter 7). For now we need only point out that for most of the youth in the study, religion was not a deeply held belief, at least no more deeply held than beliefs about money, family, sex, or relationships—and teenagers had plenty to say about each of these subjects.

Smith and Denton make a pointed observation here. "We do not believe that teenage inarticulacy about religious matters reflects any general teen incapacity to think and speak well," since many youth interviewed were impressively articulate about other subjects. Rather, Smith and Denton hypothesize that the youth we interviewed were inarticulate in matters of faith because no one had taught them how to talk about their faith, or provided opportunities to practice using a faith vocabulary. For a striking number of teenagers, our interviews seemed to be the first time any adult had asked them what they believed, and why it mattered to them.[34]

4. A minority of American teenagers—but a significant minority—say religious faith is important, and that it makes a difference in their lives. These teenagers are doing better in life on a number of scales, compared to their less religious peers

Forty percent of all young people deem religion important enough to practice regularly—a minority, but a very significant minority. One in twelve (8%) can be described as "highly devoted" (e.g., they attend religious services weekly or more, they feel very close to God, they participate in a religious youth group, they read Scripture, pray frequently, and say faith is very important in their lives). These were the teenagers I studied most closely for this book, in order to learn why faith is more significant for them than for their peers.

Mormon teenagers attach the most importance to faith and are most likely to fall in the category of highly devoted youth, a phenomenon explored in chapter 3. In nearly every area, using a variety of measures, Mormon teenagers showed the highest levels of religious understanding, vitality, and congruence between religious belief and practiced faith; they were the least likely to engage in high-risk behavior and consistently were the most positive, healthy, hopeful, and self-aware teenagers in the interviews. After Mormon youth, the greatest religious understanding, vitality, and salience appeared in conservative Protestant and black Protestant teenagers, followed (in order) by mainline Protestant, Roman Catholic, Jewish, and nonreligious teenagers.[35]

On the whole, teenagers who say religion is important to them are doing "much better in life" than less religious teenagers, by a number of measures.[36] While religious youth do not avoid problem behaviors and relationships, those who participate in religious communities are more likely to do well in school, have positive relationships with their families, have a positive outlook on life, wear their seatbelts—the list goes on, enumerating an array of outcomes that parents pray for.[37]

Here we must insert two caveats: (1) participating in *any* identity-bearing community, religious or otherwise, improves young people's likeliness to thrive; and (2) human ideas of "doing better" usually require conforming to social norms that sometimes contravene religious teachings. Using religion to anesthetize teenagers in order to make them nice or compliant enough to fulfill adult expectations, or involving them in a youth group to take advantage of religion's prophylactic benefits against risky behavior, could be confused with doing much better in life (even while compromising the gospel's prophetic nature). Spiritually sensitive youth often cause trouble in their communities (religious or secular) *because* of their alertness to the sacred. It is hard to imagine researchers, interviewing Jesus after he turned over the tables in the temple, ascribing the act to religious maturity—but in Christian theology it is a story of righteousness and divine purgation.

Smith and Denton recognize these risks and warn against encouraging children to participate in religion for instrumental reasons. When they find "sizable and significant differences in a variety of important life outcomes between more and less religious teenagers in the United States," they identify a wide swath of social scientific research associating religion with healthy outcomes that include, but far exceed, safety.[38]

5. Many teenagers enact and espouse a religious outlook that is distinct from traditional teachings of most world religions — an outlook called Moralistic Therapeutic Deism

Moralistic Therapeutic Deism, a tacit religious outlook that is quite distinct from Christianity, Judaism, Islam, or any of the world's major religions, helps people be nice, feel good, and leaves God in the background. It serves as the "default position" for adolescent religiosity in the United States. This is especially true when religious communities' engagement and education of youth is weak. But there is more to the story: young people seem to be barometers of a larger theological shift that appears to be taking place in the United States. The qualities of this "new mainstream faith" are taken up in chapter 2, and explored throughout the remainder of this book.[39]

THE TERRAIN AHEAD

The deepest dimensions of faith always elude measure; sociology leaves the task of theological reflection on religious research to practical theologians, people brazen enough to jump from certainty into hope. This book represents precisely that leap of faith. Whatever else they accomplish, religions offer teenagers paths to ultimate purpose, stories of self-transcendence, and ways to relate to others, both human and divine—fields for working out questions of love, work, and ideology that contribute to the integrated identity of adulthood. For Christians, identity is not an achievement but a theological as well as a developmental gift, the result of the Holy Spirit's work in and through teenage brains and human communities. What is missing from the National Study of Youth and Religion is the central interest of *this* book: how can the twenty-first-century church better prepare young people steeped in Moralistic Therapeutic Deism for the trust-walk of Christian faith?

The pages that follow will explore that question in three sections. Part 1, "Worshipping at the Church of Benign Whatever-ism," explores the NSYR's contention that American Christianity is being "colonized" by a substitute religious outlook that most American teenagers implicitly practice and that functions as the unacknowledged creed of American culture. Part 2, "Claiming a Peculiar God-Story," places the sociologist Ann Swidler's cultural toolkit theory in conversation with some of the most highly devoted teenagers in the study, who seem to share a consistent set of cultural tools that make faith meaningful. Specifically, highly devoted teenagers have an articulated God-story (their stated or unstated "creed"), a deep sense of belonging in their faith communities, a clear sense that their lives have a God-given purpose, and an attitude of hope that the world is moving in a good direction because of God. These tools seem to help young people resist Moralistic Therapeutic Deism and supply scaffolding for "consequential" faith—a faith that matters enough to issue in a distinctive identity and way of life.

For Christians, however, consequential faith cannot be reduced to the work of cultural tools. Christians view faith as God's gift, and the church's cultural tools help us own and consolidate our identities as people who follow Jesus Christ, and who enact his love for the world. In Christian tradition, mature faith bears fruit. But this kind of generative faith requires a missional imagination, which is strikingly absent from Moralistic Therapeutic Deism. Historically, the spread of Christianity itself enacts the missional rhythms of the gospel, causing the missiologist Andrew Walls to see the Incarnation's *indigenizing* and *pilgrim principles* reflected in the transmisssion of the gospel across cultures. Yet these missional principles describe the way we ferry faith across generations as well. In fact, the church's ministry with adolescents suggests that a third missionary principle may be discerned in the Incarnation— what I call a *liminal principle*—which is revealed with particular poignancy in the lives of teenagers.

Part 3, "Cultivating Consequential Faith," explores broad sets of practices that help congregations cultivate mature faith in young people—faith that is so infused with desire for God and love for others that it becomes generative. Here I introduce three categories of practices from missionary history that have become rusty from disuse in Christian formation, but that can help us refocus self-indulgent Christianity in the direction of missional faith: practices of *translation, testimony*, and *detachment*. Throughout Christian history these practices have served as vehicles that carry God's saving grace into the world "incarnationally"—i.e., through human lives—as we cross geographic, cultural, and even generational boundaries with God's infinitely abundant love. Of course, young people cannot add these practices to their cultural toolkits unless they see adults use them first.

Translation provides us with a working model of catechesis, the "handing on" of lived faith from one generation to the next. Translation begins with those already integrated into "a community of practice" (in this case, adults in a congregation) who share their lives with youth to help them become familiar with the church's language and practices, so young people can participate as fully integrated members of the faith community. *Testimony* helps young people articulate and confess their identity as Christians in the presence of those who are "other." Testimony confesses; it does not convert. It points out God's grace in the world without seeking to co-opt it. *Detachment* is an old word from ascetical Christianity that describes the experience of being de-centered by practices like outreach, hospitality, and prayer. De-centering practices open us to the Other, human or Divine, and cultivate empathy and reflexivity as we learn to focus on Christ instead of on ourselves.

THE EMPEROR'S UNDERWEAR

So here is a reckless claim. If churches practice Moralistic Therapeutic Deism in the name of Christianity, then getting teenagers to come to church more often is not the solution (conceivably, it could make things worse). A more faithful church is the solution to Moralistic Therapeutic Deism. That is going to take more than hiring a youth minister, though that is an excellent place to begin. Since the National Study of Youth and Religion repeatedly points to adolescents' tendency to mirror the religious lives of their parents, nurturing faith in young people means investing in the faith of their parents and congregations. Christian adults can no longer treat Jesus like an embarrassing relative, someone we introduce with apologies to alleviate others' (or is it our?) discomfort—that is, if we introduce him at all. To be sure, God needs no introduction; in Jesus Christ, God burst through the membrane separating heaven and earth and is "on the loose" among us (and usually in spite of us).[40] So some teenagers recognize God's fingerprints in their lives even without the usual advantages of religious parents, active youth programs, attentive pastors, or functional congregations. God finds a way, with or without our help. But American churches do not seem to be offering much assistance, maybe because we are serving the stew of Moralistic Therapeutic Deism to teenagers in the name of Christianity—maybe because we can no longer tell the difference.

To treat adolescents as a separate species instead of as less experienced members of our own was one of the twentieth century's largest category errors. Teenagers, obviously, are people too, and youth ministry is as much about being the church as it is about working with adolescents. If teenagers consider Christianity inconsequential—if American young people find the church worthy of "benign whatever-ism" and no more—then maybe the issue is simply that the emperor has no clothes, and young people are telling churches that we are not who we say we are. If we fail to bear God's life-altering, world-changing, fear-shattering good news (which, after all, is the reason the church exists in the first place)—if desire for God and devotion to our fellow human beings is replaced by a loveless shell of religiosity—then young people unable to find consequential Christianity in the church absolutely *should* default to something safer.

In fact, that is exactly what they are doing.

2

The Triumph of the "Cult of Nice"

Most American youth faithfully mirror the aspirations, lifestyles,
practices and problems of the adult world into which they are being
socialized. In these ways, adolescents may actually serve as a very
accurate barometer of the condition of the culture and institutions
of our larger society.
—*Christian Smith with Melinda Denton*

A world of nice people, content in their own niceness, looking no
further, turned away from God, would be just as desperately in
need of salvation as a miserable world and might even be
more difficult to save.
—*C. S. Lewis*

Alicia's email started out, "Dear Dave":

*You know what? Adults really tick me off (present company excluded, of
course). I was reading an article on this Moralistic Therapeutic Deism. . . .
I'm kinda curious as to how the researchers went about asking all these crucial questions about faith. For one thing, if some random person came up to
me and started asking all these questions about my faith, my innate teenage
response would probably be "Whatever" as well, because that's really none
of their business, is it? So I am admittedly offended at the following, to
quote:*

*"Most religious teenagers either do not really comprehend what their
own religious traditions say they are supposed to believe, or they do understand it and simply do not care to believe it. Either way . . . most religiously
affiliated U.S. teens are not particularly interested in espousing and*

upholding the beliefs of their faith traditions, or their communities of faith
are failing in attempts to educate their youth, or both."[1]

I'm not sure if they're trying to say I have no faith or what, but that's
what it sounds like. Now, if having faith means I have to buy into the Old
Testament fire-and-brimstone-step-out-of-line-and-be-smoted [sic] *busi-*
ness, well then I guess I don't. I'm more inclined to believe in a God that
understands that I am imperfectly made, that I mess up, and sometimes
even pray for what isn't ultimately in my best interest. I don't believe in a
"feel-good God." . . . *God is who you have when everything and everyone else*
seems to be lost to you, when there's nothing else left. God is there to guide
you through the tough times, to remind you that life, as tragic, as chaotic, as
frustrating as it can be, is worth every precious second.

Anyway, it seems to me that the "lack of faith" they're so worried about
is nothing more than a lack of communication; both a lack of words to
express the faith that everyone—teens included—has, and a lack of forum to
discuss faith issues besides what we are told to believe. So there you have it.

Alicia

Dave, Alicia's youth minister, is a friend of mine, so he asked her
permission and sent me her email. Dave had just been to a seminar
where he heard about the National Study of Youth and Religion, and he
did what any good youth pastor would do: he got a reality check from
the kids in his church. He described Alicia as an exceptionally articulate
graduating senior, with a deep faith and the kind of intellectual curiosity that makes her look up articles online after youth group. My first
thought after reading Alicia's email (after wondering how to recruit her
for seminary) was to wish she had been one of the teenagers I had interviewed. She clearly bucks the norm of most young people in terms of
her ability to articulate God's role in her life and her general theological
awareness. Furthermore, Alicia's methodological concerns are good
ones. The research team raised them as well.[2]

My second reaction to Alicia's email was a simultaneous wash of
gratitude and discomfort. Alicia is lucky: Dave, her family, and her
South Dakota congregation have created a faith-supporting ecology,
giving her tools to articulate and defend her religious identity. Alicia's
refusal to submit to a "feel-good God" suggests that she experiences
God as a source of challenge and mystery, and not simply as a means of

personal affirmation, which distinguishes her from most teenagers in the NSYR. But her email also left me curious. What is the content of Alicia's faith in God? It would be reasonable to expect an articulate Christology from a lifelong churchgoer, but Alicia doesn't offer one. Yet without an explicit role for the Incarnation, a life that "imitates Christ" will be difficult to sustain. Alicia suspects that teenagers would say more about faith if they had more chances to talk about it. She might be right.

After the first wave of research for the NSYR was completed, I did my own reality check with focus groups of youth from a Presbyterian (PCUSA) congregation in my town. One high school senior—who, significantly, had grown up in Namibia—echoed Alicia's indignation at being so neatly "categorized." But most of the others defended Moralistic Therapeutic Deism as a worldview they were proud to own, a fair representation of what Jesus intended, if not what he actually said. Tom, a seventeen-year-old lifelong Presbyterian, wondered: "Doesn't the church want us to treat people fairly, be happy, solve our own problems, and get along?"[3] Some considered Moralistic Therapeutic Deism an improvement over what Christianity has come to symbolize in much of the world, as people increasingly identify "Christian" with "American." Shawn, a sophomore on the church youth council, exclaimed: "Do I believe that God wants people to be nice and fair to each other? Yeah, I'd stake my life on that!"

The issue is less whether God wants us to get along (affirmative on that) than whether that is all there is to Christianity, whether a personal decision to be an agreeable neighbor constitutes Christian identity, and whether enacting such a decision is even possible on a purely human level. Most young people who say religion is important to them come from families who have intentionally invested in their children's religious formation, and come from congregations where they feel at least superficially connected to God, even when their theology does not live up to church teachings. A husky eighteen-year-old Catholic from Los Angeles told us: "I think, you know, church is where God lives, and it's a nice thing to get to do communion. You feel that connection."

The other 60%—the majority of American teenagers, who disproportionately call themselves mainline Protestant or Roman Catholic—harbor an attitude toward religion that one researcher described as "benign positive regard."[4] While teenagers agree that religion is good, even important (even if it is not particularly important to them), they cannot explain how or why this is so, and many of them believe religion makes no difference to them personally. As Smith and Denton write, "Most religious communities' central problem is not teen rebellion but teenagers' benign 'whatever-ism.'"[5] Most teenagers (three out of five) say they attend worship, and often youth ministry and Christian education programs, regularly. But they possess little understanding of historically orthodox Christian doctrine, few religious practices, and virtually no religious language to either critique or construct a worldview informed by (much less infused with) Christian faith.[6] In short, American teenagers may engage in substantial amounts of youth ministry and Christian education, but they do not seem to be spending much time in communities where a language of faith is spoken, or where historically orthodox Christian doctrines and practices are talked about or taught.

GRANTING WISHES AND WRITING
HALL PASSES

American young people are devotees of nonjudgmental openness, self-determination, and the authority of personal experience. Religion stays in the background of their lives, where God watches over them without making demands of them. God, above all else, is "nice":

> "What do you think God is like?"
>
> "I would imagine he's a very nice guy." (Evan, seventeen-year-old Mormon)
>
> "I think he's nice, but I don't know because I haven't actually met him before." (Michael, thirteen-year-old Lutheran)
>
> "[God is] like a really great father who cares about all of us, stuff like that. Like a really nice person." (Sam, thirteen-year-old Baptist)

It comes as no surprise, then, that teenagers tend to equate Christian identity with niceness as well. To Dana, a sixteen-year-old Church of Christ member, being religious or spiritual means "doing the right thing and acting right and doing nice things and helping other people out." Sixteen-year-old Toby, a black Baptist, thinks that being a Christian at school means to "just try to be nice to everyone and help everyone out when someone needs help." He thinks his faith has "made me a lot nicer to everyone." Apart from "being nice," teenagers do not think religion influences their decisions, choice of friends, or behaviors. It does not help them obey God, work toward a common good, compose an identity, or belong to a distinctive community. Teenagers do value religion as being personally useful: in addition to helping people be nicer and feel better about themselves, religion can provide comfort amid turmoil, and support for decisions that (by and large) teenagers want to make anyway.[7] Otherwise faith stays in the background.

A COMMON CREED AMONG AMERICAN TEENAGERS

Yet in spite of this, many American teenagers do share a tacit common creed, with or without substantial exposure to faith education, that spans all social classes, developmental stages, and religious traditions. It is particularly evident in mainline Protestant, Catholic, Jewish, and nonreligious youth.[8] Seldom discussed, it is commonly practiced; never acknowledged, it functions as a powerful moral compass in many adolescents' daily lives. Moralistic Therapeutic Deism has little to do with God or a sense of a divine mission in the world. It offers comfort, bolsters self-esteem, helps solve problems, and lubricates interpersonal relationships by encouraging people to do good, feel good, and keep God at arm's length. It is a self-emolliating spirituality; its thrust is personal happiness and helping people treat each other nicely.

Here is where the NSYR drops a bombshell on American churches. Why do teenagers practice Moralistic Therapeutic Deism? Not because they have misunderstood what we have taught them in church. *They practice it because this is what we have taught them in church.* In fact, American teenagers are barometers of a major theological shift taking place in the United States.[9] Smith and Denton observe: "Our religiously conventional adolescents seem to be merely absorbing and reflecting religiously what the adult world is routinely modeling for and inculcating in its youth."[10] To be sure, churches neither intend nor acknowledge this religious position, despite its considerable appeal. Moralistic Therapeutic Deism makes no pretense at changing lives; it is a low commitment, compartmentalized set of attitudes aimed at "meeting my needs" and "making me happy" rather than bending my life into a pattern of love and obedience to God. Like the Spiderman symbiote, Moralistic Therapeutic Deism cannot exist on its own. It requires a host, and American Christianity has proven to be an exceptionally gracious one.

NAVIGATING OTHERNESS

It is easy to see Moralistic Therapeutic Deism's homogenizing appeal. Growing up in a global village makes it impossible for most American young people to retreat into the enclaves of sameness that once kept religions apart. Today, cultural pluralism is a fact of life, increasing young people's access to once unimaginable social networks.[11] While history is rife with examples of religion's polarizing potential, the NSYR finds little evidence of such polarization in American teenagers. Their experience of religion is homogenizing, not polarizing; in fact, what makes American churches such cozy places for Moralistic Therapeutic Deism is our easy, uncritical fusion of the "other" with ourselves—which, of course, dismisses others' identities by subsuming them in ours.

Smith and Denton compare Moralistic Therapeutic Deism to American civil religion. Moralistic Therapeutic Deism accomplishes on a personal level what civil religion accomplishes through public discourse.[12] Both Moralistic Therapeutic Deism and American civil religion involve commonly shared, apolitical symbols and values aimed at making dialogue easier with people who may not share our views. Unlike interfaith dialogue, which structures conversations aimed at preserving the integrity of the religions involved, Moralistic Therapeutic Deism lubricates interpersonal relationships for the immediate moment at hand. While civil religion aims for public unity, Moralistic Therapeutic Deism aims for interpersonal benefits like making people feel good, easing social relationships, helping people get along by sticking to shared, religionless ideas about the sacred. Listen to this conversation in the backseat of my car last week, between my thirteen-year-old daughter, Shannon, and her Hindu friend, Lali:

SHANNON: So how many gods do you have?

LALI: [*laughing*] A lot! But—it's complicated. They take different forms.

SHANNON: Like a cow. You don't eat a cow because it could be God.

LALI: No, everybody thinks that. The god rides on a cow. He doesn't become a cow.

SHANNON: [*relieved*] That would be bad, to eat your God. I think all religions' gods are part of the same god.

LALI: Yeah, we need a lot of gods. One religion can't do everything.

You can appreciate the motivation behind such slippery theology. The purpose of this conversation was not doctrinal fidelity but establishing common ground between friends. Some Hindus do venerate cows, and Christians have been accused of eating their God (word got out in the first century that Christians were cannibals, eating the "body and blood" of Jesus Christ in the Eucharist). But what mattered to Shannon and Lali in the car that day was easing the potential tension of confronting a friend's "otherness"—a particularly disquieting prospect in early adolescence, a developmental period when teenagers project themselves onto their friends to preserve the hard-won beginnings of a fragile identity. The resolution is not a mutual understanding of Shannon and Lali's respective religions but a blurring of the boundaries between them. Shannon co-opts Hinduism into her Christian monotheism ("I think all religions' gods are part of the same god") and Lali, a good Hindu, splits God apart again ("Yeah, we need a lot of gods"). But both of them feel as though they have come to a common understanding—and they have. This understanding grows out of their identity as American teenagers, who have been marinating in the ideals of personal autonomy and individual freedom long enough to know that getting along gives them license to adjust any particularist claims their religions may make.

LEARNING TO BE OURSELVES

Of course, for American young people who call themselves Christian—and three out of four of them do—the freedom to jettison Christian spirituality's distinctive faith claims raises serious questions.[13] In the first place, Christianity *is* particular. The Triune God communicated in the Bible is Christianity's calling card, and only in light of the life, death, and resurrection of Jesus Christ does the Christian story cohere. Second, Christianity is radically oriented to the *other,* both the Other who is God and the other who is neighbor—which means all parties in a relationship need to retain their integrity. In Judeo-Christian tradition, the fusion of self with other (or Other) is sin, with devastating effects on our relationship with God. At Babel, the attempt to become Godlike led to *con*fusion—literally, against fusion—as languages emerged as boundaries to clarify who we are, and who we are not (Gen. 11:1–9).

Arguably, issues of identity and openness pose the most daunting challenges facing American Christianity in the twenty-first century.[14] Where is the line between identity and openness? Who are my people, and who is the "other"? If I proclaim Jesus as Lord, am I indicting those who do not? If my religion matters to me—if I am willing to stake my life on one Truth against which I measure all others—does that make me a person of faith or an ideologue? If I believe that God loves everyone, does that make every religion equal or all religions irrelevant?

Teenagers, who mingle daily in the cultural stir-fry of American pluralism, know that answering these questions is dangerous. One slip could offend a friend, risk a label, box them into a particularistic corner that isolates them from their peers. A few months into the adolescent natural selection process (read, the American high school) and most young people have already begun to hone the twin survival skills of pigeonholing others while evading being pigeonholed. Successful teens—i.e., those who win adult approval—instinctively apply a veneer of noncommittal niceness to the process that gives a permissive shrug to difference ("whatever") and avoids particularities hinting at ultimate loyalties. What niceness masks, however, is our tendency to reduce others to replicas of ourselves, which contradicts the nature of Christian discipleship. Following Jesus requires, not the avoidance of particularity but *radical* particularity, which—along with genuine openness to the other—is made possible only by taking part in God's particularity and openness through Jesus Christ. The conundrum confounding twenty-first-century youth ministers (and the church as a whole) is not, "Do we align ourselves with otherness or particularity?" but, "How can we do both?"

WHAT'S WRONG WITH NICE?

As a social lubricant, "nice" is a cheap and versatile adjective; it offers a nod without a commitment, in religion as in other spheres. Edward, a Hispanic seventeen-year-old from California, described his church as a place that is "warm and welcoming and people are nice. Little groups . . . send you get-well cards and stuff." Teenagers may criticize "the church" in general, but few complain about *their* churches. In everybody else's churches, people are judgmental and hypocritical; but in *their* congregations, people are "nice."[15] Few teenagers experience religion as a source of family conflict; but they do not view it as a source of identity, either. Faith is not a boundary either to claim or repudiate. As we have mentioned, American teenagers "tend to view religion as a Very Nice Thing"[16]—meaning that religion may be beneficial, even pleasant, but it does not ask much of them or even concern them greatly, and as far as they can tell it wields very little influence in their lives.

For all its incipient niceness, Moralistic Therapeutic Deism's superficial pleasantness pales beside Christian teaching on hospitality and compassion. In the practice of hospitality, God sends me to strangers in the name of Jesus Christ, who calls me to recognize God's image in them and, because we share divine parentage, to acknowledge them—in all their glorious strangeness—as my brothers and sisters. The Bible has much to say about kindness and compassion but says nothing at all about being nice. In Judeo-Christian teaching, God is far less concerned with religion than with identity and relationship: Do we know ourselves to belong to the One who made us, who loves us too much to lose us, and do we live as though this matters? The God of Abraham and Mary is personally and morally concerned about creation and desires not just our obedience but our love. As we discover the God who came among us but is also radically "other" than us, we learn that we are God's beloved, "other" than God and adored as such. For this reason, Jews and Christians have always viewed faith as a way of life born out of love for God, rather than as a set of religious propositions to which we subscribe.

In Chaucer's day the word "nice" meant ignorant or foolish, an etymology that cuts both ways for Christians. If we approach nice like Dr. Seuss's Thidwick (the big-hearted moose)—if the church accommodates all manner of sycophants without asserting our own identity because "a host above all must be nice to his guests"[17]—then we inevitably become a haven for symbiotes who take up residence in our antlers. In this case, the church's accommodating impulse does not stem from God's call to us to share our lives with the stranger or to share God's love with others. Instead, it grows out of our need as a church to be liked and approved.

On the other hand, if we approach nice as the foolishness of the cross, then Chaucer's definition may suit us after all. Becoming "fools for the sake of Christ" (1 Cor. 4:10) requires an identity grounded in *God's* accommodation to human culture, not ours—namely, God's choice to become human in Jesus Christ. Foolish faith comes from the security of knowing that we live in God's embrace, and with that knowledge comes a peculiar kind of courage. Foolish faith flies in the face of the self-fulfilling norms of consumerism and addresses issues of identity and openness, not by avoiding the cross, as Moralistic Therapeutic Deism would have us do, but by clinging to it. As G. K. Chesterton pointed out, "A man who has faith must be prepared not only to be a martyr, but to be a fool."[18] Moralistic Therapeutic Deism prepares young people to be neither.

REAPING WHAT WE SOW

What explanations can we give for Moralistic Therapeutic Deism's hold on American teenagers? One possibility is that the research is wrong—that teenagers' faith is less superficial than it seems. Interviews can be unreliable methods for unearthing deep commitments; our most cherished convictions surface more naturally in stories than in propositional answers to interview questions.[19] As Alicia surmises, just because teenagers do not talk about faith does not necessarily mean they do not have any. After all, something makes large numbers of American teenagers go to church; statistics on adolescent religiosity in the United States would make church leaders in many other parts of the industrialized world weep for joy. It is heartening to know that young people, who take cultural pluralism for granted, are deeply tolerant of one another's religions (one of my colleagues exulted after reading the study: "We should be celebrating that teenagers aren't *killing* each other!") So perhaps the issue is not religious disengagement, but a a kind of spiritual constipation that prevents young people with religious leanings from communicating them to researchers.

The hitch in this explanation is that, if we assume that teenagers did not represent themselves accurately when answering questions about religion in the NSYR, then we must also assume that they did not represent themselves accurately in questions about families, relationships, future plans, and other subjects they cared about. Furthermore, since interviews are the most common means of obtaining qualitative research, to invalidate teenagers' responses in the NSYR would call into question most sociological research on adolescents.

Perhaps a better explanation would accept the NSYR conclusions as accurate but blame young people's superficial Christianity on youth ministry, not on the broader struggles of congregations. Critiques of youth ministry in postmodern American churches abound. Most forms of youth ministry were conceived more than a century ago (e.g., Sunday school and youth groups); surely it is unrealistic to expect them to adequately support today's teenagers, who must withstand the pressures of globalized, postmodern culture. This is the position of much of the published literature on youth ministry and Christian formation. Youth ministry could combat mutant Christianity, so the reasoning goes, by updating, streamlining, or shoring up our methodologies, and by beefing up our educational efforts so they legitimately compete with lifestyles and activities that discourage postmodern young people from prioritizing faith.

Smith and his colleagues offer some alternative explanations for the data themselves. They note that external factors may disrupt adolescents' religious commitments. For example:

- *Inadequate supply*: Some religious communities provide few resources for nurturing faith in young people, or have only weak versions of them;
- *Failure to appropriate*: Some youth in religious communities that do offer constructive religious influences choose to remain detached, marginal, and uninvolved, and so they cannot benefit from the religious formation being offered;
- *Disruptive events*: Some youth who are constructively influenced by religious involvement may have that influence disrupted by "detrimental events" (e.g., divorce, abuse, unreconciled fallings-out with people in the religious community, etc.);
- *Competing influences*: Some youth who are positively influenced by religious involvement are overwhelmed by "counterinfluences" from other social activities (sports, the media, school, etc.) that promote competing moral orders and practices.[20]

Clearly, these factors affect the faith formation of some adolescents. Yet God regularly surprises us by reaching through such external circumstances, drawing young people to faith who, statistically, should not have any. Meanwhile, teenagers with every apparent religious advantage remain practically numb to God's presence in their lives. Why?

The most plausible explanation is more insidious. Even if teenagers participate fully in youth ministry programs, are involved in churches, and manage to dodge disruptive life events and overwhelming counterinfluences, youth are unlikely to take hold of a "god" who is too limp to take hold of them. Perhaps young people lack robust Christian identities because churches offer such a stripped-down version of Christianity that it no longer poses a viable alternative to imposter spiritualities like Moralistic Therapeutic Deism. If teenagers lack an articulate faith, maybe it is because the faith we show them is too spineless to merit much in the way of conversation. Maybe teenagers' inability to talk about religion is not because the church inspires a faith too deep for words, but because the God-story that we tell is too vapid to merit more than a superficial vocabulary.

The elephant in the room in the discussion about the National Study of Youth and Religion is the muddled ecclesiology of American churches, a confusion present, not only in young people but in congregations themselves. Put simply, churches have lost track of Christianity's missional imagination. We have forgotten that we are not here for ourselves, which has allowed self-focused spiritualities to put down roots in our soil. When practices intended to reflect God's self-giving love are cut off from their theological taproot in the *missio dei*—God's sending of God's own self into the world in human form—these activities lose their ability to reflect outward, which weakens our resistance to spiritualities like Moralistic Therapeutic Deism.[21] In the process, we confuse Christianity with self-preservation, which is the very opposite of Jesus' own witness, and the antithesis of his call to his disciples to take up their crosses and follow him.

It would be unlikely for teenagers to develop any religious framework besides superficial Christianity if churches have supplanted the gospel with a religious outlook that functions primarily as a social lubricant, with a "god" who supports teenagers' decisions, makes them feel good about themselves, meets their needs when called upon but otherwise stays out of the way. If this is the god we offer young people, there may be little in Christianity to which they object, but there is even less to which they will be devoted. By contrast, the God portrayed in both the Hebrew and Christian Scriptures asks, not just for commitment, but for our very lives. The God of the Bible traffics in life and death, not niceness, and calls for sacrificial love, not benign whatever-ism. If the God of Jesus Christ is a missionary God who crosses every boundary—life and death and space and time—to win us, then following Jesus is bound to be anything but convenient. Jesus Christ doesn't tinker; he tears down walls, draws up new plans, makes demands: "Have no other gods before me. Love one another as I have loved you. Leave your nets, and follow me."

The most likely explanation for Moralistic Therapeutic Deism is simply that we reap what we sow. We have received from teenagers exactly what we have asked them for: assent, not conviction; compliance, not faith. Young people invest in religion precisely what they think it is worth—and if they think the church is worthy of benign whatever-ism and no more, then the indictment falls not on them, but on us.

FROM NICENESS TO HOLINESS

The fruit of a consequential Christian faith is holiness, not niceness, which is not a course for the faint of heart. If the Bible is any indication, holy people make us uncomfortable. They take sacrificial risks on behalf of others; they are disarmingly wise and, often, disconcertingly weird. They expose us with their honesty. Teenagers on this trajectory find ninety-five things wrong with the church, nail the list to the door, and call the press. Yet in their faith is the passion of God, who empowers them for mission and calls them out of their comfort zones so they can call us out of ours. Holiness—a word that implies justice, kindness, and humility before God (Micah 6:8) but that somehow got shrink-wrapped inside twentieth-century Protestant piety—means to be "set apart" for God. Holiness is another word for sanctification, a life conformed to the self-giving love of Jesus Christ, God-made-flesh who came into the world to save it. Holiness enacts the gospel's missionary impulse, the result of news too life-giving to keep to ourselves. True love begs to be shared.

I do not want to overlook the importance of the NSYR's discovery that teenagers harbor no hostility toward religion, but the fact remains that "benign whatever-ism" is a far cry from holiness. I do not pray with my children or call on young people in crisis or or lead confirmation retreats because I long for teenagers to have "an absence of hostility" toward religion (especially when this "absence of hostility" is not because they love their neighbors as themselves, but because they don't care one way or the other). Instead, I ache for them to know Christ's love in their bones, to belong to a community that bathes them in grace, and to experience the kind of communion that weds them to God and to all humanity. The love God shows young people in the cross is passion, a love worthy of suffering, not an absence of hostility. God's love is consequential love, which calls for a consequential faith, which calls for communities where holiness—not niceness—rules the day.

GOOD ENOUGH CHRISTIANS

Jesus would caution against criticizing the speck in teenagers' faith before scrutinizing the log in our own (Matt. 7:5). If teenagers are

members of the Church of Benign Whatever-ism, it is because we are
too. The National Study of Youth and Religion's most incontrovertible
finding is that parents generally "get what they are," in religion as in
most things. This is as true in churches as it is in families, which means
that we can expect the faith of the young people we love to reflect the
faith we show them. So we need to ask before going further: Do we practice the kind of faith that we want our children to have?

I think the honest answer might well be, "Yes, we do." The simple
truth seems to be that young people practice an imposter faith is because
we do—and because this is the faith we want them to have. It's that not-
too-religious, "decent" kind of Christianity that allows our teenagers to
do well while doing good, makes them successful adults without turning them into religious zealots, teaches them to notice others without
actually laying their lives down for any of them. If this is the faith they
see lived out by their parents, their pastors, and their churches, how
would they know it's a sham? In a world crazed with violence and intol-
erance, isn't being "good enough" good enough?

Not according to Jesus, who radically reframed the question. Goodness belongs to God; Jesus calls us to be *holy*—which changes the equation substantially. Line up the Apostles' Creed beside the assumptions
of Moralistic Therapeutic Deism sometime: they bear little resemblance
to one another in either tone or substance. The Apostles' Creed is a dramatic, sweeping description of God's wildest ideas (born of a virgin?
raised from the dead? resurrection of the body?) while Moralistic Therapeutic Deism sounds like the Declaration of Independence in Sunday
School (God wants us to be fair in our pursuit of happiness, but generally plans to stay out of the way except to open heaven's gates if we're
good). The Apostles' Creed never mentions requiring us to be good
simply because the creed is about God, not about us. But Moralistic
Therapeutic Deism is all about us. God's primary role in Moralistic
Therapeutic Deism is to stand back and approvingly watch us evolve.

FROM THE CULT OF NICE TO SUFFERING LOVE

Moralistic Therapeutic Deism is what is left once Christianity has
been drained of its missional impulse, once holiness has given way to

acculturation, and once cautious self-preservation has supplanted the divine abandon of self-giving love. Yet the gospel is God's invitation to young people—to *all* people—to participate in the divine plan of salvation in Jesus Christ and to rely on God's goodness, not our own. Only grace makes this kind of faith possible. Imitating Christ makes people lay down their wallets, their reputations, their lives for the sake of others, which is why parents rightly fear it for their children. The cult of nice is so much safer; God is friendly and predictable, offering little and asking less. Moralistic Therapeutic Deism does not ask people to lay down their lives for anyone, because niceness does not go that far. *Love* goes that far—and true love is neither nice nor safe.

The majority of American young people seem to have no intention of seriously worshipping the flimsy God of a co-opted Christianity. The offhand religiosity of many American teenagers suggests that young people may recognize—perhaps better than we do—the impotence of the symbiote's story, and simply take it for what it is worth. As stories go, there are worse ones. So Moralistic Therapeutic Deism acts as a sort of social placeholder, a decent dance partner who "will do"—although if you ask them, what most teenagers really long for is someone who will sweep them off their feet.

THE EXCEPTIONS: HIGHLY DEVOTED TEENAGERS

The National Study of Youth and Religion found one group of teenagers who were exceptions to this rule—youth who really were swept off their feet by the Holy, and who consistently managed to avoid Moralistic Therapeutic Deism. They were the study's highly devoted youth, representing the 8% of American teenagers who are deeply anchored in their religious traditions and their faith communities, who practice their faith holistically and who find coherence, significance, and self-integration in knowing they belong to God.

As I read the interviews of these teenagers more closely, I began to notice common threads across theological traditions. For one thing, these youth readily talked about faith, in ways that suggested they had thought about it before the interview itself. Also striking was the way

TABLE 2.1. Four Religious Ideal Types in the National Study of Youth and Religion

THE DEVOTED **8%** of American youth	• Attends religious services weekly or more • Faith is very or extremely important in everyday life • Feels very or extremely close to God • Currently involved in a religious youth group • Prays a few times a week or more • Reads scripture once or twice a week or more
THE REGULAR **27%** of American youth	• Attends religious services weekly or more • Attends religious services 2–3 times a month or weekly • Faith is very or not very important in everyday life • Closeness to God, youth group involvement, prayer, and scripture reading are variable but less religious than for the "devoted"
THE SPORADIC **17%** of American youth	• Attends religious services a few times a year to monthly • Faith is somewhat to not very important in everyday life • Closeness to God, youth group involvement, prayer, and scripture reading are variable.
THE DISENGAGED **12%** of American youth	• Never attends religious services, or attends many times a year and identifies as not religious • Faith is somewhat, not very, or not important in everyday life • Feels only somewhat close to God or less • Not involved in a religious youth group • Prays 1-2 times a month or less

they talked about faith. They portrayed God as loving, powerful and active in the world; they talked about their church communities as spiritually and relationally significant. They sensed a divinely appointed purpose for their lives, and they bore witness to a hopeful future. Although these teenagers were disproportionately Mormon, conservative Protestant, and black Protestant, these four notes were sounded, in slightly different keys, in religiously mature teenagers across the theological spectrum.

These teenagers did not belong to the Church of Benign Whatever-ism. They belonged to families and faith communities that shaped and supported their understanding of who God is, who they belong to, why they are here and where they are going—support beams that helped them construct a religious framework for their lives. Their identities were grounded in an articulated "God-story" that, along with the support of their faith communities, filled their lives with purpose and hope. These four theological accents—a creed to believe, a community to belong to, a call to live out, and a hope to hold onto—were pronounced in the faith of these teenagers. In the next two chapters, we will meet some of them and examine how some highly devoted teenagers, from very different religious communities, use such cultural tools to compose religious identity. Are these young people faithful or brainwashed? And what do they teach us about resisting Moralistic Therapeutic Deism?

PART 2

Claiming a Peculiar God-Story

Christianity, if false, is of no importance, and if true, of infinite importance. The only thing it cannot be is moderately important.
—C. S. Lewis

3

Mormon Envy

Sociological Tools for a Consequential Faith

Certain religious traditions in the United States appear more or less capable of eliciting serious, multifaceted religious devotion in their teenagers. Conservative Protestantism and Mormonism seem especially likely and Catholicism appears particularly unlikely to produce highly religiously devoted teenagers (all compared to mainline Protestantism).
—*Christian Smith with Melinda Denton*

Never be discouraged. If I were sunk in the lowest pits of Nova Scotia, with the Rocky Mountains piled on me, I would hang on, exercise faith, and keep up good courage, and I would come out on top.
—*Joseph Smith Jr.*

Sitting on the bleachers of adolescent life about as far from benign whatever-ism as you can get is Juliana Rencher, a senior at West Linn High School in Portland, Oregon. "Some of my friends are shocked that I can say no to alcohol," she told the reporter who interviewed her for a local newspaper after her morning "seminary" studies. Every weekday morning for the past four years, Juliana—like thousands of Mormon teenagers across the United States—has roused herself at dawn to make her way to seminary to study Mormon doctrine and history before school starts. Seminary is a daily ritual for Latter-day Saints teenagers, designed to help them learn sacred texts and foster a lifestyle consistent with Church expectations. In addition to learning the Book of Mormon, seminary advises Juliana to shun adolescent rituals like swearing, smoking, watching R-rated movies (not to mention drugs, sex, and alcohol). Yet socially, Juliana counts her non-Mormon, party-going peers among her friends. Juliana muses, "Why is it so shocking? . . . My friends who do a lot of drinking are grateful that they can come to me in a time of need. They know I'm stable."[1]

Stable hardly covers it. A distinctive feature of Mormon identity is the ability to use the tools of the surrounding culture without losing your "Mormon-ness" in the process. Remember the Osmonds? While conservative Protestants fled the popular music scene in the 1970s to create a "parallel Christian universe" of popular music with evangelical lyrics, teenagers Donnie and Marie Osmond sifted through popular culture, found songs they could reasonably interpret with Mormon values, and performed them—investing the popular music industry (and the celebrity myth that accompanies it) with Mormon standards of wholesomeness. Utah church leaders exempted Donnie Osmond from the missionary commitment expected of nineteen-year-old boys because they felt he was already doing missionary service for the church in his role as a pop star.[2]

Likewise, teenage fans of 2005's super-geek movie *Napoleon Dynamite* (the brainchild of Brigham Young University film school graduates) made a number of Mormon cultural practices, including Napoleon's use of "gosh" and "darn" (standard LDS substitutions for swear words) part of the mainstream code for cool. On the DVD director's cut, Mormon star Jon Heder joked that Napoleon and love interest Deb might be "sealed in time and all eternity"—a reference to the Mormon belief in eternal marriage. In the Mormon world, religious identity influences everything from adolescents' caffeine intake to heavenly reward to their views on God, community, vocation, and hope—coordinates that highly devoted teenagers in the National Study of Youth and Religion seemed to share.

THE DISPROPORTIONATELY DEVOTED

Moralistic Therapeutic Deism is part of the story told by the National Study of Youth and Religion—but it is not the whole story. Forty percent of the teenagers we interviewed said religion was an important part of their lives, and one in twelve (8%) attended religious services weekly or more often, participated in religious youth groups, prayed and read the Bible regularly, *and* said they felt very close to God and that faith is extremely important in their lives.[3]

These were the highly devoted teenagers in the study (see table 2.1, page 41), and they stand out in a number of ways. Highly devoted young people are much more compassionate, significantly more likely to say they care about things like racial equality and justice, far less likely to be moral relativists, to lie, cheat, or do things "they hoped their parents would never find out about."[4] They are not just doing "okay" in life; they are doing significantly better than their peers, at least in terms of happiness and forms of success approved by the cultural mainstream.[5] Religious devotion in teenagers correlates positively with other youth-supporting variables. For example, highly devoted teenagers tend to have highly devoted parents who are married and well-educated. They are more likely than other youth to say their parents love, accept, understand, and closely monitor them—all of which contribute to adolescent well-being.[6] So it comes as no surprise that young people who reported positive relationships with parents and peers, success in school, hope for the future, and healthy lifestyle choices were also more likely to be highly committed to faith as well.[7]

For highly devoted young people, faith *is* a big deal. They "own" their traditions, possess articulate and integrated theologies, and draw significantly from their religions' faith stories to influence their decisions, actions, and attitudes. While religious devotion spans the theological spectrum, the NSYR found significantly more highly devoted teenagers in conservative Protestant and black Protestant communities than in mainline Protestant and Roman Catholic ones (who had higher percentages of religious devotion than Jews or atheists).[8] But topping the charts—in religious devotion, in overall well-being, in integration of faith and life—were the Mormons (see appendix C). In Smith and Denton's words, when belief and "social outcomes" are measured, "Mormon kids tend to be on top."[9]

A SOCIOLOGICAL EXPLANATION: CULTURAL TOOLKITS

"Culture, to use a computer analogy, is humanity's operating system," explains the sociologist Tim Clydesdale. "And like a computer operating system, culture gets installed with certain 'default' settings that, unless overridden, determine how humans view their world and structure their everyday behavior."[10] Those default settings led the sociologist Ann Swidler to propose her theory of the "cultural toolkit." Cultural tools are the symbols, stories, rituals, relationships, and worldviews that we pick up from our experience of the world around us—our default operating system—and we use them to construct meaning and guide our actions in the world (see table 3.1).[11] They are, to use Pierre Bourdieu's phrase, what people "like us" do, and we use our tools the way people "like us" use them.[12] Of course, we pick up cultural tools selectively, mostly unreflectively, depending on which tools seem to be favored by people around us. Mormon young people hold a particular view of God, belong to a distinctive community of faith, articulate an explicit life purpose, and adhere to a worldview typical of the followers of Joseph Smith. In short, their cultural toolkits include a creed, a community, a call, and a hope that reinforce what Mormons believe, who they belong to, why they are here, and how they should live.

The cultural toolkit theory offers one explanation for why patterns of behavior in communities persist over long periods of time. The persistence of poverty, southern hospitality, the cyclical pattern of child abuse all stem from differently stocked cultural toolkits. Helpful or harmful, our first impulse is to reach for the cultural tools—the language, stories, relationships, practices, and worldviews—that we see people "like us" using to navigate the world. Comedy makes the most of these cultural

TABLE 3.1. Types of Cultural Tools Made Available by Religion

Moral order	• moral directives
	• spiritual experiences
	• religious role models
Learned competencies	• community and leadership skills
	• coping skills
	• cultural capital that is transferable to other contexts and situations
Social and organizationalties	• social capital from experience in communities that are not rigidly age-stratified
	• network closure (teens and parents know each other's friends)
	• extracommunity links

tools, including the awkwardness of learning new ones that may become available (ever watch *The Beverly Hillbillies*?). Without access to new cultural tools, or equally important, without a way to picture ourselves using a tool that becomes available (like education or money), we capitulate to the gravitational pull of the familiar, replicating the world we know best.

So our toolkits do important things: they help us construct certain kinds of selves, mark us as members of certain groups, provide ideas and images for certain worldviews, and give us skills and habits so we fit into particular social worlds.[13] But they also limit us; we could use more culture than we do, and we seldom add new tools to our toolkits unless someone we trust shows us how. Every religious convert goes through this process when joining a faith community, and religious formation involves teaching young people how to use religious tools in the ways that are distinctive to that community, thereby establishing young people as members who belong to a particular faith tradition. Highly devoted young people seem adept at using at least four cultural tools in ways that mark them as members of their traditions: (1) they confess their tradition's *creed*, or God-story; (2) they belong to a *community* that enacts the God-story; (3) they feel *called* by this story to contribute to a larger purpose; and (4) they have *hope* for the future promised by this story. In addition, these youth seem to have families and churches that model—convincingly—that these tools matter: something is at stake in using these cultural tools "as we do," and something is lost in not using them at all.

To be sure, the mere presence of such cultural tools does not guarantee faith. Every teenager needs a governing ideology, a significant community, a life purpose, and a source of hope—religious or not—since these tools help young people construct stable ego-identities, at least in the West.[14] It is our perceived access to cultural tools, not their quality, that leads us to include them in our toolkits as we look for ways to cobble together a coherent sense of self. That is important, for some young people brandish these tools in dangerous but nonetheless identity-forming ways. Tantalized by Hitler's charisma and promise of a united Germany, German youth in the 1930s found solidarity with their peers as well as an illusory sense of purpose by joining the Hitler Youth. Today the Palestinian group Hamas galvanizes young people around fundamentalist Islamic teachings, reinforced in Hamas settlements, that call young people to jihad and martyrdom, complete with the hope of heavenly reward.

Across the United States, gangs initiate new members, sharing gang lore and impressing upon them absolute loyalty to the gang, where a sense of purpose (often revenge) and long-term hope of "respect" in the streets unites group members. Young people in these organizations also claim a creed, belong to a community, pursue a purpose, and harbor hope in ways that utterly oppose the gospel.

Cultural tools, therefore, are not "magic bullets" for faith formation. The "form" implied in Christian formation is Jesus Christ. Christian communities employ cultural tools in order to imitate Christ, believing that the Holy Spirit's presence in human communities can alter these human tools into vehicles of divine grace and transformation. Still, because faith does take shape in human communities, we cannot ignore the sociological dimensions of religious identity. Before mature faith can emerge, young people must learn what the cultural tools available in their faith communities mean, how to employ them, and why they are significant for "people like us."[15] And that requires the people nearest to teenagers—parents, youth leaders, pastors, congregations, interested adults—to use these cultural tools as well.

Few religious communities are more insistent on modeling the use of their cultural toolkits for teenagers than the Church of Jesus Christ Latter-day Saints. Mormons invest heavily in teaching young people to exemplify and promote Mormon beliefs and behaviors. By intentionally reinforcing the significance of Mormonism's particular God-story, by immersing young people in a community of belonging, by preparing them for a vocation and by modeling a forward-looking hope, Mormons intentionally and consistently create the conditions for consequential faith—so much so that Mormon teenagers are more likely than teenagers from any other group to fall in the category of young people the NSYR called highly devoted.

CONDITIONING FAITH: LEARNING FROM LATTER-DAY SAINTS

Mormons remain a homogeneous bunch, ideologically and demographically—which makes them ideal for sociological research, and as a result, social science has amassed reams of data documenting the health and well-being of Mormon young people, compared to other sectors of the population.[16] NSYR researcher John Bartkowski points out: "The story we tell about Mormon youth is not that all is well, but compared with other teens they're more knowledgeable about their faith, more committed to their faith, and have more positive social outcomes associated with their faith."[17] In the general culture, most people are more familiar with Mormon behavior than theology; in the NSYR (as in numerous other studies) Latter-day Saints teenagers were less likely to drink, smoke, or engage in risky behavior. For example, Mormon teenagers postpone first intercourse longer than most teenagers (to age eighteen versus sixteen and a half). One in eight Mormon teenagers (compared to one in five teenagers in the general population) admits to not being a virgin.[18] Meanwhile, Mormon teenagers rank ahead of other youth in terms of spiritual vitality, hope for the future, and overall health and well-being.

The "good kid" mentality of Latter-day Saints teenagers is not merely the result of impressing upon them rules for good behavior. The Mormon way of life is invested with personal substance; young people see it modeled by families and congregations. Latter-day Saints teenagers are significantly more likely than their peers to hold religious beliefs similar to their parents' (73%), attend religious services once a week (43%), and talk about religious matters in their families more than other teenagers (80% once a week or more).[19] They rate the importance of religious faith in shaping their daily life as "extremely important" (43%), and engage in practices like fasting and other forms of self-denial (68%). Compared to other teenagers, Mormon youth participate in more religious practices of all kinds, and are much more articulate about church teachings.[20] Mormon teenagers receive a "regular presentation of religious motifs in a way that many other people, even conservative Protestants, ordinarily don't get," explains the sociologist Benton Johnson. "They have a more religiously articulated home life culture than even evangelical families."[21]

Intense religious socialization and teaching in Mormon communities comes at a price. Mormon teenagers tend to be the "spiritual athletes" of their generation, conditioning for an eternal goal with an intensity that requires sacrifice, discipline, and energy. Long before their classmates are smacking their snooze alarms, more than half of Mormon teenagers are rolling out of bed at 5:00 a.m., every single school day for four years straight, in order to attend seminary. Seminary is frequently taught by a parent and typically involves reflexive practices like journaling about one's life and spiritual growth, as well as practical advice on how to plan and save for a two-year mission commitment to service and evangelism.[22]

Mormon families also commonly practice family devotions and family home meetings, thereby prioritizing religious conversation at home as well as in church. While seminary serves as a significant rite of passage for Mormon teenagers, the premiere rite of passage into Mormon adulthood is missionary service, encouraged (not mandated) for all Mormon males before they finish college. All of these experiences—demanding programs of religious education, peer accountability for living according to Mormon norms, family activities that emphasize Mormon distinctiveness, participation in Mormon missions—impress on Latter-day Saints young people that Mormonism is not an activity they choose nor a church they attend. It is literally a way of life, and affects every choice they make.

The imminent prospects of missionary service and early marriage for Mormon teenagers invests Mormon religious education with an urgency lacking in many other religious cultures. Mormon formation is less focused on adolescent conversion or God's transformation than on preparing Mormon young people to be fully engaged, articulate, and participative church members. For parents teaching seminary classes, the payoff of four years of early morning teaching (an act of solidarity not lost on teenagers) is its immediate relevance for sons and daughters who will embark on mission or marriage soon after high school. Religious formation for Mormons is not simply a way to encourage teenagers to make good choices in high school, or a way to invest in their eternal well-being—although it is both of those. Young people's ability to succeed in the Mormon community's signature rites of passage, and to maintain their Mormon identities in the broader culture once they leave the Mormon enclave, depends upon this education. Parents take to heart their responsibility to get young people ready.

A TEXTBOOK CASE: MOLLY

The research on Mormon young people is not unproblematic. One disconcerting footnote in the data is Mormon teenagers' almost preternatural level of religious certainty: 91% reported "few or no doubts" about religious beliefs in the past year (the next most certain group of teens, surprisingly, were mainline Protestants; 84% reported "few or no doubts" about religion in the past year).[23] This news may sound heartening, but adolescents lack the life mileage necessary to truly develop Paul Ricoeur's "second naivete" or James Fowler's "conjunctive faith," those views of religious confidence associated with maturity, experience, and interestingly, a sense of peace with religious doubt and mystery. Religious certainty in highly devoted adolescents could mean confidence in God, or it could signal a "foreclosed" religious identity instead of an "achieved" one.[24]

It is also possible that the "textbook" faith and well-adjusted outlooks of highly devoted teenagers—for Mormons and others—may be a better indicator of these teenagers' ability to win adult approval than an indicator of mature faith. We generally approve of teenagers who let us socialize them into younger versions of ourselves. Mormon young people get along well in American culture in part because their use of cultural tools perpetuates so-called American values like wholesomeness, family, patriotism, and hard work. Yet religion often challenges the tendency to "go along" with culture; many highly devoted religious teenagers throughout history—Joseph Smith included—were notorious for scandalizing their religious communities and for challenging the dominant culture's idea of success. Whether highly devoted teenagers in the NSYR had more integrated religious identities than their peers, or whether they were simply better at conforming to adult expectations, was not always clear.

For the most part, however, the highly devoted young people we met were like Molly, a lively fourteen-year-old from Idaho, the youngest of three sisters in a warm, close Mormon family, whom we met (ironically) in a coffee house. Molly readily demonstrates how being Mormon structures her developing selfhood around a view of God, a religious community, a sense of call, and an eternal hope. These cultural tools bear the marks of Molly's "peculiar God-story" and yield numerous practices and convictions that set her apart from her peers. When asked what made her religious, Molly described both actions and beliefs: "Well, I go to church and I believe in God, I believe in Jesus Christ, you know . . . I have a testimony at my church and I read my scriptures and I pray. I know a lot of kids don't do any of that."

Claiming a Creed

Unlike most Mormon youth—but like most of her highly devoted peers—Molly said she felt "very close" to God, and described God in terms that were both personal and powerful. When she thinks about God, Molly said, "I think about my father. . . . He knows who I am and he knows who you are. He's kind of the controller of everything."

Mormons have a distinctive take on divine power—namely, that it is something humans (especially men) acquire, evidenced in the vision given to church prophets to inspire all people to progress toward the "celestial kingdom."[25] In Mormon tradition, God became God by developing and progressing, and humans are called to follow this pattern.[26] Mormons perceive no ontological gap between God and humans, so practices of repentance and reconciliation have social benefits but only indirectly contribute to salvation. In fact, unlike classical Christianity, Mormon theology has little transcendence, asserting that "God is not of another species."[27]

But make no mistake: what God lacks in omnipotence, God makes up for in grandeur. God may not be transcendent in Mormon theology, but the celestial kingdom is, and its sweeping (some would say totalizing) vision prevents God from being contained in Moralistic Therapeutic Deism's shrink-wrapped God-images. Instead, God creates heaven for God's beloved, a vision communicated in shocking physicality and detail. For Mormons, God's power is relational, akin to the father-child relationship of human families. Most highly devoted teenagers used father imagery for God, but Molly's father image also reflects the importance of familial relationships stressed by Latter-day Saints. The theologian Blake Ostler explains that for Mormons, "Religious faith is more a function of intimacy than of ultimacy, more a product of relationships than of logical necessities."[28] Thus, Molly sees no contradiction in seeing divine power as an intimate relationship, like the one she has with her dad.

Belonging to a Community

The most important faith community in Mormon life is the family. Devotion begins at home (literally), and parents view part of their mission as the faith formation of their family. Belonging to a Mormon family simultaneously means belonging to the Church, which presents eternal kinship as a binding condition. Separating family and church is inconceivable in Mormon culture. Congregations function as extended families (church members address each other as "brother" and "sister"). The intimate connection between a teenager's family and her congregation bears directly on religious salience, since the number of adults teenagers can turn to for help and support increases proportionately with teenagers' religious devotion.[29] Molly blurs the line between kin and congregation, describing her church as

> just like our family. Some of our family friends, they'll always come up to you and [say], "How are you doing, you know, what's going on with you?" . . . And a lot of the members are young married couples with children and so I babysit for a lot of them, so I talk to them when I'm babysitting their kids. So it's really welcoming.

She especially likes the bishop, who interviews each youth "just to see if we're doing all right":

> Those are always a lot of fun 'cause, you know, I don't do anything wrong so I just get to talk to the bishop. He's a really great guy and he's funny and, you know, we'll just sit there and talk, and we'll just be laughing. . . . They really focus on the youth because they're going to be the next generation of leaders, so you need to make sure they're all right. You know, on the right page. And that's a lot of fun 'cause sometimes they come and they do stuff with us in our youth activities, like squirt gun fights and stuff like that.

Molly's sense of belonging in this community is palpable. Family and church are bound up in each other, and Molly feels joyfully bound to both.

While religiously devoted teenagers in the NSYR all have practices that set them apart from their peers (standing up for injustice, attending church regularly, reading the Bible, and dressing modestly are common), Mormon youth also described practices distinctive to LDS life. Mormon teenagers belong to a highly participatory church structure; more than half of all Mormon teenagers (53%) reported giving a presentation in church in the past six months (fewer than one in seven Southern Baptists, and only one in twenty-five Catholic youth had done the same). Nearly half (48%) of Mormon teenagers had attended a meeting in the past six months where they were part of making decisions, compared to about one in four Southern Baptists and one in twelve Catholic teenagers.[30] Mormon youth assume that their contributions matter, and frequently mentioned taking part in church rituals like public testimony, fasting, baptisms and blessings, which—along with upholding community norms like abstaining from alcohol and premarital sex—they deemed important to their identity as Mormons.

Since the family is the primary "community of belonging" in the Mormon church, taking part in family practices like Monday family home nights and tithing is as significant as taking part in church activities is for Protestants and Catholics.[31] Mormons are almost twice as likely as other teenagers to pray with their parents at times other than meals or worship (79%) and to talk about God or religion as a family almost every day (74%).[32] In 1970, LDS officials mandated Monday nights as family home evenings, forbidding Monday evening temple and ward activities and creating curriculum for nuclear families to gather for devotions, religious instruction, and wholesome activities. These practices underscore the Mormon dialectic between individual and corporate religiosity. As one reviewer put it, "Ultimate salvation, in Mormon terms, is a corporate venture; it depends on relationships to other people, especially those to whom one is 'sealed.' "[33] In other words, Molly's individual religious practices tangibly contribute to her family and her faith community in ways that make a difference to their eternal well-being.

Pursuing a Call

For Molly, the purpose of faith formation is mission. Take any Mormon educational endeavor to its logical conclusion, and you wind up with a more informed, thoughtful, and skilled missionary of Mormonism. This is no coincidence, since mission work is not limited to a few church members who are gifted or called to special service. Nor are parents the only missionaries in the Latter-day Saints community. Every Mormon teenager is literally, not just rhetorically, a potential missionary. Like many Mormon teenagers we interviewed, Molly naturally assumes that life's purpose is to fulfill, in her words, "the mission you were supposed to come here for: help whoever you were supposed to help, . . . be the example you're supposed to be."

Mormon youth are vastly more likely than other teenagers to participate in mission trips (70%), share their faith with someone not of their faith (72%), participate in religious youth groups (75%), and speak publicly about their faith in a religious service or meeting (65%).[34] Sharing one's religious faith is simply part of Mormon life; Molly told us that she invites her friends to church because "I know my church is true, so I just want to share it with everybody . . . 'cause I wish they could have the happiness I have." The emphasis on sharing the faith sharply focuses the doctrine of vocation for Mormon teenagers. From a very early age the church fosters in Molly the skills that help her talk about her faith and participate in faith-sharing practices, starting with regular religious conversations at home, shared leadership practices in youth ministry, and frequent opportunities for public testimony in worship.

Nowhere is the Mormon emphasis on vocation more evident than in the expectation of missionary service for boys and marriage for girls after high school. While not universal, missionary service is held up as a Mormon ideal, and returned missionaries are held in high esteem. (Girls are permitted to serve on a mission for eighteen months after they are twenty-one, but they frequently marry instead.) Missionary service, an evangelistic endeavor aimed at Mormon baptisms that sometimes includes other forms of service, is widely regarded as a practice that solidifies and intensifies Mormon identity. For Molly, missionary work bears directly on her future plans, even as a woman. Modifying her ambitions to be a "field agent" (which she viewed as incompatible with marriage and raising children), Molly says she wants to marry "a good person who will take care of me who's a member of the church, and hopefully a returned missionary, because they learn so much on their mission [that] they become different people. . . . They come back as really good people." Asked about her own missionary ambitions, Molly explained: "If I was not married and I was done with a certain [amount of] schooling, I would go. . . . They really don't encourage girls to go as much as boys . . . [because] girls can't baptize the people." She noted that one of her older sisters "really want[ed] to go on a mission," but had not; both sisters "got captured [by marriage] before they got a chance to go."[35]

Confessing Hope

Few American religious communities have eschatologies as explicitly developed as Latter-day Saints.[36] Mormons believe that salvation resurrects the body, effected by Jesus' death and atonement, which is God's gift of grace to all people, of any religion, without condition. Yet ultimate salvation, or "exaltation" (what some refer to as moving toward godhood) takes effort, and is accomplished only in the celestial kingdom as a result of specific actions, including secret temple rituals designed to emphasize the boundaries between Mormons and "gentiles" (non-Mormons). As Richard Ostling explains, "By keeping God's covenants, Mormons believe God promises them they will be a 'peculiar treasure unto me above all people' (Exod. 19:5 [KJV])."[37]

The Mormon hope of entering the celestial kingdom represents the unifying goal of Mormon life; it affects what a Mormon teenager eats and drinks, how she spends her money, what clothes she will (and will not) wear, who and where she will marry. Molly justifies marriage on eschatological grounds: "You jump, like, another step when you get married . . . it's kind of like baptism. You jump another covenant step." Many of the Mormon teenagers we interviewed echoed Molly's eschatological worldview. Richard, a seventeen-year-old Mormon from Utah, explained how the very purpose of life itself is tied to the hope of heaven: "Life is like a testing period for us. If we choose the right, then we can go back . . . to our heavenly father, and live with him."

Mormon eschatology offers a way for teenagers to be engaged with their surrounding culture without sacrificing their subcultural identity, because they are free to invest aspects of mainstream culture with religious meaning.[38] Deeply aware that their ancestors paid a high price for their cultural differences, contemporary Latter-day Saints follow a pragmatic path, participating fully in American public life.[39] So Mormon teenagers do not hold themselves apart from culture (Molly was fully involved in school activities, and she told us how excited she was about her church youth group's upcoming dance) as much as they reframe culture in terms of its potential to contribute to passage into the celestial kingdom. As Molly told us, "We have dances, but it's good music and it's good dancing" (i.e., not obscene or provocative). Molly's parents will allow her to date at sixteen, per church teaching, but they adjust dating norms to allow for significant parental supervision. While some churches deplore proms' sexual overtones or consumer excess, Mormon congregations often encourage girls to wear their prom dresses to church the morning after prom (which has the effect of promoting modesty in dress, and earlier prom evenings). Reframing prom couture with a Mormon theology of baptism, one Latter-day Saints journalist advised girls: "As you and I were baptized, we made a covenant. We promised to 'stand as witnesses to God at all times and in all things and in all places' (Mosiah 18:9). We might also add the phrase, 'and in all prom dresses.' "[40]

GRACE: A MONKEY WRENCH IN THE CULTURAL TOOLKIT

It may be difficult for a "gentile" or non-Mormon to read Mormon views on God, community, vocation, and eschatology without raising an eyebrow—but it is just as difficult to read the data on Mormon teenagers without feeling a hint of awe. To be sure, Mormons have their share of Moralistic Therapeutic Deists, though in smaller numbers.[41] But Mormon young people offer a window on how to use cultural tools, bolstered by a number of faith-supporting variables, in the service of consequential faith.[42]

Chief among these faith-supporting variables is the religiosity of Mormon parents. Since Mormons are known for tightly knit, intact, and religiously devoted families—and since we know that teenagers mirror their parents' faith to a high degree—it stands to reason that Mormon communities would have higher-than-average rates of religious devotion among teenagers. Even the extended family of the congregation, as the bishop's interview with Molly suggests, takes teenage faith extremely seriously, and opportunities for young people to take part in education, mission trips, youth groups, and worship abound.[43]

Finally, since teenagers are more likely to be highly devoted if their closest friends also participate in religious activities, the fact that many Mormon teenagers say most of their friends are also Mormons has a strong positive affect on religious devotion as well.[44] Molly picks up cultural tools from other highly devoted Mormon young people, in part because people like her show her how to use them.

But now we must change our lens back from sociology to theology. At some point, a peculiar God-story must *set the terms* for how teenagers use religion's cultural tools.[45] Mormons rigorously and unapologetically plunge teenagers into a peculiar God-story, and surround them with religiously articulate adults who demonstrate how to approach their creed, community, and understandings of vocation and hope to enact a Mormon way of life. Christian teenagers also have these cultural tools at their disposal, but the terms for their use are very different. In Christian tradition, Christ does not simply bless our cultural toolkits; he enters the world through them. The goal of Christian formation is not church membership, but more perfect love of God and neighbor. Jesus did not call people to come to church; he called people to follow him.

The Christian God-story emphasizes a God so smitten with creation that God chooses to enter creation with us, and stops at nothing—not even death—to win us back. Christian formation is less about acquiring cultural tools than surrendering them, placing ourselves—cultural tools and all—at the disposal of a God who transforms them, and us, into means of grace. In Christian tradition, a creed, community, call, and hope are not just tools we pick up along the way because people like us use them. They are tools God uses to enter the world, and to enter us—resulting in a very different imagination than the one Moralistic Therapeutic Deism assumes.

4

Generative Faith

Faith That Bears Fruit

Most religious teens in the United States appear to engage in few
religious practices. But even basic practices like regular Bible reading
and personal prayer seem clearly associated with stronger and deeper
faith commitment among youth.
—*Christian Smith with Melinda Denton*

Attentiveness to peculiar narrative identity seems to me an urgent
practical enterprise for a religious community that is often so bland
that it loses its raison d'être. The issue is to practice a peculiar identity
that is not craven in the face of the moralisms of the right or the left.
—*Walter Brueggemann*

You remember the flux capacitor, Doc Brown's trippy invention that
makes time travel possible in the *Back to the Future* trilogy. The flux
capacitor was the mythical contraption that powered the DeLorean time
machine, sending Marty McFly back in time to save his parents and
therefore ensure his own birth. Once Marty and Doc are safely ensconced
back in 1955, however, a problem arises: where to find the 1.21
"jigowatts" of electricity needed to propel Marty home again to 1985?
Only lightning packs that kind of wallop—which is when Doc remembers (great Scott!) that a bolt of lightning stopped time on the town
clock at precisely 10:04 on a Saturday night in 1955. "This is it! This is
the answer!" Doc tells Marty. "If we can somehow . . . harness this lightning, channel it into the flux capacitor . . . it just might work!" As Marty
climbs into the driver's seat for his trip "back to the future," Doc reas-
sures him: "*As long as* you hit *that* wire with the connecting hook at

precisely 88 mph the *instant* the lightning strikes the tower . . . everything will be fine."

No pressure.

THE PROBLEM WITH PASTORAL
FLUX CAPACITORS

Every Christian parent, pastor, youth worker, and educator has a little bit of Doc Brown in us. We spend a lot of time hunting for flux capacitors: gadgets, curriculum, methods, and even cultural tools that we hope will somehow (we're not sure how) convert human practices into holy fire. As long as we use the proper tools in the proper way with the proper timing, we tell ourselves, we can convert parental determination and pastoral energy into electrifying faith for the young people we love: "As long as you hit *that* wire with the connecting hook at *precisely* 88 mph . . ." As long as youth ministry provides the right equipment, as long as parents create the correct conditions for learning, as long as churches provide the right relationships and experiences . . . everything will be fine.

The delusion that human effort can generate mature faith—in young people or anybody else—is as old as fiction itself. Trying to channel God, like trying to channel lightning, kept countless false prophets in business throughout the Hebrew scriptures. Today, we are more likely to view God as a source of fuel than a source of awe as we try to harness divine power for our own use. But ancient people had it right: they hid their faces at the Lord's approach, and prayed for mercy.

In the end, cultural tools can provide support beams for, but not the content of, consequential Christian faith. Christians believe that faith depends on the electrifying presence of the Holy Spirit, who gives cultural tools their holy momentum. Churches can (and must) help by plunging teenagers into Christianity's peculiar God-story, and by inviting young people to take part in practices that embody it. For centuries, these two strategies—telling God's story and enacting it—comprised the heart of Christian formation, or catechesis, the "handing on" of a faith tradition from one generation to the next.

Catechesis shapes missional imaginations, which help us recognize God's activity in Jesus Christ and in us, as Christ calls us to participate in his redemptive work in the world. Catechesis clarifies the church's understanding of who God is; shapes our ability to participate in the Christian community; provides the means for discerning our call as disciples and for claiming our hope in God's future. Catechesis, therefore, gives teenagers cultural tools that stake up young faith, improve teenagers' exposure to the Son and therefore the likelihood that their faith will mature and bear fruit. Catechesis makes young people—and the rest of us—more combustible before God. Yet catechesis does not guarantee that teenagers will follow Jesus. Only the Holy Spirit ignites faith, transforming human effort into holy fire that comes roaring into our lives at the first hint of welcome, insistent on igniting us, sharing us, and being shared.

THE GOSPEL'S MISSIONARY IMPULSE

It is no accident that Christians have long associated fire with the Holy Spirit. An insular church is an oxymoron; churches "on fire" with the Spirit cannot contain themselves, any more than a forest fire can stop itself from catching. Fires spread, not according to plan but according to the availability of combustible tinder. Christianity likewise has a boundary-crossing, outward-reaching, other-oriented impulse modeled by Jesus himself, formally taken up by the church when the disciples "caught fire" with the Holy Spirit at Pentecost. But the first sparks occurred weeks earlier, when Jesus mysteriously appeared to the disciples behind locked doors on that first Easter evening, leaving them with the astonishing command: "As the Father has sent me, so I send you" (John 20:21).

A less likely church, then or now, is hard to imagine, and these are all the instructions we get. Christian identity is a stated goal of nearly all church youth programs—an identity that involves following Jesus into the world and not just amassing church activities.[1] As Douglas John Hall notes, "The whole purpose of [a] theology of the cross is to engender a movement—a people—that exists in the world under the sign of the cross of Jesus Christ: a movement and people called into being by his Spirit, and being conformed to his person and furthering his work."[2] Disciples are people who participate in God's movement toward the world, and who are empowered by the Holy Spirit to represent Christ in the process.[3]

This is the root of the church's missionary identity. Etymologically, a missionary is one who is "sent," especially one who is sent across boundaries—which makes God the original missionary, crossing every human boundary imaginable in the Incarnation of Jesus Christ. Mission originates in God, not in a church committee. The *missio dei* is God's sending of God's own self into creation, making God both the sender and the one who is sent. A church that fails to respond to the Holy Spirit's boundary-crossing impulse, that fails to share the love of Jesus Christ—God's own self in the world—is unthinkable. As the Swiss theologian Emil Brunner observed, "The church exists by mission as fire exists by burning."[4]

Brunner's simile expands our understanding of John 20:21 in a subtle but crucial way. Mission is not just a matter of geography—i.e., *where* Jesus was sent, into the world. It is also a matter of identification—i.e., *as* Jesus was sent, as a person, and specifically as a person whose love for humanity was of such divine proportions that he chose to share human suffering in order to overcome it with God's death-shattering power. "As the Father has sent me, so I send you," Jesus tells the disciples. In other words, Jesus not only sends the church *where* he was sent; he sends us in the same way that he was sent, as human translations of divine love, people whose words and actions do not grasp for God as much as they reveal a God who grasps for us.

The missionary nature of the church rules out Moralistic Therapeutic Deism as a substitute for Christian faith. In contrast to Moralistic Therapeutic Deism's agenda of personal fulfillment, Christian discipleship enacts the inside-out logic of a self-giving God, whose power is weakness, who deems love worthy of suffering and who promises that life will spring from death. Hall reminds us that the New Testament's portrayal of the church's suffering has more to do with solidarity with those outside the church than with our own "personal or ecclesiastical suffering."[5] Christian scriptures insist that for the church to be true to the story we proclaim, sacrificial love must be part of the equation. Hall believes that this concept of the church is, unfortunately, "so foreign to the average North American congregation that it is hard for us to appropriate or even to hear."[6] Yet every teenager recognizes the equation: True love inspires sacrifice. True love is "to die for." Anything less is not true love.[7] The gospel's central message—that God loves us enough to die for us—severs self-serving spiritualities like Moralistic Therapeutic Deism at the root. Christian identity comes from worshipping a God who loves us enough to suffer on our behalf, and who calls us to enact this kind of love for others: "As the Father has sent me, so I send you."

A FARM WITH NO FENCE

Resisting cultural ideologies like Moralistic Therapeutic Deism is not a matter of keeping these ideologies at arm's length as much as maintaining our focus on Jesus Christ despite pressure to focus on ourselves. An African Christian described it to me this way: "You Americans think of Christianity as a farm with a fence. Your question is, 'Are you inside the fence or outside of it?' We Africans think differently. We think of Christianity as a farm with no fence. Our question is, 'Are you heading towards the farm, or away from it?'" The church's identity is not defined primarily by its edges, but by its *center*: focused on Christ, the sole source of our identity, no intruder poses a threat. No alien hops a fence, because there is no fence. Boundaries are determined by proximity to the Holy Spirit's centripetal pull, not by arbitrary human borders. The truth is that two thousand years of Living Water sloshing over the church's walls has done more to erode than defend them, leaving chinks and gaping holes that let wind and strangers in and that allow the Christian community to go out. The more churches lose our ability to barricade ourselves off from one another, the more God's grace flows through us into the world.

A missional imagination calls us to rethink the nature of the church and the relationship we expect young people to have with Christianity. A missional church follows Christ into the world, and is dispersed but not dissolved into the host culture. The Christian story proclaims a God whose love and forgiveness are so achingly profuse that a human life cannot hold it all. God's love in Jesus Christ is simply not something we can keep to ourselves. As individuals and as a church, the sheer magnitude of divine love bursts our walls of resistance, as God's self-giving love surges into the world through us.

This story of excessive, life-giving grace is the peculiar God-story to which highly devoted Christian teenagers subscribe. The Christian God-story is peculiar both in the sense that it is distinctive and because it is passing strange. The Hebrews clung to a God who delighted in and anguished over creation, to the point that the Jews organized history around God's repeated acts to save them. Christians extend this pattern through Jesus Christ: loving us too much to lose us, God entered human history to save us, once and for all, from ourselves. God paid the ultimate price to win us back, only to trump death in the next hand. But the gospel's distinctiveness does not end there. Equally strange is the gospel's assumption that Christians should love others to this degree. Self-giving love counters every human instinct for self-preservation. It contradicts American culture's insistence on self-fulfillment. Moralistic Therapeutic Deism protects for both self-preservation and self-fulfillment, whereas imitating Christ subverts both.

What matters is not that young people belong to a peculiar story, but to a peculiar story about *God*. Christian identity is not determined by our oddity as a religion, but by Jesus Christ, whose Incarnation is evidence that God is not a distant, disinterested entity but a living, invested, passionate Being who relentlessly loves us, forgives us, and drenches our lives in grace. Christian tradition maintains that the Word of God is not a text, but a person, the divine *Logos*, Jesus Christ. In Christ's hands, the cultural tools of highly devoted teenagers become fields for divine-human interaction, vehicles God uses to enter the world through young people themselves.

Young people like Kelsey.

BECOMING SENT: KELSEY

Kelsey, an upbeat sixteen-year-old Hispanic Baptist from Idaho, talks about her faith with ease. Like other highly devoted teenagers, Kelsey is comfortable relating daily activities to her understanding of the Christian story. A lifelong conservative Protestant, Kelsey thinks the gospel encourages her to engage in actions that reflect the life, death, and resurrection of Jesus Christ. She views her mother as an example of this way of life.[8]

Kelsey's early years were marked by tragedy: at six, she found her father dead from a self-inflicted gunshot wound. One of five children, Kelsey matter-of-factly remembers her mother responding to the suicide by drawing on religion in a way that "really helped our family:"

> You know, God used it in a great way . . . to shape my mom. People were saying . . . you know, those kids, they need counseling, but my Mom just . . . trusted in God and went to the Word. . . . We homeschooled for three years and we did some, like, really good, great curriculum and it was just all focused on the Bible. . . . She [taught us that] God is the father to the fatherless and she really didn't let us become, um, depressed over what had happened. . . . She really kept us going and looking forward.

Kelsey frames both the painful events of her childhood and her outlook on life in general in terms explicitly gleaned from her church. She reads the Bible daily, believes in "not forsaking the fellowship of Christian believers," and helps out with children's programs in her congregation. She talks frequently with her mother about religion. Kelsey's Christian self-understanding sometimes deviates from standard conservative Protestant teaching, especially as she reflects on faith with her mother. At first glance, Kelsey's faith seems superficial, like something she memorized in Sunday School:

> I believe that Jesus is God's son and that he came and he died for me and for everyone else because we're all sinners, and that he didn't stay dead but he rose again and he wants us to come live with him. We just have to admit that we're sinners and believe that he came and died on the cross and rose again, and just choose to follow him.

On first read it is unclear whether Kelsey "owns" these views or has borrowed them from the adults around her. As the interview continues, however, the answer seems to be: both. Kelsey's vocabulary reflects her conservative Protestant repertoire, but unlike most teenagers we interviewed, *because* she uses language to confess her faith, she can examine it—and she does. Because she talks to her mother about religion, she knows her mother's theological commitments and feels permission to make some of her own. She recalls talking with her mom about people unaware of the gospel, and—still drawing on norms of Scriptural authority common among conservative Protestants—she concludes that God must be knowable apart from the church: "In one of the verses in the Bible it says that all the creation shouts 'God,' and so, you know, people can find him through that."

Kelsey articulates no single "conversion experience" but consciously adopts the religious outlook of her family; her attitudes and lifestyle are consistent with the norms of most conservative Protestant congregations. In Eriksonian terms, her identity is maturing but is not yet mature, since she articulates no "crisis" of identity formation (although a case could be made that the ripples from her father's suicide created an extended period of family crisis that enveloped most of her formative years). Kelsey views herself as a child of God and is secure enough to question sacred texts without worrying about losing her spiritual footing. Like other highly devoted teenagers, Kelsey turns especially to an articulated God-story, her church community, and church teachings on vocation and hope as the coordinates for making meaning in her life. For her, the Bible (especially the New Testament) provides an all-embracing narrative of divine care that includes her, her father's death, her family's response to tragedy, and even mundane decisions like health decisions and which CDs to buy. She understands her entire being—body and soul—to be surrendered to God: "If you're saved, you have Christ living in you and so you want to be a good example and . . . our bodies are not our own anymore."

Kelsey's family, her church, and her (Christian) school are faith communities that all enact the Christian story by multiplying opportunities to share Christ's love with others (for instance, Kelsey joined an after school "mission club" that gives water bottles to the opposing team after home games). Like many conservative Protestants, Kelsey equates mission with evangelism, which includes (but is not limited to) "telling people about God." She notes: "I think we're here because God put us here and our ultimate goal . . . is to tell other people about him." But, Kelsey adds, "There's so much more that plays around [telling people about God], in how we should act and what we should do, and why." Her view of Christian service is neither instrumental nor self-serving; she seems shocked that some Christians would undertake service projects primarily because helping others "feels good." When we asked her if her religion had anything to do with her willingness to volunteer in the community, she seemed surprised: "I mean, it's biblical, how can it not be? And so it's not just like, oh, if it feels good do it."

Kelsey's views on God, the church, vocation, and the future bear the marks of the formation she has received from her family, church, and school. At the same time, her faith seems genuinely her own. Christianity is central to her sense of who she is and how she engages the culture around her. She approaches religion neither as an intellectual exercise nor as the uncritical acceptance of a tradition. It is unclear how Kelsey came to appropriate Christianity for herself, though she clearly projects herself into a Christian future. She interprets God's purpose for her life matter-of-factly through her desire to be a teacher, noting simply that Christian faith requires attentiveness to others.

Finally, while Kelsey borrows her mother's theological outlook and her church's theological language, she also shows a willingness to stand her own ground ethically and theologically, and an awareness of—and eagerness to live into—her own agency as a person of faith.[9] (We will return to the importance of such reflexivity in chapter 8.) At this point, she seems to accept her faith community's guidance on matters of love, work, and ideology. She takes for granted Jesus' presence in the world and in her life, and assumes that people who love Jesus are recognizable through practices that demonstrate this love for God and others. The primary example of such a person is her mother, whose sacrifices for her children were, in Kelsey's mind, motivated by faith and made possible by God. At the same time, Kelsey poses questions to the Bible (the presumed authority for conservative Protestants) and does not think such questions threaten her Christian identity. At least one faith community— her family—seems to be a place where such questions may be safely explored.

CHRIST AND THE CULTURAL TOOLKIT

"For the committed adolescent religion is not simply a matter of general identity or affiliation or cognitive belief. Faith for these teenagers is also activated, practiced, and formed through specific religious and spiritual practices."[10] The NSYR did not define religious practices, but studied teenagers' participation in both personal and communal activities that express and strengthen their faith. For our purposes, we can consider faith practices the ongoing human activities of Christian communities by which centuries of people have "imitated" Christ, enacting and taking part in the mystery of his life, death, and resurrection. As we have seen, cultural tools may include attitudes, relationships, symbols, and stories as well as practices. Highly devoted Christian teenagers approach faith as a way of life, not just a system of beliefs—and specifically, as a way of life that practices an ethic of self-giving that reflects Christian views on the nature of God.

Claiming a Creed

Creeds are articulated beliefs. The theologian William Placher defends the importance of creeds by citing Lionel Trilling: "It is probably true that when the dogmatic principle in religion is slighted, religion goes along for awhile on generalized emotion and ethical intention—morality touched by emotion—[but] then it loses the force of Its impulse and even the essence of Its Being." Placher elaborates:

> Even if I have a warm personal relationship with Jesus, I also need an account of what's so special about Jesus to understand why my relationship with him is so important. If I think about dedicating my life to following him, I need an idea about why he's worth following. Without such accounts and ideas, Christian feeling and Christian behavior start to fade to generalized warm fuzziness and social conventions.[11]

When I talk about the "creeds" of highly devoted Christian teenagers, I am referring to what they think and say about God, whether or not it is formally summarized. In other words, do teenagers describe a God who is worth following? Highly devoted Christian teenagers espouse creeds that are unabashedly personal; more often than other teenagers, they describe God as being personally concerned *for* them and powerfully involved *with* them—a stance precisely opposite that of classical deism. If most NSYR teenagers viewed God as a cosmic lifeguard, highly devoted Christian teenagers thought of God more as a divine swimming teacher, powerful enough to save them but also "down in the water with them," buoying them up as they learn to stay afloat. While Moralistic Therapeutic Deist teenagers swapped divine power for divine approval, highly devoted Christian youth refused to separate divine love and power. They commonly described God's power as parental discipline, a justified form of judgment because it is motivated by parental care. "[God is] very forgiving and he's a loving God but he's also a disciplining God," observed Danny, a freshman conservative Protestant from Delaware. Kelsey echoed this theme herself: "[God is] a father. . . . Even though you may not have a Dad, [God] is still a father. He disciplines like a father . . . because he's a friend, he's a provider, he cares."

Unlike most Americans—who overwhelmingly believe that God loves them but who have little confidence in divine power[12]—highly devoted Christian teenagers had varied soteriologies but saw no contradiction between God's transcendence and God's desire for human relationship. Aaron, a sixteen-year-old black Protestant from California, insisted that a personal relationship "between you and God" is the most important thing about religion: "[God] is, like, the highest of the highest, like [it] doesn't go no higher than him."[13] For Teresa, an eighteen-year-old black Baptist from New Orleans, the convergence between divine power and divine love became a way to come to terms with a horrific rape: "[The rapists] had the opportunity to kill me but something just didn't let them. . . . That just opened my eyes. God really loved me because he spared my life. He knew it wasn't my time to go right now, he got something else in store for me."[14]

In contrast to the "divine butler/cosmic therapist" views of God that dominated the NSYR interviews, the parent-like God-images of highly devoted Christian teenagers are significant. Who we are and what we do as religious people are decisively shaped by the kind of God we worship.[15] Israel viewed the God of Abraham and Sarah, Moses and Mary to be worthy of praise because Yahweh's irrefutable power and passionate care warranted their love and respect. Frustrated by social science's tendency to equate religion with rituals and practices, the sociologist Rodney Stark states the obvious: "Gods are the fundamental feature of religions."[16] Stark's cross-cultural analysis of world religions found that religions involving *personal* god-images (gods with personal consciousness who are morally concerned with the universe) influenced the social arrangement of societies more than religions with distant, impersonal god-images. Likewise, religions where people worshipped *powerful* gods influenced social behavior more than religions with friendly, affectionate god-images.[17] In short Stark's research suggests that god-images help sustain the moral order of societies only if people perceive God to be responsive and dependable—or if they think God is powerful enough to reward or punish them.[18]

Stark's study lays bare the impotence of the "nice guy" gods of Moralistic Therapeutic Deism. Christianity solves the dichotomy between personal and powerful god-images by positing a God who is *both*. In Christian theology, (a) God wants to save us, and (b) God can save us (though the word "save" may carry a number of theological accents, from healing to rescue to existential transformation). Christians insist that the God who willingly shared our humanity in Jesus Christ is the same God who vanquishes sin and death. Significantly, love *is* power in Christian tradition. God's love overcomes death in Jesus Christ—and "intoxicated with love" for us, as Catherine of Siena put it, God suffers betrayal, endures crucifixion, and raises the dead.[19]

Belonging to a Community

Sociologists consider a young person's sense of belonging in a religious community to be a more accurate predictor of his or her adult religious involvement than regular church attendance.[20] Caring congregations help teenagers develop what social scientists call "connectedness," a developmental asset accrued from participating in the relational matrix of *authoritative communities*—communities that provide young people with available adults, mutual regard, boundaries, and shared long term objectives.[21] Highly devoted teenagers readily defended Christianity's communal aspects. Aaron, the sixteen-year-old black Protestant we met earlier, said bluntly: "Christianity . . . is not something you just live. You have to practice. You can't live it all by yourself, you need to go to church."

CHARACTERISTICS OF THE
AUTHORITATIVE COMMUNITY

1. It is a social institution that includes children and youth.
2. It treats children as ends in themselves.
3. It is warm and nurturing.
4. It establishes clear limits and expectations.
5. The core of its work is performed largely by nonspecialists.
6. It is multigenerational.
7. It has a long-term focus.
8. It reflects and transmits a shared understanding of what it means to be a good person.
9. It encourages spiritual and religious development.
10. It is philosophically oriented to the equal dignity of all persons and to the principle of love of neighbor.

Congregations are important sources of both interpersonal and spiritual support for highly devoted Christian teenagers. Peer relationships matter. Religious teenagers' closest friends tend to be other religious teenagers (nonreligious teenagers' closest friends are usually other nonreligious teenagers, suggesting that peers reinforce religious identity in both directions).[22] Yet equally important are adults who befriend teenagers. Compared to their peers, young church-attenders are far more likely to have adults in their lives with whom they enjoy talking, and who give them lots of encouragement (79% versus 53% of nonattending teens).[23] Darla, a seventeen-year-old conservative Protestant from South Carolina praised her congregation's "range of age," commenting: "I know if I couldn't talk to my parents about something, I'm pretty comfortable with [other adults in the congregation]." In Indiana, fourteen-year-old Jenni, also a conservative Protestant, agreed: "Since I don't have any grandparents, [older people in our church] are kind of like [that]."

Highly devoted Christian teenagers mentioned pastoral friendships with special affection. While most teenagers in the NSYR (81%) told us they had never talked to a pastor or youth pastor about a personal issue or problem, most highly devoted teenagers did so frequently.[24] Teresa, the eighteen-year-old black Protestant mentioned earlier, said she really liked her pastor's sermons, but later in the interview casually mentioned, "He helped me pass my 'LEAP' . . . the exit exam [for graduation]."

> Besides being a reverend, he's a professor and he deals in business and accounting, so he's good at math. So he said he'll take his time out, maybe like once or twice a week—I'll go over there and he'll help me go over stuff and say, "Look, this is how you do it." . . . He'll be, like, "Now, you try." So he helped me pass my exit exam.

Apparently, Teresa talked to her pastor about many subjects, including her struggles in school. By embodying a holy refusal to let her fall through the cracks, Teresa's pastor symbolized the confidence that she could not muster for herself—and the Christian community's support when other institutions had given up on her.

Yet highly devoted Christian youth viewed their congregations as more than interpersonal support systems.[25] Overwhelmingly, they valued their churches' spiritual as well as social connections. They wanted to be valued by the people in their congregations, but they also longed to belong to God. So they found in their churches evidence of God's confidence in them—a confidence mediated by people who loved and trusted them. Libby, a buoyant, over-involved seventeen-year-old Baptist, rattled off a daunting list of church activities that she apparently loved (and often led). Libby's church provided her with a network of social connections, but she also valued her church for the sense of spiritual belonging it offered:

> [I go to church] a lot of hours a week, like even when there's no church or no one in the church, I still go. I don't know why. I feel so at home in the sanctuary. Um, it's where I belong. I know it is. I can honestly say that. At school, I don't. . . . At church, I can go there and no one is there and I can be by myself and I feel like I've got, I've got a crowd just watching me, and like I know that crowd is angels. I just, you know, you just feel loved. It's great.

Libby experienced an almost primal sense of connection to the cosmos (angels included) in her church, a kind of existential security that comes from being on holy ground. Libby participated in choir tours and mission trips partly because she enjoyed being with friends, but also, she said, because she was on a holy mission, participating in the work of Christ: "We still do a lot of witnessing, like passing out water bottles to people," she said, adding that no one told her to do this. "They're not encouraging us to witness or anything . . . but why pass up an opportunity? You know, you're traveling for the Lord, why not spread it?" Her church was a staging area for being "sent out" to others in Christian love. Having experienced radical acceptance from her faith community, Libby felt morally bound to share this acceptance with others.

Pursuing a Purpose

The NSYR revealed a strong link between young people's levels of religious commitment and the type of moral universes they occupy. Highly devoted teenagers lived within what Smith and Denton describe as a "morally significant universe," in which one's life is "inescapably bound up to a larger framework of consequence."[26]

> One's own single life finds its significance not in relation to itself, but by becoming connected to this larger moral order, by living a life in tune with and reflecting that order. . . . [T]he living out of one's life really means something significant because of the role it somehow plays in helping to perform the larger dramatic narrative. In a morally significant universe, actions really do embody and reflect bigger challenges, struggles, failures, and victories—and all things really are finally going somewhere important.[27]

In short, a morally significant universe is one in which our choices have meanings and consequences beyond themselves. Since being bound to Christ simultaneously means being bound to others, highly devoted teenagers recognize that their decisions have consequences for others, and that the church has a moral responsibility to look after others' well-being.

One surprise in the NSYR was the weak association between Christianity and vocational purpose for mainline Protestant and Catholic young people, whose denominations traditionally emphasize social justice and transformation. Yet mainline Protestant and Catholic youth in the NSYR were less likely to equate moral responsibility with following Jesus Christ, and less likely to occupy "morally significant universes" than their conservative and black Protestant peers. Mainline Protestant and Catholic teenagers, for example, were the *least* likely to report helping others in need (38%), while black Protestant youth (51%) and teenagers with no religious affiliation (47%) were the *most* likely to report helping needy people.[28] The social gospel zeal that has historically characterized mainline Protestant and Catholic theologies seems mostly absent in young people raised in these communities.

Highly devoted Christian teenagers, on the other hand, explicitly sought ways to respond to Christ's mandate to sacrifice on behalf of others: "This is my commandment, that you love one another as I have loved you. No one has greater love than this, to lay down one's life for one's friends" (John 15:12–13). They talked about discovering God's direction for their lives, sometimes associating their future careers with a "calling" (a term mostly used by conservative and black Protestant teenagers). They were quite likely to think about the ethical components of discipleship in terms of concrete, immediate forms of ministry, participating in "mission trips" and "service projects," and living with a general attentiveness toward God and others.[29] Some teenagers shared Kelsey's view that responding to Christ carries specific moral obligations, like "telling people about God." Others had more general ideas about vocation. Libby told us: "I want to make a change. . . . I want people to know that it's okay to step up and make a difference." The important distinction between the objectives of highly devoted Christian teenagers and their peers was simply that highly devoted Christian teenagers did not think about their actions or their futures simply in terms of what *they* wanted. They considered themselves morally bound to contribute to God's purpose in the world.

Harboring Hope

Moralistic Therapeutic Deist teenagers are not a particularly hopeful lot. Their horizons are close; their vision extends as far as personal happiness but not much further (in the NSYR interview transcripts, the specific phrase "feel happy" appeared more than 2,000 times).[30] These youth value churches not as venues for furthering Christ's work on earth or as signs of God's coming reign, but as useful communities that help them feel good about themselves—accomplished largely by communicating a sanitized, culturally cooperative but wildly truncated version of Christianity. Smith and Denton's conclusion is unsurprising: "The actual dominant religion among U.S. teenagers is centrally about feeling good, happy, secure, and at peace, . . . about attaining subjective well-being, being able to resolve problems, and getting along amiably with other people."[31]

Most of the teenagers we interviewed, therefore, were not concerned that they would fail God or suffer consequences for failing God. On the contrary, they assumed that God might fail *them*, so they lowered their hopes accordingly. As long as God demands little, teens are free to invest little; everyone is happy. Smith and Denton pointedly observe,

> It is thus no wonder that so many . . . teenagers are so positive about religion, for the faith many of them have in mind effectively helps to achieve a primary life goal: to feel good and happy about oneself and one's life. It is also no wonder that most teens are so religiously inarticulate. As long as one is happy, why bother with being able to talk about the belief content of one's faith?[32]

Once again, highly devoted Christian teenagers proved the exception to this rule. They countered the hopelessness and cynicism of their peers with a confidence that the world (and their lives in particular) are "going somewhere" good. In fact, this is what Christian eschatology teaches. Because God's future is wide and remarkable, it provides a worthy direction for our lives. For Christians, eschatology is less a story that explains the end of the world than a key to interpreting the present with confidence and hope because God controls the outcome.[33] When a Steelers fan knows that her team has already won the Super Bowl, she can watch reruns of bungled plays without anxiety.

The content of Christian hope was unexplored by the NSYR, but highly devoted youth were far more likely to "think about and plan for the future" compared to religiously disengaged teenagers (87% versus

60%, respectively), and far more likely to never think life is mean-ingless (56% versus 30%).[34] Many highly devoted Christian teenag-ers, especially those from conservative or black Protestant churches, come from faith communities where eschatology is openly discussed. Of course, an articulated eschatology does not mean a theologically sophisticated one; teenagers often sounded like facile optimists (Chris's remark, "I see good things with God in my life" and Libby's flip comment, "[The future] is gonna be great, I know it" were typi-cal). Sometimes they ventured into more reflective territory on the relationship between hope and hardship; Libby told us about pass-ing a church sign while her father was fighting his way back from a near-fatal fishing accident: "[The sign] said, 'God promised a safe landing, not an easy flight.' And I was like, wow, that's so true. And from that moment on, we've had so many more hardships and I know . . . God brings you to it, and he'll get you through it. So my faith is everything." Like most highly devoted teenagers, Libby had little interest in the mechanics of hope; what mattered was her con-fidence that God is actively involved in time, and therefore can be trusted to steer the future—including her personal future—in a good direction.

In short, highly devoted Christian teenagers operationalized Chris-tian hope as a generalized trust that God has the future under control, without showing much familiarity with (or interest in) traditional teachings associated with Christian eschatology, like the return of Jesus Christ, the promise of heaven, and so on. Hope, for the most part, pro-vided highly devoted teenagers with a resource for getting through the present—which in turn gave them confidence that they had the tools necessary to face whatever hardships may lie ahead.

FAITH THAT BEARS FRUIT: MARKS OF CHRISTIAN MATURITY

It seems obvious that one reason highly devoted teenagers may be "doing better" than their peers is that participating in a faith tradi-tion exposes them to cultural tools that have helped generations of people "like them" produce the integrated identity associated with

American adulthood.[35] Christian teenagers are no exception. The Triune God espoused by Christianity is both personal and powerful, qualities associated with moral influence. Churches function as authoritative communities, significant sources of "connectedness" for young people. The call to discipleship invokes a morally significant universe in which actions have consequences for others, and a hopeful future—because God has designed it—is worth investing in.

Yet faith is not measured by the standards of identity formation. Some young people (teenagers with Down syndrome, for instance) face significant developmental challenges yet are remarkably clearheaded about matters of faith. And, of course, it works the other way too. "Foreclosed" religious identities (faith identifications that are imposed, and are neither self-critical nor self-chosen) can masquerade as religious maturity, since identity foreclosure is often a move to appease authority figures.[36] Human development is rarely a straight shot. Most of us lurch our way to maturity, in height and intellect and social awareness—and in matters of faith as well. The adolescent's ego, by definition, is a "work in progress," making adolescents more likely to adopt a "provisional" identity, subject to ongoing revision, than a foreclosed one. Ego exploration depends upon this process of trial and error. Adolescents establish trial selves as a matter of course, discarding or reconstructing the ones that do not fit. Add Christian faith into the equation, and identity is no longer simply a matter of what we do to maintain a coherent sense of self; it is a matter of what Christ does to incorporate us into the coherence of the divine self, transcending the shifting sands of culture and the human lifecycle with a story of divine love offered on our behalf.

How, then, do we assess Christian maturity in young people? One common approach, favored by research like the 2004 Exemplary Youth Ministry study of congregations, is to identify faith *attributes*. Using descriptions of highly committed Christian young people from prior research, the Exemplary Youth Ministry study tried to ascertain qualities of "mature" Christian faith in teenagers. Researchers identified forty-four "assets" (theological commitments, qualities of ministry, and congregational practices) common to 350 theologically and demographically diverse Christian congregations where adolescents consistently demonstrate mature Christian identities (see appendix D). The study concluded that mature Christian young people:

- *Seek spiritual growth, both alone and with others*; they pursue questions, guidance, and commitment through conversation, study, Bible reading, prayer, small groups, retreats, etc.
- *Are keenly aware of God,* and view God as active and present in their own lives, in the lives of others, and in the world
- *Act out of a commitment to faith in Jesus Christ,* privately and publicly, through regular worship, participation in ministry, and leadership in a congregation
- *Make Christian faith a way of life* by recognizing God's "call" and integrating their beliefs into conversation, decisions, and actions in daily life
- *Live lives of service* by being involved in caring for others and addressing injustice and immorality
- *Reach out to others* who are different or in need through prayer, hospitality, conversation, and support
- *Exercise moral responsibility* by living with integrity and utilizing faith in making considered moral decisions
- *Speak publicly about faith* by speaking openly about Jesus Christ and God's participation in their own lives and in the world
- *Possess a positive, hopeful spirit* toward others and toward life.[37]

Yet while these faith attributes offer helpful markers for religious maturity, *Christian* identity is conferred primarily in baptism, not the accumulation of assets. For Christians, identity is a gift, not an achievement, which is why we refer to it as being "born anew." We did not ask to be children of God; baptism merely claims for us what God has already determined, that we are God's beloved, and no human transgression can change that. In baptism, we agree to participate in God's restoration of the divine image in the world, but Christ has already begun this process. All of this makes Christian maturity more complex—and more straightforward—than either cultural tools or Christian attributes imply.

The essential mark of maturity in Christians—as in peach trees—is generativity. Mature faith bears fruit. Mature Christians are branches on which God's love is multiplied and offered for the nourishment of others. As Jesus pointed out, "My Father is glorified by this, that you bear much fruit and become my disciples" (John 15:8). By nurturing and offering the life-giving fruits of the Spirit (e.g., love, joy, peace, patience, kindness, goodness, faithfulness, gentleness, and self-control [Gal. 5:22–23]), we become branches of divine grace, vehicles Christ uses to extend himself to others.

GOD'S PREFERENTIAL OPTION FOR
THE UNLIKELY

This "ethic of giving," as the Catholic theologian Jean Luc Marion calls it, is the telltale sign that God's image is under construction in us. Marion believes that Jesus' suffering love on the cross is an act of God's giving, not an expression of God's being; God's giving precedes God's Being. In fact, for Marion, giving constitutes God's being in the world.[38] The evidence that God's image is being restored in us, as individuals and as a church, is the fact that we give—we give *Christ*, who established the church to bear his fruit in the world. We are, to be sure, flimsy boughs for such abundant fruit. Yet Scripture repeatedly describes God's preferential option for the unlikely as God calls people not for what they have, but for what they lack. Empty hands can receive, empty wombs can be filled, empty tombs can proclaim resurrection—and the unformed selves of adolescents can make room for Christ in ways that are difficult for hardened, formed egos. In fact, God does not ask us to give ourselves to others. God asks us to give *Christ*—who transforms us, dwells within us, fills us with his self-giving love. "It is no longer I who live, but it is Christ who lives in me," says Paul (Gal. 2:20). In the fruits of the Spirit, we offer Christ to others, not some holier version of ourselves.[39]

When we blithely hope that young people will "grow" in their faith, what we usually mean is that we hope that soon their faith will look like ours. The NSYR suggests that we have gotten our wish: the faith of American teenagers *does* look like the faith of their parents, which as we have seen is not an unmitigated blessing. Strangely, the gospels contend that mature believers have more in common with children than adults. "Unless you change and become like little children," Jesus tells his hearers, "you will never enter the kingdom of heaven. Whoever becomes humble like this child is the greatest in the kingdom of heaven" (Matt. 18:3–4). To the puzzled Nicodemus, Jesus says: "No one can see the kingdom of God without being born from above" (John 3:3). Even Paul, who urges us to "put away childish things" in favor of adult-sized righteousness (1 Cor. 13:11; Heb. 5:13–14), recognizes that this kind of maturity comes from relinquishing our selves to Christ, rather than from clinging tightly to who we think we are. What the gospel and Pauline views of spiritual maturity have in common is the theme of increasing surrender, not escalating accomplishment. Emptied of self-importance, poured out for others, the church makes room for Christ, whose grace pulses into the world through those who love Him.

Faith in Jesus Christ is neither a vehicle to cultural power nor to spiritual self-improvement. God has far bigger plans for young people than that. The nineteenth-century journalist and theologian George MacDonald famously compared God's work in human restoration to renovating a cottage (the masculine language is original):

Imagine yourself as a living house. God comes in to rebuild that house. At first, perhaps you can understand what He is doing. He is getting the drains right and stopping the leaks in the roof and so on: you know that those jobs needed doing and so you are not surprised. But presently he starts knocking the house about in a way that hurts abominably and does not seem to make sense. What on earth is He up to? The explanation is that He is building quite a different house from the one you thought of-throwing out a new wing here, putting on an extra floor there, running up towers, making courtyards. You thought you were going to be made into a decent little cottage: but He is building a palace. He intends to come and live in it Himself![40]

Christ's goal is to make us new, not just better—and new life, in saplings or teenagers, has surprising flexibility, strength and resilience.[41] Generative faith possesses unnerving power; churches where young people exhibit highly devoted faith look and act differently than those colonized by Moralistic Therapeutic Deism. Among other things, they are more likely to have full time youth ministers, a variety of programs for teenagers, and opportunities for youth to participate in religious practice and leadership.[42] According to the Exemplary Youth Ministry study, these congregations are also more likely to:

- portray God as living, present and active
- place a high value on scripture
- explain their church's mission, practices and relationships as inspired by "the life and mission of Jesus Christ"
- emphasize spiritual growth, discipleship, and vocation
- promote outreach and mission
- help teens develop "a positive, hopeful spirit," "live out a life of service," and "live a Christian moral life."[43]

These congregations view young people, not as moralistic do-gooders, but as Christ's representatives in the world. Teenagers in faith-supporting congregations do not describe God as a Pez dispenser, delivering good feelings on demand, but as a "living and active presence" in their lives. Adults in these congregations till the soil for consequential faith in young people. Pastors and adult leaders model "the transforming presence of God in life and ministry," and parents engage "in conversations, prayer, Bible reading, and service that nurture faith and life."[44] These congregations invite, cultivate, and nurture faith that bears fruit, yielding new life in and beyond the church.

HOLY MIRRORS

When Robert Fulghum (the Unitarian minister who wrote *Everything I Need to Know I Learned in Kindergarten*) attended a conference where the peace advocate Alexander Papaderos was speaking, he raised his hand when Papaderos asked if there were any questions: "Dr. Papaderos, what is the meaning of life?" Fulghum remembers people laughing as they gathered their belongings to leave.

But Papaderos took the question seriously. He fished out a small round mirror from his wallet as the room shushed. He began to tell about a day when, as a small child in a poor, remote village during World War II, he found the pieces of a broken mirror from a German motorcycle. "I tried to find all the pieces and put them together," he said. "But it was not possible. So I kept only the largest one. This one." He held up the mirror.

> I began to play with it as a boy and became fascinated by the fact that I could reflect light into dark places where the sun would never shine—in deep holes and crevices and dark closets. It became a game for me to get light into the most inaccessible places I could find. I kept the little mirror, and as I went about my growing up, I would take it out in idle moments and continue the challenge of the game. As I became a man, I grew to understand that this was not just a child's game, but a metaphor for what I might do with my life. I came to understand that I am not the light or the source of the light. But light—truth, understanding, knowledge—is there, and it will only shine in many dark places if I reflect it.

Papaderos then looked at Fulghum and concluded, "I am a fragment of a mirror whose whole design and shape I do not know. Nevertheless, with what I have I can reflect light into the dark places of this world. . . . This is what I am about. This is the meaning of my life."[45]

In Christian tradition, cultural tools are more like mirrors than flux capacitors. God has already given the church what we need to reflect Christ to the young people we love. Yet our creed, our communities, our sense of call and hope are useful only if they reflect Christ's Light into the dark places of the world (2 Cor. 3:18). Young people will not develop consequential faith simply by being absorbed into a so-called "Christian" culture (if such a thing is even possible). As we have seen, churches are quite capable of developing deformative cultures of their own, while washing down the gospel with large gulps of rationalization. Consequential Christian faith reflects Christ who, as the missionary historian Andrew Walls explains, "sends his people as he was sent: to be the light to the world, to give healing and hope to the ill, and the weak and the unwanted, to suffer, perhaps unjustly, on behalf of others."[46] With this kind of missional imagination, consequential Christianity turns self-focused spirituality on its head.

5

Missional Imaginations

We Are Not Here for Ourselves

We have no simple answers.
—*Christian Smith with Melinda Denton*

If we are to reach . . . youth, it is precisely this sort of missional
imagination that we need to cultivate and encourage in leaders. Insights
(both good and bad) from cross-cultural mission hold the clues as to
how we go about mission in our own cultures, and not just overseas.
—*Jonny Baker*

Some would argue—maybe you are among them—that Moralistic
Therapeutic Deism is not worth such a fuss. History has seen worse
heresies. We want young people to be happy and feel good about themselves; it is good to help people get along. In an age of global pluralism,
living out religious faith beyond our own spiritual enclaves might cause
insensitive if not perilous divisions. Maybe we should be grateful that
Christianity matters to some young people and stop expecting it to
matter to anyone else.

Maybe. But then ESPN reports a story like this one.[1]

Grapevine, Texas—one of *Money Magazine*'s top 100 "best places to
live" in 2007[2]—is almost 90% white, has a $90,000 median family
income, and award-winning schools like Faith Christian School. Like
most towns in Texas, Grapevine takes its high school football seriously.[3]
Faith's football team, for example, has seventy players, eleven coaches,
the latest equipment, and hordes of involved parents. In November
2008, the Faith Lions were 7–2 going into the game with the Gainesville
State Tornados.

Gainesville State, on the other hand, headed into the game 0–8, having scored only two touchdowns all year. Gainesville's fourteen players wore seven-year-old pads and dilapidated helmets and were escorted by twelve security guards who took off the players' handcuffs before the game. Gainesville State, a maximum security prison north of Dallas, gets its students by court order. Many Tornados have convictions for drugs, assaults, and robberies. Many of their families have disowned them. They play every game on the road.

Before the game, Faith's head coach Kris Hogan had an idea. What if, just for one night, half of the Faith fans cheered for the kids on the opposing team? "Here is the message I want you to send," Hogan wrote in an email to Faith's faithful. "You are just as valuable as any other person on Planet Earth." The Faith fans agreed.

When the Gainesville Tornados took the field, they crashed through a banner made by Faith fans that read "Go Tornados!" The Gainesville players were surprised to find themselves running through a forty-foot spirit line made up of cheering fans. From their benches at the side of the field, the Gainesville team heard two hundred fans on the bleachers behind them, cheering for them by name, led by real cheerleaders (Hogan had recruited the JV squad to cheer for the opposing team). "I thought maybe they were confused," said Alex, a Gainesville lineman. Another lineman, Gerald, said: "We can tell people are a little afraid of us when we come to the games. . . . But these people, they were yellin' for us! By our names!" Gainesville's quarterback and middle linebacker Isaiah shook his head in disbelief. "I never thought I'd hear people cheering for us to hit their kids. . . . But they wanted us to!"

At the end of the game (Faith won, 33–14), the losing team practically danced off the field with their fingers pointing #1 in the air. They gave Gainesville's head coach Mark Williams what ESPN sportswriter Rick Reilly described as the first Gatorade bath in history for a 0–9 coach. When the teams gathered in the middle of the field to pray, Isaiah surprised everybody by asking to lead. ("We had no idea what the kid was going to say," remembers Coach Hogan.) This was Isaiah's prayer: "Lord, I don't know how this happened, so I don't know how to say thank You, but I never would've known there was so many people in the world that cared about us."

As guards escorted the Tornados back to their bus, each player received a bag filled with burgers, fries, candy, a Bible, and an encouraging letter from a Faith player. Before he stepped onto the bus, Williams turned and grabbed Hogan hard by the shoulders: "You'll never know what your people did for these kids tonight. You'll never, ever know." The Gainesville players crowded onto one side of the bus, peering out the windows at an unbelievable sight—people they had never met before smiling at them, waving goodbye, as the bus drove into the night.

It was, in Reilly's words, "rivers running uphill and cats petting dogs"—or, as another Isaiah put it:

The wolf shall live with the lamb, the leopard shall lie down with the kid,
the calf and the lion and the fatling together,
and a little child shall lead them. (Isa. 11:6)

CHURCH IS A WASTE

The church's first witness, as the theologian John Howard Yoder reminds us, is the way we live before the eyes of the watching world.[4] You may recall that, two nights before the Passover, Jesus was having supper at the house of Simon the leper, when in walked a woman with an alabaster jar. She smashed it and poured its precious contents of nard—worth about $35,000 in today's dollars—over Jesus. Biblical scholars widely read her anointing both as a sign of Jesus' impending death and of his reign as Lord, but the disciples missed the symbolism. Thinking about what such a sum would have meant for a local non-profit, the disciples were aghast: "Why was the ointment wasted in this way?" (Mark 14:4).

The word "waste" is important. Presbyterian pastor Emily Anderson reminds us that we hear it again, from the same Greek root, a few chapters earlier, though in that passage the Greek is usually translated as "lose": "Those who lose [waste] their life for my sake, and for the sake of the gospel, will save it" (Mark 8:35).[5] Those who waste their lives for Jesus, who squander their talent on the church, who throw away their lives in ministry—in *youth* ministry, for goodness' sake—will gain it. Following Jesus is a waste. The Bible tells us so.

Yet the history of the church is one of backwards, disproportional influence. A wasted jar of nard, a lamb among wolves, the Faith Lions cheering the Gainesville Tornados, cats petting dogs—these are not the result of some kind of religious magical thinking. They are the impossible yet real consequences of what Daniel Berrigan calls the "upside down" hermeneutic of the gospel that participates in the suffering love of Jesus Christ.[6] We don't know why Christ gave himself in this way. We don't know how to say thank you. We never would have known we were cared for this much—enough to be worth sacrificing for, enough to be worth dying for.

Wasteful love transforms us into bearers of such love for others. As God pours out God's own self in Jesus Christ, the Holy Spirit floods us, flowing into the world through us (and often in spite of us). When we realize what God has done, when we discover that Christ has bound himself to us so radically that nothing can separate us from him, when we gratefully reciprocate by fastening our lives to his life, death and resurrection in baptism, the Holy Spirit empowers us to consciously participate in the life of God. Where Jesus goes, we go; when Christ suffers, we suffer; what God gives, we give. Our lives are so bound up with Christ that the Holy Spirit gives us more of God's love than we can fathom or hold. This is how we become Christ's witnesses: awash in God's wasteful love, overwhelmed by divine grace, we cannot keep quiet and we cannot keep it to ourselves. Such reckless, Godly giving is wasteful, but never wasted. This is how God enters the world: through people like us.

Witnessing to Christ, in these terms, presents a rather stark contrast to Christian attempts to dump Jesus onto people or to hand him over (as though he is ours to give) like a family heirloom that has historical or sentimental significance but is otherwise inert. Mission means participating in the very life of God, taking part in the "to die for" love of Jesus Christ, which is the purpose of the church. Tradition calls the church the Bride of Christ because, at our missional best, the church acts like a smitten lover: overwhelmed with awe at being loved in this way, our words and actions overflow with gratitude that Christ has bound himself to us and invited us—us!—to bear God's fruit in the world.

Missional churches invest in the gospel's wasteful, reckless grace. This is no guarantee of happy endings, at least not in the short run; the Greek word for "witness" is *marturia* (martyr), an etymology that is terrifyingly contemporary. While Christian witness never entails harming others, it does mean accepting Christ's invitation to "come and die," as Bonhoeffer put it—not always metaphorically.[7] Instead of lowest-common-denominator Christianity in which everyone is happy if people just get along, missional churches ratchet up expectations by consciously striving to point out, interpret, and embody the excessive nature of God's love. They intentionally, willingly, joyfully practice Jesus' last-shall-be-first ethic of giving and purposefully refrain from doing much in the way of institutional self-preservation. For the record, missional churches are also happy when people get along, though Christianity's tendency to upset social roles with unmerited grace inevitably ruffles feathers (especially the feathers of people in charge). The Christian story reminds us that the price of practicing Jesus' last-shall-be-first ethic of love can be execution. Nothing undercuts the human instinct of self-preservation like sacrificial love.

Christian love is messy and risky. It is a kind of indecorous love, like the prodigal father who literally throws himself on his smelly, wayward son who returns home; an imprudent love, like that of a shepherd who leaves ninety-nine sheep in order to go search for one directionally challenged one; a spendthrift love, like the kind that makes people deny themselves and take up their crosses to follow Jesus. Once, people could not talk about the church without meaning this kind of self-giving love, in which Christ is the self offered (Acts 2:41–47). Once, the church was known for lavish grace, reckless hospitality, utter devotion to Jesus Christ as God-with-us. Once, people viewed the church as being shackled to the *missio dei*, the extraordinary measures God took to woo us back into God's arms through the Incarnation. Yet as the NSYR dramatically demonstrates, today it is not only possible to think about the church apart from the mission of God, it is now *normative* to do so—even for young people who call themselves Christians.

MISSION AS INCARNATION

Every church is called to be a "missional church." The fact that we have turned the word "mission" into an adjective testifies to the American church's frayed ecclesiology. A nonmissional church is not a church in the first place, but in a culture largely devoid of a theological vocabulary, this language has become necessary to remind us that the church exists not for ourselves, but for the world. Karl Barth called the church "the missionary community," and viewed witness as the litmus test for determining "whether the Christian is really a Christian and the Christian community the Christian community."[8] Yet we persistently view mission, not as the identity of the church but as an instrument of it. The practical theologian Alan Hirsch points out that while "we frequently say 'the church has a mission,' according to missional theology a more correct statement would be '[God's] mission has a church.'"[9] The church's identity, in other words, is revealed in our fidelity to the mission of God.

I've been told that when FBI agents are learning to detect a counterfeit bill, they do not spend most of their time studying counterfeits. Instead, they memorize the original. By internalizing the weight, smell, and look of a real dollar bill, they can spot a fake almost intuitively, without having to stop and analyze it. Christian formation requires a similar familiarity with the God-story of Jesus Christ: young people who know the shape, feel, and look of the gospel can discern the cruciform pattern of God's activity in the world—just as they can readily spot spiritual counterfeits that masquerade as vaguely comforting creeds, communities, calls, and hopes, but that fall short of the gospel. For the church to convey the Christian story with fidelity, we must first become the church this story calls for. As missiologist Lesslie Newbigin explains, the church's most convincing witness is our authenticity:

> If the gospel is to be understood. . . . if it is to be received as something which communicates the truth about the real human situation, if it is as we say "to make sense," it has to be communicated in the language of those to whom it is addressed and it has to be clothed in symbols which are meaningful to them. And since the gospel does not come as a disembodied message, but as the message of a community which claims to live by it and which invites others to adhere to it, the community's life must be so ordered that "it makes sense" to those who are so invited. It must, as we say, "come alive." Those to whom it is addressed must be able to say, "Yes, I see."[10]

Newbigin's concern was that the church never separate mission from Incarnation, God-made-flesh sent into the world. The point of God's Incarnation was mission, the sending of God-as-love into creation, which created the template for the church's missional way of life. As far back as Tertullian, the early church enacted such a curiously counter-cultural way of life that when nonbelievers saw the way Christians lived as a community, they were compelled to see Christianity's "brand" as the practice of a special love. Tertullian described nonbelievers' reaction to the early Christian community: "'See,' they say, 'how they love one another.' . . . We who have become mingled in mind and soul have no hesitation about sharing what we have. Everything is in common among us—except our wives."[11]

Because the church in the second and third centuries maintained a parallel existence with other faiths in a multireligious culture, Christian identity depended upon a radical focus on Jesus, even while maintaining contact with people of other worldviews. The Christian community's distinctive eschatological focus, and specific practices that maintained this focus by enacting a cruciform-shaped way of life patterned on Jesus' life, death, and resurrection, took for granted the idea that embodying God's love was a vehicle through which the Holy Spirit worked in the world. Living as "little Christs," as Luther later put it, made the word mission all but unnecessary, until the sixteenth-century missionary movement claimed it for Christendom.[12] Originally, church *implied* mission; it was impossible to think of one without the other. Not until mission became a political instrument did it acquire the territorial connotation (and provincial baggage) that soon overshadowed its identification with God's sending of Jesus Christ.

MISSION FOR POST-CHRISTENDOM: TRANSLATION, NOT CONQUEST

American young people's experience of religious culture is less like the overarching Christendom of the Roman Empire, dominated by one religious perspective to the point of rendering most other religions invisible, and more like the Hellenistic pluralism of the New

Testament, or the multireligious world of ancient Israel. Both the Hebrew and Christian scriptures describe a culture where multiple religious communities coexisted, converged, and diverged as Israel continually renegotiated her relationship with the surrounding culture in light of her distinctive understanding of Yahweh.[13] As the missional historian Lamin Sanneh explains, "The one God was a part of, rather than apart from, one's formation in culture and society. . . . Human beings were given a double heritage, an earthly and a heavenly one." As a result, says Sanneh, being a Christian in the Roman Empire involved a "reciprocal encounter of give-and-take, not a prickly exceptionalism."[14]

Many missiologists notice parallels between the cultural pluralism surrounding ancient Israel and the early church, and the cultural milieu of twenty-first century American Christianity—suggesting that contemporary churches can learn from the cultural attitudes of our ancestors. Andrew Walls sees today's cultural pluralism as an opportunity for churches to reconsider colonial (mis)understandings of mission as territorial, theological, or ideological conquests:

> The territorial "from-to" idea that underlay the older missionary movement has to give way to a concept far more like that of Christians within the Roman Empire in the second and third centuries: parallel presences in different circles and at different levels, each seeking to penetrate within and beyond its circle. This does not prevent movement and interchange and enterprise . . . but it forces revision of concepts, images, attitudes and methods that arose from the presence of a Christendom that no longer exists.[15]

In the Anglican bishops' 2004 report *The Mission-Shaped Church*, British church leaders proposed recasting the future of the Church of England exactly as Walls describes. "Inviting people back to the church as we know it may be an effective mission strategy for reaching [some of] the population," the report ventured, but "it is misconceived to assume that this represents a coherent mission approach for the majority of the population for whom church as we know it is peripheral, obscure, confusing, or irrelevant."[16] The bishops explicitly sought to reframe mission in terms of culture, not geography:

[We] aim to follow the pattern of the incarnation—to be with people where they are, how they are. The word "where" in that sentence suggests geography and territory—being in a particular place and location. . . . Today, it might help to say that we must be with people how they are. "How" is a word that suggests connection beyond geography and locality—connecting with people's culture, values, lifestyle and networks, as well as with their location. . . . A geographical approach alone is not sufficient.[17]

Interestingly, youth ministry has already made this shift. Recognizing postmodernity and popular culture as the natural habitats of teenagers, missional language finds a ready hearing among youth leaders. Adults in youth ministry have long viewed themselves as missionaries to an alien culture, a special breed of theological anthropologists who must learn the language, taboos, artifacts, and rituals of the teenage universe in order to make the gospel accessible to them.[18] Seeking to imitate God's own missional strategies, youth ministers (and youth ministry literature) overwhelmingly advocate incarnational ministries with young people—with varying degrees of theological sophistication and success. What these efforts share is the conviction that God employs human beings as vehicles of divine love. Just as God came alongside us in the person of Jesus Christ, we best represent Christ with young people by coming alongside them as envoys of his unconditional love.[19]

Not every youth ministry does this well, of course; the strategy easily devolves into pointing to ourselves instead of Jesus, or into thinly-disguised efforts to co-opt teenagers into coming to youth group or taking up "our" brand of Christianity. Most youth ministries—even those with strong missional leadership—capitulate to the culture of the sponsoring congregation over time (between the high percentage of short-term volunteers, the high turnover of youth ministers, and the graduation rates of teenagers themselves, pastoral continuity is extremely difficult to maintain in youth ministry). Still, youth ministry offers the American church a well-stocked laboratory for experimenting with incarnational missiology at home, as we seek to follow Jesus into the developmental and cultural spaces of adolescence.

If you were to visit Outreach Red Bank (ORB), a youth outreach-turned-congregation on the Jersey shore, you would see one such experiment under way.

A COMMUNITY OF GRATEFUL PEOPLE

You have to look hard to find a Moralistic Therapeutic Deist among the youth—or the adults—who worship at ORB. What began as an outreach to homeless teenagers in a downtown park now supports a pastoral staff, a church nursery, and seminary interns; on Sunday mornings an eclectic congregation of retirees, working-class families, young professionals, and teenagers straight out of detention worship together in a borrowed movie theater.[20] Curious about the ministry's appeal to teenagers, parents began to visit ORB as well, and many of them stayed. Last summer, the pastor spoke to me about his biggest problem in youth ministry: "We've got too many parents involved."

ORB is a missional church. To be clear, ORB did not set out to become a missional church or a church at all; most people in the congregation would not know the term "missional." ORB grew out of a small band of praying Presbyterians, young adults from a local congregation who discerned a call to befriend struggling teenagers in their town. ORB's participants consciously look for ways to confess Christ with young people in Red Bank, both in word and deed.[21] Shunning the term "youth church" (ORB's goal has never been to entertain disaffected teenagers), ORB refers to itself as a "grateful community" where people of all ages pray together to discern where Christ is leading them—and so far, that has meant extending Christian friendship to marginalized young people, whether or not youth return the favor.

ORB's ministries tilt unmistakably toward teenagers (as I write this, their website is advertising "The Prom from Outer Space"). But ORB considers itself a mission more than a youth group, a ministry more than a church. ORB has no members, owns no building, operates on a shoestring, and generally earns its reputation for being on the edge organizationally, liturgically, and financially. Much of ORB's appeal lies in the inspired passion of the pastor, Christian Andrews, whose part-time job during seminary evolved into a full-time pastorate as ORB blossomed into a multigenerational congregation. Andrews keeps his vocation (and the attention ORB regularly receives from curious researchers and reporters) in perspective by devouring Karl Barth's *Church Dogmatics* and the Bible, cover to cover, a couple of times a year.

And this is key. In practice, Andrews serves less as the pastor-in-charge than as chief bard, a storyteller-in-residence who is more interested in creating a culture than a congregation as he immerses young people in the origin stories of the Christian community. Andrews and his wife Michelle (a seminary graduate with pastoral smarts of her own) invest heavily in teaching, preaching, prayer, and welcome, cultivating a voracious theological curiosity—and a contagious affection for Karl Barth—in ORB's teenagers and young adult leaders. It does not seem to occur to anyone that teenagers do not normally lead churches; young people at ORB routinely initiate ministry and are integral to the community's leadership. For most of these youth, ORB is the only church they have ever known, and like teenagers everywhere, they assume that their church is like all churches. Doesn't every church gather as a community of effusively grateful people? Don't all youth come together to study Barth and the Bible, and don't all youth leaders lavishly befriend teenagers, whether or not kids come to church? Don't all Christians invite strangers home for dinner, raise money for fire victims, and prayerfully serve the sad, the sick, and the lonely to the point of personal sacrifice? Isn't every church a missional church?

ORB is not yet a decade old, and it remains to be seen if it can weather the pressures of becoming a mature Christian congregation. But so far the community seems to have sidestepped Moralistic Therapeutic Deism, countering the narcissism of American culture with a strong missional ecclesiology. Faith at ORB is "consequential" because no one at ORB is there for his or her own entertainment. Teenagers' cultural toolkits are regularly stocked with Christianity's peculiar God-story, and young people belong to a body of believers that tries to enact the Christian story in their community. Most teenagers at ORB come away convinced that God is up to something good in the world, through Christ and through them.[22]

Missional churches like ORB seldom spring from church growth strategies. Their purpose is not to *grow* the church or to *serve* the church, but to *be* the church. Many missional congregations begin like ORB did, somewhat by accident, thanks to a handful of Christians who try out a shared way of life that they hope reflects the gospel as they address a particular set of needs in their community. Because missional churches tend to be structurally agile, they often rub shoulders with other local youth-serving institutions like schools, law enforcement, the media, and politics. At the same time, their communal life is intentionally patterned after Christ's life, death, and resurrection. Both liturgically and pastorally, missional churches cultivate the cruciform practices of Christian communities everywhere: worshipping, praying, studying Scripture together, reaching out to strangers, resisting injustice and sharing meals and livelihoods.

In short, the goal of missional churches is to imitate Christ in context, to participate in *anamnesis*, a sacramental term that means "re-membering" (putting back together something that has come apart). As communities of memory, missional churches seek to re-member God's overwhelming love by enacting it in human form, whenever the community gathers and wherever God's people are sent. The model for this re-membering is the Eucharist, the church's celebration of the One who re-members us by incorporating our lives into the life of God. What we do "in remembrance" of Jesus Christ in the Eucharist puts us together again as well, transforming our brokenness into Christ's one Body. And here is the missional part: every time we do this, God enters the world again in human form, this time through us.

MISSION IS NOT A TRIP

While ministries like ORB point us in the direction of a missional imagination, in practice most of youth ministry's missiological leanings are too haphazard to operate as a coherent approach to discipleship formation, and too intuitive to avoid getting absorbed by other congregational agendas. Like all research and development departments, youth ministry's experiments with mission have a high failure rate. So while youth ministry provides a promising laboratory for test-driving missional ecclesiologies, it may also unwittingly perpetuate anemic understandings of mission and witness. Ask teenagers in a church youth group what they mean by mission, and most of them will tell you about a hot week in July when they traveled to a poverty-stricken community to do home repair, lead Bible school, and (theoretically) help those who are culturally and/or economically "other."

For all of their benefits (and I am among those who think they have some), we would do well to admit that these trips' primary beneficiaries are the middle-class teenagers who can afford to take them (more on this in chapter 8). Mission is not a trip or a youth activity, a silent cousin to evangelism, or an optional model of youth ministry. Mission is the business that congregations are in.[23] Christ views young people as participants in God's mission rather than as targets of ours. God does not send out a few teenagers in a church van to represent Christ in the world on behalf of the church; God sends the whole church. A missional imagination assumes that young people take part in the church's mission—that every Christian teenager is a missionary called to translate the gospel across boundaries, not because she is capable or even interested, but because she is *baptized* and is therefore sent into the world as Christ's envoy. The more teenagers tell this story, the more it starts to "tell them." In other words, as the Holy Spirit aligns young people's lives with the gospel and empowers them to proclaim and enact Christ's embrace, a missional imagination takes root: teenagers begin to view the world as a place where God acts, and to see themselves as participants in God's action.

This is what an incarnational view of mission looks like: the human translation of divine action in the world. If we take the Incarnation seriously, mission becomes more like translation than ideological, territorial, or even spiritual conquest. God models translation by pouring out the divine self into human form; as Walls puts it, "The Incarnation is God's perfect translation."[24] God is an unapologetic locavore, using local means (human biology, local customs and languages, and cultural institutions like families and religious communities) to translate the good news of salvation into human form. And then, Christ sends us into the world as translations of God's love as well—"lesser translations, to be sure," says Walls—but translations nonetheless.[25]

Walls picks up the incarnational significance of translation. While words matter to Christian faith (see chapter 7), communicating the gospel has never relied solely on linguistics, which allows the church to put down anchor in any culture. Lamin Sanneh views the gospel's translatability as one of Christianity's signature qualities. Unlike Islam, he observes, "Christianity spread as a religion without the language of its founder":

Without a revealed language and without even the language of Jesus, Christianity invested in idioms and cultures that existed for purposes other than Christianity. . . . Being a translated religion, Christian teaching was received and framed in the terms of its host culture; by feeding off the diverse cultural streams it encountered, the religion became multicultural. The local idiom became a chosen vessel. . . . Local versatility animated the mission movement.[26]

For missiologists like Walls and Sanneh, mission simply means translating God's love in human form, putting every cultural tool—stories, symbols, attitudes, language, practices, patterns of life—at the gospel's disposal. To be "little Christs" means allowing God to become Incarnate in our own lives as we smuggle divine grace into the world.

The reason parents, pastors, and youth ministers should take Walls's theory of mission-as-translation to heart is simple: it is not just about witnessing to the gospel in new locales. Translation is how we hand on faith to our children. The principles that describe the gospel's transmission across cultures could just as easily describe the way we ferry faith across generations. Unlike other great world religions, Walls points out, the gospel has no native culture—or generation. The church freely follows the Holy Spirit's movement across boundaries, disestablishing itself in one culture as it becomes established in another. Of course, Walls is a historian, not a youth minister (and no one is more surprised than Walls to find himself advising the church on youth ministry).[27] Yet Walls's depiction of the "trans*mission*" of faith throughout the world also describes catechesis, the three-dimensional handing on of the gospel to faith's newcomers, as they hear the gospel reframed for their own cultural toolkits.

Here is where youth ministry offers hope to a church desperate for a voice that can speak to global postmodernity. In a culture where a domain refers to a webpage, not a kingdom, understanding mission geographically is not enough. God calls the church to bear Christ across every boundary, which includes but exceeds topography. We are called to follow Christ not only into the "where" but into the "how" and "who" of human existence—into the cultural toolkits we use to make sense of our lives. Parents, youth ministers, and congregations embody the church's missional imagination by transmitting the gospel across generations as well as cultures, translating God's self-giving love for young people through the medium of our own lives—lives that are remembered by Christ every time we remember him.

TRANSLATING FAITH: THE MISSIONARY PRINCIPLES OF THE GOSPEL

For Andrew Walls, the movement of faith in Christian history—the translation of the gospel, both literally and figuratively—replicates two "missionary principles" of the Incarnation itself: the *indigenizing principle* and the *pilgrim principle*. The indigenizing principle maintains that Christ makes his home among us, accepting us as we are, becoming "one of us," fully translated into human terms, fully participating in human culture. In this way the Incarnation enacts God's radical acceptance of humanity, and exhibits a divine willingness to "meet us where we live," sinners that we are. As Walls notes, God does not wait for us to "tidy up our ideas" or our behavior before accepting us into God's family.[28] God's unexpected arrival in our neighborhood—God-as-human, born into poverty as a Jew in Judea, with relatives and friends and trips to the synagogue for religious instruction—demonstrates the divine acceptance of the human condition, suffering included. Left to our own devices, the indigenizing principle would fall into uncritical enculturation; yet the basic premise of Christ's unconditional acceptance is inescapable. God takes us as we are, along with all our partners, our biases, our blind spots, and our baggage. God works with all of it. (see table 5.1)

At the same time, Christ does not leave us as he finds us. "Not only does God in Christ take people as they are," writes Walls. "[Christ] also takes them in order to transform them into what He wants them to be."[29] The pilgrim principle, therefore, ejects us from our comfort zones so we can follow Jesus into new terrain. Unsettling though it may be, no locked door, and no locked heart, can stop Christ's decision to come to us. Ignoring the bolted entry, Jesus entered the Upper Room on Easter evening not to settle the disciples but to send them: "As the Father has sent me, so I send you" (John 20:21). The pilgrim principle represents God's radical challenge to us to follow Jesus by going out of our comfort

TABLE 5.1. Missional Practices for Youth Ministry

Missional principle	Indigenizing principle	Pilgrim principle	Liminal principle
Divine action enacted	Christ's acceptance	Christ's call	Christ's transformation
Discipleship goal	Translation	Testimony	Detachment
Educational strategy	Participative learning	Situated learning	Transformative learning
Congregational practices	"Behind the wall" conversations *e.g., teaching for catechesis* "On the wall" conversations *e.g., teaching for cultural literacy*	Spiritual apprenticeships *e.g., mentoring* Faith immersions *e.g., camps, retreats*	Creating space for human encounter *e.g., hospitality, outreach* Creating space for Divine Encounter *e.g., prayer, pilgrimage*

zones to others who inevitably see Jesus from a different perspective—which has the effect of enlarging our perspective as well. In human hands alone, the pilgrim principle would disintegrate into triumphalism, encouraging our tendency to enter new situations as sanctimonious know-it-alls. Yet the pilgrim's job is to confess, not convince. As the missiologist Darrell Guder puts it, "The biblical emphasis is upon sowing, not harvesting. It is upon testifying, not sentencing. Witnesses remain witnesses, and they do not move over to the judge's seat."[30]

To participate in God's own sending of Jesus Christ, youth ministry must attend to both missionary principles of the Incarnation: God's coming to us and God's sending of us, God's blessing and God's calling, God's radical acceptance and God's radical challenge. Let's read this passage again:

> When it was evening on that day, the first day of the week, and the doors of the house where the disciples had met were locked for fear of the Jews, Jesus came and stood among them and said, "Peace be with you." After he said this, he showed them his hands and his side. Then the disciples rejoiced when they saw the Lord. Jesus said to them again, "Peace be with you. As the Father has sent me, so I send you." When he had said this, he breathed on them and said to them, "Receive the Holy Spirit. If you forgive the sins of any, they are forgiven them; if you retain the sins of any, they are retained." (John 20:19–23)

There it is, in the middle of verse 20: "*Then.*" An unnoticeable word, maybe, unless you are a parent, or a pastor, or anyone who works with teenagers—but there it is, a delayed reaction, the lapse that occurs between telling a teenager she is beautiful and having her believe it; the interval between showing up at the high school gym and having your player, ready for a free throw, notice that you are there; the space between hearing the good news and responding to it. Jesus shows up, speaks up, shows the disciples his scars—*then* they reacted. A liminal nanosecond in John 20, but a season of life for many of us: the gap between recognizing Christ's coming and Christ's sending. Jesus could have grabbed the disciples (or us) by the scruff of the neck, flinging them into the world to proclaim his resurrection right then and there, but he doesn't. He waits. Between Christ's coming and Christ's sending, Jesus waits for us to recognize him, and for us to rejoice that God's good news, after all that we have done to deny it, has come to *us*. As the dispirited disciples dangle in their God-given in-between, Jesus waits . . . and *then*: rejoicing! It dawns on them that God's promise is true, the One they love is alive, the story they are part of is far, far bigger than they ever imagined.

The very fact that the gospel writer records this less-than-immediate recognition (it is more prominent in the story than that tricky business of how Jesus slipped in through the locked doors) underscores the moment's significance. It must have been part of what people remembered, and recounted, when they retold the story of that Easter night. In this moment of grace, of divine waiting—the gospel's *liminal principle* in action—God remains with us. This paradoxical place, where Christ woos us as he waits for us, is marked by revelation, recognition, and rejoicing—and it is where an enormous amount of youth ministry takes place. Teenagers dangle daily in liminality; every adolescent is suspended between childhood and adulthood, not quite the person he was but not yet the person he will become. In postmodern circles, many argue that young people experience liminality as a more or less permanent state.[31] Yet God is active in this unclaimed, interstitial moment. The gospel's liminal principle represents Christ's ongoing revelation as he expectantly waits for us to recognize him and rejoice.

Postmoderns are quick to notice that experience trumps authority in the scene. When no one reacts to Jesus' presence in the Upper Room, he does not raise his voice or resort to theatrics (or loud music or humorous skits) to get the disciples' attention. He shows them God's wounds. It takes a first-hand encounter with Jesus' suffering to do what Jesus' miraculous entry and assuring words did not do: awaken the disciples to the fact of Jesus' resurrection and presence. To be sure, evidence is not devotion's highest form of proof; later in the passage Jesus admonishes Thomas for believing only after touching Jesus' wounds (John 20:29). But for Christians, revelation begins not with lofty assertions of God's power but with the fact of God's suffering in the world. Ultimately, coming to terms with the resurrection requires facing the fact of crucifixion, which explains why young people often recognize Christ's presence most clearly when they confront God's wounds in human suffering.

For a moment in the passage, Jesus waits as the disciples seem to experience him as a disorienting but unrecognized presence—probably a fair description of most divine-human encounters, at least as they are portrayed in the Bible. Revelation often accompanies a decentering experience that jars us from our habituated religious expectations and ecclesial comas. Like us, the disciples do not seem to notice Christ, although he is present; they do not seem to hear his words, although he is speaking directly to them. Interestingly, the passage is situated between the church's archetypal story of faith (Mary recognizing Jesus in the garden by the tomb) and the church's most famous story of doubt (Thomas's refusal to believe the news of the risen Christ unless he sees Jesus' wounds for himself). Maybe the disciples are just dolts, ignorant of what is unfolding before them. Or maybe, like us, they simply cannot fathom that Jesus would desire them so deeply that death and betrayal cannot keep him away. Maybe we, the church, miss the Holy standing right in front of us just because we are too nearsighted to notice that in between faith and doubt, in between God's call and our response, Jesus waits.

Liminal spaces are known for their blurry transience and ambiguity. We think of liminal spaces as shadowy interludes like dusk and dawn, foggy moments between waking and sleeping, boundaries like horizons and waters' edges, places where we reach for shells that disappear, moments when we forget our most vivid dreams. Yet wherever two worlds collide, unexpected gifts wash up on shore. So liminal spaces are also places of creativity, insight, and celebration, and in many cultures, they are revered as sites of divine inbreaking and transformation. When we accompany young people through decentering experiences like acts of prayer and mercy—contexts in which they glimpse, however briefly, God's wounds—we invoke the gospel's liminal principle. As Christ waits, we wait, hoping they will recognize and rejoice at Christ's presence. We already know what young people are still discovering: Jesus is prone to meeting us while we are "in between" or *en route*—whether the road we travel is to Damascus or Emmaus or adulthood, whether we recognize Jesus as our companion or not.

MISSIONAL IMAGINATION: AN ANTIDOTE TO MORALISTIC THERAPEUTIC DEISM

Moralistic Therapeutic Deism is the unholy residue of a church that has lost its missional imagination. In stark contrast to institutions colonized by Moralistic Therapeutic Deism, missional communities do not exist primarily to perpetuate themselves. But without the antidote of God's self-giving love revealed in the life, death, and resurrection of Jesus Christ, our culture of self-fulfillment inevitably seeps into congregations and clouds our missional imaginations. No wonder consumer-oriented American teenagers accept Moralistic Therapeutic Deism as the product churches peddle, unaware that it represents an emaciated faith, a flimsy facsimile of the grace-full life that participates in the mission of God.[32] To the extent that Moralistic Therapeutic Deism represents a so-called religious point of view, teenagers do not object to it; nearly half of them find religion personally useful and most laud its social benefits. A religion aimed at self-fulfillment, if not compelling, is at least understandable.

Yet Christianity's peculiar God-story urges self-relinquishment not self-fulfillment, sacrifice not stature—an ethic of love "which seeketh not its own," as Reinhold Niebuhr observed.[33] Only self-emptying faith makes room for the overwhelming grace of God, patterned after Jesus himself: "Let the same mind be in you that was in Christ Jesus," Paul counseled the Philippians, "who, though he was in the form of God, did not regard equality with God as something to be exploited, but emptied himself, taking the form of a slave, being born in human likeness" (Phil. 2:5–7). Faith does not mean mimicking Jesus, but participating in his self-giving love—not because we have somehow chosen to be like him, but because, incredibly, God has chosen to become like us.

THE RISKS OF TRANSMISSION

As we will see in chapter 6, to view mission as translation, to communicate God's excess in the name of self-giving love, requires profound humility. Translation does not seek to insert new information into a conversation; it aims to make plain a conversation already in progress. Handing on faith with young people is not a matter of giving them Jesus, as though he were ours to give, or as though Christ's presence in their lives depends on us. Approaching mission as translation assumes Christ is already present in their lives, even those without noticeable faith, long before we arrive on the scene. Nor is translation lifeless replication. The gospel of Jesus Christ is God's living translation—and requires living translations as well, people who offer us fresh perspectives on Jesus, on young people, and on the church itself.

If you had attended the Faith Lions–Gainesville Tornados game in November 2009—a year after Kris Hogan's missional brainstorm—you would have seen a tradition beginning to take shape. The Gainesville Tornados still ended the season 1–8. But when they came to Grapevine, they ran through a one hundred and fifty foot spirit line, found "GSS" painted in team colors in one of the end zones, and played the game before four thousand cheering fans (not to mention television and film crews). Just as important, several other high schools on the game roster, having read about Faith's generosity, replicated the gesture when the Tornados played at their schools. The missional imagination of the parents and students at Faith Christian High School bore fruit; game after game multiplied Christ's self-giving love. As sportswriter David Thomas put it, "If a Texas high school football field can be a place where unconditional love can be offered—and received—then any place can."[34]

At the end of the day, making disciples requires *incarnation*, not cultural adaptation. Walls acknowledges wild disparity in gospel translations; using a now-famous analogy, he wonders aloud how a time-traveling space visitor would ever guess that eleventh-century Celtic monks singing in ice water, nineteenth-century Bible-brandishing Protestants in England, and twenty-first-century dancing Pentecostals in Nigeria (or high school football fans in Texas, for that matter) all belong to the same tradition? His answer: every Christian community shares a certain amount of ecclesial DNA, which emerges in ways that are unique to every body of believers. We follow the same sacred writings, pray to the same Triune God, use bread, wine, and water in the same special ways, and claim to be mystically related to one another. Above all, concludes Walls, one unvarying theme unites communities that call themselves Christian: "The person of Jesus called the Christ has ultimate significance."[35] Any cultural practice or ideology, including Moralistic Therapeutic Deism, that compromises the ultimate significance of "the person of Jesus called the Christ" compromises the church's missional identity.

The good news is that congregations do have tools for cultivating consequential faith, even if they are rusty from disuse. Practices like *translation, testimony*, and *detachment* figure prominently in missionary history. As the next three chapters demonstrate, these practices help young people resist Moralistic Therapeutic Deism by seeding the missional imaginations necessary for consequential Christian faith. In so doing, they remind us how to be a church that sends young people out rather than ropes young people in.

PART 3

Cultivating Consequential Faith

When opportunity knocks the wise will build bridges while
the timorous will build dams. It is a new day.
—*Lamin O. Sanneh*

6

Parents Matter Most

The Art of Translation

The best way to get most youth more involved in and serious about
their faith communities is to get their parents more involved in and
serious about their faith communities.
—*Christian Smith with Melinda Denton*

It is always a "miracle" when the conversation behind the wall
decisively impinges on the conversation at the wall, when the
imagination of the community can break the dominant rationality.
Miraculous turns are, in fact, what church education is about.
—*Walter Brueggemann*

In April 2005, when the youth center at the Lutheran Church in Katzwang, Germany, needed a new coat of paint, the church's teenagers
planned a fund-raiser. They decided to make a calendar depicting
modern-day biblical scenes that they could sell to the local community,
and they would pose as the models themselves. Nude.

The Katzwang youth calendar fund-raiser was neither hastily conceived nor covertly executed. The youth director—church member,
husband, father, and amateur photographer—wanted to do things
right, so he received approval from the church board, collected permission slips from parents of all youth under eighteen, and asked the
pastor for suitable Bible stories for the project. "It's just wonderful
when teenagers commit themselves with their hair and their skin to the
Bible," Pastor Bernd Grasser told the BBC. The youth carefully staged
twelve scenes. Without so much as a fig leaf, Eve stood in the sanctu-
ary aisle and proffered an inviting apple to the camera. King David

(a peeping tom in the sauna) secretly watched a woman bathing. Rahab (unclad save for garters and stockings) lingered in a motel room door-way. Salome danced in body paint and a thong, and a topless Delilah trimmed Samson's locks. The teenagers planned to unveil their photo-graphs at an exhibition in the church hall on the second Sunday in Advent.

Fearful that no one would attend (*really?*) Pastor Grasser notified two local church news outlets, and the avalanche began. Reuters picked up the story, beaming it around the world with the church website. Three days and six million hits later, the youth had sold all 5,000 calendars and the church's Internet server had crashed. The overwhelmed youth leader removed the order form from the website, but orders poured in anyway, from India, Korea, the United States, Latin America. The BBC, Russian news services, and radio stations from as far away as Colombia con-tacted the pastor. Television news stations beamed the story across Europe. Within two weeks, the youth of Katzwang's Lutheran Church had earned more than forty thousand Euros.[1]

WE GET WHAT WE ARE

One wonders what Martin Luther might have said to the Katzwang con-gregation's enthusiastic support of their young people—or to American congregations, for that matter, who support scores of less dramatic but equally questionable forms of Christian witness among teenagers. It is hard to imagine the Katswang debacle in an American congregation, but every church has its share of pseudo-Christian youth activities exe-cuted for the sake of good intentions. Ski trips and candy sales, perfor-mance choirs and martial arts teams, confirmation "statements of faith" and Youth Sundays can turn into opportunities for teenagers to feel good about themselves, or for congregations to feel good about teenag-ers, or occasions to celebrate middle-class values of achievement, self-expression, and self-determination. No wonder young people have trouble distinguishing the teachings of Jesus from American culture; not even congregations can tell them apart—a long-standing problem for Christian churches. Luther complained in the 1529 preface to his *Small Catechism*:

The deplorable, miserable conditions which I recently observed when visiting the parishes have constrained and pressed me to put this catechism of Christian doctrine into this brief, plain, and simple form. How pitiable, so help me God, were the things I saw; the common man, especially in the villages, knows practically nothing of Christian doctrine, and many of the pastors are almost entirely incompetent and unable to teach. Yet all the people are supposed to be Christians, have been baptized, and receive the Holy Sacrament even though they do not know the Lord's Prayer, the Creed, or the Ten Commandments and live like poor animals of the barnyard and pigpen. What these people have mastered, however, is the fine art of tearing all Christian liberty to shreds.[2]

Luther was convinced that Christian formation began with youth ministry, and he was convinced that youth ministry started at home. Even before his break with Rome, Luther wrote: "If ever the church is to flourish again, one must begin by instructing the young."[3] One of his first goals as a reformer was to teach children the basics of Christian religion. Borrowing the medieval assumption that all things precious are known "by heart," Luther developed a method of instruction-by-memorization he called catechism, from *catechize*, to "echo back," or teach out loud.

Luther's *Small Catechism*, widely regarded as an educational masterpiece, was noteworthy for another reason as well. It located teaching out loud in households, not congregations, which had the effect of locating Christian formation in the intimacy of families, where children drew direct connections between religious instruction at the dinner table and the lives of people who loved them. Luther admonished pastors to preach from the catechism and advised all Protestants to "pray the catechism," but the *Small Catechism* itself was intended for parents (especially fathers). The instructions explicitly indicate "How the Head of the Family Should Teach His Household." It was an educational stroke of genius, since it effectively ensured that parents, children, and servants learned the core teachings of the church together.

Luther would not have been surprised by the National Study of Youth and Religion's conclusion that the best way for youth to become more serious about religious faith is for parents to become more serious about theirs. (Interestingly, in the NSYR's longitudinal interviews, parent religiosity during the teenage years was an even stronger predictor of young people's faith in emerging adulthood.)[4] Research is nearly unanimous on this point: parents matter most in shaping the religious lives of their children.[5] This is not to say that parents determine their children's spiritual destinies. Even the Bible has apostate parents with spiritual children, and vice versa, which only underscores the importance of supplementing teenagers' religious formation with congregational education—consistently the second most important variable on adolescent religiosity.[6] Yet there is no doubt that teenagers' appreciation of a life-orienting God-story, and their ability to discern God's ongoing movement in their lives and their communities are heavily influenced by *adults'* appreciation of such a story, and *adults'* ways of discerning and responding to the Holy Spirit's presence in their lives. Proximity matters. Teenagers' ability to imitate Christ depends, to a daunting degree, on whether *we* do.

Herein lies the rub. Many adults lack confidence in articulating, much less teaching, their own faith. What if parents and volunteers are no more religiously prepared than teenagers are? How do we speak with conviction about faith that we have trouble explaining ourselves? What if we accept church teachings but then discover, as we rub shoulders with different cultural perspectives, that we have questions about God too? Even allowing for Jesus' radical redefinition of the family in which he adopts the entire church, not just biological kin, as his spiritual family (Matt. 12:50), we often feel, as Luther's pastors did, "incompetent and unable to teach" the young people in our care. How do we translate our faith with conviction when we are not always convinced ourselves?

NURTURING A BILINGUAL FAITH

Walter Brueggemann argues that the cultural conditions of postmodernity require the church to function as a bilingual community, conversant in both the traditions of the church and the narratives of the dominant culture. Metaphorically, "bilingualism" lies at the heart of God's mission in the Incarnation. God became what God loved, translating the divine self into human form, sending Jesus to become like us so we could become like him. Christian formation requires a similar but admittedly imperfect move, translating words of faith into lives of faith, as the church provides young people with resources necessary for maintaining their alternative worldviews while they interact with a persuasive dominant culture.

Brueggemann offers 2 Kings 18–19 as a model of community particularity that converses with the broader culture, but also refuses to give in to the dominant culture's demands. Here is the story: The Assyrians have surrounded Jerusalem, and now all attention is on the wall of Jerusalem that stands between the Jews and the culture that seems destined to overwhelm them. The Assyrian negotiator stands at the wall, taunting Yahweh and shouting conditions for surrender. Israel responds with a tactical move of its own. While negotiations on the wall with the Assyrians are being conducted in Aramaic (the official imperial language of those who dismiss Yahweh), Israel's leaders were immersed in a behind-the-wall conversation in Hebrew, the language of Judah, where Yahweh is addressed.

The behind-the-wall conversation turns out to be pivotal. Within their own community, the people of Judah speak and grieve openly in Hebrew, the intimate language of family and friendship, of worship and prayer. Speaking Hebrew behind the wall, the people of Judah recount stories of God's faithfulness to them, remembering that their salvation is in Yahweh's hands. Behind the wall, the people of Judah remember who they are—a people whom Yahweh has promised to save, whom Yahweh has called to be a blessing to all nations (Gen. 12:2–3). As the sociologist Nancy Ammerman observes, "Any community that wants to sustain itself must have space behind the wall to tell its own primal narrative and imagine its own future in relationship to that narrative."[7] These behind-the-wall conversations are decisive for what happens on the wall. Remembering God's faithfulness, Judah's leaders enter the on-the-wall conversation with different assumptions about the world from those of the empire—which allows them to negotiate on the wall, using the language of the realm, emboldened by an alternative vision of their future.

Brueggemann maintains that taking part in both conversations is crucial for people of faith, and Christian formation must result in a bilingual consciousness. God calls God's people both to converse fluently behind the wall, using the Christian community's distinctive language, perceptions, and assumptions, *and* to take part in the conversation on the wall, which requires competence in the language, perceptions, and assumptions of the broader culture. The controlling conversation, however, is the one behind the wall. If we lose this language and its distinctive view of reality, "there is nothing to do inside the wall but concede that the Assyrians' view of God and life is the true one."[8] Without the behind-the-wall conversation, "the language of the Empire prevails."[9] Within the holy community, where everyone speaks the language of faith, our identity as God's people is reinforced. There we gain cultural tools that critique the dominant culture's vision of reality, and that remind us that we need not capitulate to the empire's demands. We know that the conversation on the wall is not the only conversation to be had.

At the same time, we need a public language for negotiating on the wall. If we *only* take part in conversations behind the wall, we risk absolutizing these intimate conversations. We begin to think that the inner conversation is the only one, that everyone must join it, and that we must "speak the language of faith '**in bold type.**' "[10] The on-the-wall conversation gives us distance from which to critique our own conversations as people of faith. It reminds us that our behind-the-wall language (for example, the language of the Bible and liturgy) is largely dysfunctional for public discourse. The purpose of scripture and liturgy, after all, is not public testimony, but "to make sure we do not lose our voice and keep alive this conversation so those who abide in it and are nurtured by it will become *translators* of the truth we hold, outside the walls, so that others who do not know our stories will begin to understand."[11] Brueggemann maintains that the "sectarian hermeneutic" nurtured behind the wall is essential to the church's public witness on the wall: "Christians must . . . be able to speak both the language of policy formation and the language of transformative imagination. There is merit in seeing these as distinct educational tasks but dependent upon each other."[12]

We can safely assume that the modern-day Assyrians (media, marketers, and other culture-makers of global postmodernity) are immersing American teenagers in the official language of the commercial empire. The empire's language dismisses Yahweh, offers tantalizing but ultimately empty promises of salvation, and hands out scripts that the empire expects teenagers to follow. Unless the church cultivates a behind-the-wall conversation that reminds young people who they are, who they belong to, why they are here, and where their future hope lies—unless we hand on a tradition that gives them cultural tools to help them lay claim to this alternate vision of reality—then the empire's conversation is the only view of reality they have.

CATECHESIS AS TRANSLATION

Catechesis translates Christian tradition into lived faith and nurtures the conversations behind the wall that anchor religious identity. Teaching the Bible is an obvious starting point, but the twentieth century's Christian education paradigm, which borrowed heavily from American schooling's reliance on information-processing and problem-solving, proved insufficient for seeding a missional imagination. Catechesis sets out to evoke trust in a person, and specifically the person of Jesus Christ, more than to inculcate religious ideas. For this reason, it submits the whole learner—not just the intellect or the emotions—to divine transformation so we will "know by heart" the ways of Christ and, empowered by the Spirit, participate in the work of God.

Some people are troubled by using the metaphor of translation as a way to describe the missional nature of Christian catechesis. The postmodern philosopher Jacques Derrida refers to the impossibility of translation, which is especially true when the object of translation is God's self-revelation.[13] The centuries old debate over where the power of translation lies, in the original text or in the interpreter, rages on.[14] Yet the missiologist Lamin Sanneh argues that "translatability" is a signature feature of the gospel, demonstrating God's equal regard for all people:

> No culture is so advanced and so superior that it can claim exclusive access or advantage to the truth of God, and none so marginal and remote that it can be excluded. . . . In any language the Bible is not literal; its message affirms all languages to be worthy, though not exclusive, of divine communication. . . . Christianity is a translated—and a translating— religion, and a translated Christianity is an interpreted Christianity, pure and simple. "Original" Christianity is nothing more than a construction.[15]

I am less interested in the intertextual dynamics of translation than in the metaphor offered by the actual practice of translating the Bible throughout history, a missional practice that "carried over" the gospel, revisions and all, into new contexts so new people could hear it. Biblical translation expanded our understanding of Jesus by giving marginalized and inexperienced believers access to scriptural sources of authority and, by introducing new points of view into the Christian conversation, offering a prototype for mission in all its forms.

Translating Scripture into the common, spoken languages of laypeople is arguably the most basic of all missional practices, and at first it was almost entirely accomplished by missionary bishops who needed a way to "indigenize" the gospel for potential converts who did not speak Latin, the language of policy in the Roman Empire. In the fourth century, a bishop named Wulfila (d. 383) created a nearly complete translation of the Bible for the Visigoths (he omitted 1 and 2 Kings because, he said, his people "needed no more instruction as to warfare").[16] Latin evolved into a special ecclesiastical language, unfamiliar even to many priests; while its strangeness enhanced the mystical quality of Scripture and the liturgy, pastors could not catechize new converts without a more indigenous approach.

So although Rome discouraged the translation of Scripture, by the fifth century, missionaries like St. Patrick did their teaching and preaching in the local tongue. By the 1500s, most known spoken languages had a Bible to call their own. During the Reformation, Martin Luther's twin emphases on *sola scriptura* and the priesthood of all believers required Protestants to have easy access to Scripture, so the first printing presses busily published Bibles and theological papers for laity who, for the first time, could read them for themselves.[17] In short, anywhere the instruction of new Christians was an issue, the gospel was translated into local forms that people could understand.

The political conditions surrounding these efforts have parallels in the church's work with young people today. Like the missionary bishops of the fifth century, youth ministers are notorious for ignoring ecclesial decorum to negotiate on-the-wall (and sometimes, we should admit, off-the-wall) conversations between the gospel and popular culture for young people who are unfamiliar with, or unconvinced by, the church's way of doing business. Carrying over God's word from one context to another resonates with handing on Christian tradition from one generation to the next. In both cases, the gospel winds up in the hands not of church powerbrokers but of people on the margins: lay people, young people, novices in faith whose newfound ability to participate in the behind-the-wall conversation sets in motion new ways of "being church."

Yet the data from the NSYR suggests that these behind-the-wall conversations are not widespread in American churches, or at least they are not happening with sufficient energy to involve young people, or with sufficient clarity for young people to be able to distinguish the conversation behind the wall from conversations elsewhere. What's more, the similarities between the religious outlooks of teenagers and their parents indicate that youth are not the only ones in need of a catechetical conversation behind the wall. Many parents feel their inadequacy, either abandoning the religious instruction of their children altogether or turning the job over to church "experts," assuming a division of labor in which parents provide a modicum of moral support (but not too much, in case soccer or homework gets in the way) while church professionals give their children information about faith.

But faith is a way of life, not only a body of information to master, which means that youth groups and church education programs, important as they are for social networks, religious information, and opportunities for spiritual reflection, play second string when it comes to the transmission of faith. A missional imagination requires the indigenizing practice of translating doctrine and rituals into vibrant public witness. This takes models, not theories. Translation requires communities that embody the tradition in three-dimensional form, and adults who can connect these traditions to daily life on the wall. As Brueggemann notes of the prophets in 1 and 2 Kings, *what* is known in the narrative is always inextricably linked to *how* it is known.[18] The fact that God revealed God's self-giving love in human form tells us that the conversation behind the wall makes no sense apart from a community of people who thoughtfully and faithfully follow the person of Jesus Christ.

ADULTS AS CULTURAL INTERPRETERS: FROM TEACHING TO TRUSTING

The conversation we are talking about most closely resembles a variety of translation called "cultural interpretation." Remember the people in period clothing at living history museums like those in Williamsburg,

Virginia, or Tombstone, Arizona? Those people are called cultural inter-preters. For the most part, they are volunteers, not professional histori-ans; they are retired teachers and history buffs, librarians and stockbrokers who love the history of colonial America or the Wild West, and who want us to love it too. They do not take our tickets, hand us a map, and wish us luck as they point us to the gardens. They travel with us through the exhibits, point out details we might overlook, highlight important events, encourage us to try out candle-making or cider-pressing or target-shooting for ourselves. They make the strange ways of colonists and cowboys meaningful and familiar by inviting us to par-ticipate in this way of life alongside them. In so doing, they hand on (or carry over, the Latin meaning of *translatus*) their passion for history to us, hoping that we will delight in it too.

Catechesis is strikingly similar. From the earliest days of the church, faith instruction involved guides (catechists) who were themselves par-ticipants in the church's behind-the-wall conversations. A catechist walked beside the novice Christian throughout the formation period, both to vouch for her character (since sometimes spies came from out-side the wall), as well as to interpret the in-house, behind-the-wall con-versation for the newcomer, showing her how to use the cultural tools of Christian tradition. The idea was to introduce her to a way of life, not just a way of believing—to translate God's radical acceptance of us in Jesus Christ into radical acceptance of one another.[19]

Catechesis is an indigenizing practice of the first order. Its aim is not primarily the formation of beliefs about Jesus but the cultivation of trust in him. It is an important distinction. When famed French tightrope walker Charles Blondin crossed Niagara Falls on a high wire in 1860, carrying his trembling manager Harry Colcord on his back, the nineteen-year-old Prince of Wales Edward Albert was there to watch. Before the stunt, Blondin asked the prince, "Do you believe that I can carry a man across the Falls on a tightrope?" Edward replied that he did. So Blondin asked: "Will you be that man?" (The prince declined.)[20]

Incredibly, Blondin died in his bed in 1897 at the age of seventy-five after an accident-free high-wire career. The facts of his feats had been widely reported. But to participate in Blondin's high-wire act required trust, not belief—a quality found almost exclusively among those close to him, which is why Blondin's stunts involved his manager (and his five-year-old daughter, until the French government prohibited it, citing "child endangerment") instead of strangers. Belief may enable us to approach Christ as a curious bystander, but our investment is abstract. Trust opens us to God relationally as we submit ourselves to divine love, which awakens our desire to know Christ better for ourselves.

Shifting the emphasis of Christian formation from religious information to a trust born out of love makes a profound difference in mobilizing faith. Faith does not ultimately depend on religious instruction, important as this is. Trust depends not on what we comprehend, but on who we love, which is why the church's initiation rites (for example, baptism and confirmation) are freely offered to people who may lack the cognitive or emotional ability to grasp their significance. What awakens faith is desire, not information, and what awakens desire is a person— and specifically, a person who accepts us unconditionally, as God accepts us. We may question what we believe, but most of us are pretty clear about who we love, and who loves us. It is such a preposterous claim—God-with-us (oh *please*)—that young people are unlikely to believe it unless we give them opportunities to do some sacred eavesdropping on us as we seek, delight, and trust in God's presence with us. The Benedictines accomplished this kind of eavesdropping in monastic communities, which included the youngest monks at every gathering of the order; Benedict's famous rule starts with the word, "Listen." In Israel, this sacred eavesdropping began in families. The Mosaic law proclaimed,

> Hear, O Israel! The LORD is our God; the LORD alone. You shall love the LORD your God with all your heart, and with all your soul, and with all your might. Keep these words that I am commanding you today in your heart. Recite them to your children and talk about them when you are at home and when you are away, when you lie down and when you rise. (Deut. 6:4–7)

Note what the Deuteronomist is actually saying here. Parents are not called to make their children godly; teenagers are created in God's image, no matter what we do to them, and no matter what they do to disguise it. The law called upon Jewish parents to *show* their children godliness—to teach them, talk to them, embody for them their own delight in the Lord, 24/7. Everything they needed for their children's faith formation, God had already given them. In the end, awakening faith does not depend on how hard we press young people to love God, but on how much we show them that we do.

WHITE CASTLE IS GOOD FOR THE SOUL

Somewhere along the way, an adult in your life—a parent, a grandparent, perhaps—shared something with you for no reason other than the sheer joy of sharing with you something he or she loved, hoping you would delight in it too. Country music. Making fudge. Fishing. Ohio State football. My father grew up near the home of White Castle hamburgers (known as sliders everywhere else), which gave him an irrational affection for those greasy little burgers. When I was five or six years old, every now and then my parents cleverly disguised a babysitting strategy as an invitation for me to "go to work" with my father. Inevitably, these outings ended at the local White Castle, where we would sit in the front seat of the car and polish off ten hamburgers between us. Today, I no longer share my dad's affection for sliders, but I never pass a White Castle franchise without thinking of those outings with my father, and remembering how good it felt to be loved by him.

This is how Christ wants us to feel about him, which means that handing on faith must mean sharing our love for him, and not just information about him. We forget that catechesis is this straightforward. We fall prey to the myth that teaching is a display of competence rather than an act of love. In one of the first churches I served as a pastor—back in the days when I was still tinkering with my flux capacitor—I convinced three dubious thirteen-year-old girls that confirmation would be a good idea, and decided on a mentor-based curriculum since the group was so small. I envisioned mentors and girls befriending one another, accompanying each other in settings where teenagers could "eavesdrop" on mature faith. I told the girls about the ancient catechumenate where sponsors vouched for their charges' faith, prayed for their souls, and held white robes while each confirmand stripped down naked to be plunged under the river for baptism. We would do this metaphorically, I assured the one girl getting baptized, since United Methodists are a sprinkling tribe who prefer to worship fully clothed.

The girls agreed, and gave me the names of their favorite adults in the congregation. I went to work playing matchmaker (the NSYR testifies to young people's willingness, even eagerness, to hang out with adults who support and encourage them).[21] I called every adult on the list, explaining how he or she could travel alongside these confirmands in their faith journeys, conversing with the girls about Christ and the church and helping them grasp the basics of Christian tradition. That was when things started to unravel. As it turned out, mentoring a confirmand had as much appeal as pinkeye. People who selflessly supported youth ministry with money, phone calls, baked goods, and prayer chains came unglued at the thought of mentoring a teenager. I knew I had hit rock bottom when one woman told me, "No, I'd rather work on the stewardship campaign."

Maybe these potential mentors were afraid of teenagers (an explanation I frequently hear when adults are reluctant to work with youth), but I don't think so. These people coached soccer teams, led Girl Scout troops, worked at the high school. What these potential mentors seemed to be afraid of was *faith*. They lacked confidence in their own faith formation and had no idea how to bring up the subject with youth. They succumbed to a common misunderstanding that teaching the gospel requires us to create a curriculum rather than translate a tradition, that we need to "make the story interesting" rather than invite teenagers to enact it alongside us. In the end, three women finally did agree to give mentoring a try, and confirmation that year included (unofficially) six people: three eighth-grade girls and three adults learning to translate beliefs into love.

A LABOR OF LOVE

Here is a crucial point: to approach catechesis as an act of love instead of as a show of expertise does not make faith formation an anti-intellectual enterprise. Far from it. Remember the cultural interpreters from Williamsburg and Tombstone? Because they love history, they have mastered an astonishing amount of it. They do not need notes for their conversations about it; they have internalized these time periods sufficiently to allow their knowledge to shape and instruct them from within, freeing them to go with the ebb and flow of tourists' questions.

We learn best what we love most. Teenagers immediately recognize this equation. A swooning tenth-grade girl tirelessly researches her beloved (who has Spanish second period, is smitten with the Lakers, dislikes carrot cake, and has a dog named Toodles). Eighth-grade boys with a "band crush" can tell you (and will tell you, given half a chance) obscure details about every band member and the group's musical evolution. Teenagers instinctively "master the culture," as ethicist Ted Smith puts it, internalizing profound levels of detail and nuance.[22]

The order matters. Young people do not research a band, and then decide on the basis of their research to enjoy the band's music. First, they are swept away by a song, and then because they love the music, they start to learn about the band. Approaching faith formation as a labor of love instead of as a collection of beliefs invites teenagers into behind-the-wall conversations about Christian tradition at this level of personal investment. When we downshift Christian education from the paradigm of expertise to a paradigm of love, we do not dilute the importance of rigorous theological reflection. On the contrary, inverting the order of instruction makes serious inquiry all the more likely. We learn best what we love most.

If translating the gospel is a standard missionary practice, it is also a humbling one; no one community of Christians tells God's story in full. Jesus does not ask parents or congregations to be theological experts. He asks us to follow him, to remember him, to love him—and to let it show. The question lurking beneath the data surfaced by the NSYR is, "Do we adults *love* Jesus enough to want to translate the Christian conversation for our children?" Handing on our faith tradition, like translating Scripture itself, is fraught with the risk of human contamination. Only God overcomes the impossibility of translation. Yet if we are not to surrender teenagers to the Assyrians, a behind-the-wall conversation must be had, and faithful parents and adults must initiate it. So perhaps a few rules to guide our translation will get us started.

GUIDELINES FOR TRANSLATING FAITH WITH YOUNG PEOPLE

1. The best translators are people, not programs.
2. The best translators are bilingual.
3. The best translators invoke imagination.
4. Translation can threaten the people in charge.

1. The best translators are people, not programs

You might have read about the computer programmers who, testing English/Russian translation software, fed the phrase "Out of sight, out of mind" into the program. The computer translated the phrase: "Blind idiot."[23] Computers are known for providing wooden translations—translations that, because they cannot adapt to context or cultural idioms do not ring true. The reason is simple: the best translators are people, not programs. When we attempt faith formation through programs instead of people (e.g., when we shuttle teenagers off to youth group without engaging them in behind-the-wall conversation about faith at home), they hear the gospel as a wooden translation, a vision of the church that, while briefly serviceable, is frequently distorted, often stilted, and usually bland.

Information is hard to translate; the impossibility of translation recognizes that there is no one-to-one correspondence between the meanings intended by your words, symbols, body language, and cultural traditions and mine. Often, adults try to replicate our own God-encounters for our children ("Camp changed my life; surely it will change yours"), but human experience also lacks one-to-one correspondence, even when it points us to Christ. As Walls points out, we see Christ differently based upon where we sit in the human auditorium, so no matter what I do to translate Christ to my children, they will always encounter him differently.[24]

So what overcomes the impossibility of translation? What communicates more clearly than information? The answer provided by the Incarnation is *love*. To be clear, catechesis requires moments of real instruction as well as opportunities for practice and reflection, in part because every effort we make to translate the gospel is tainted. We confuse love with control, distort it with fear, limit it with our short-sighted imaginations. With the best of intentions, we offer ourselves instead of Christ, finite good will instead of God's unbounded grace. In short, we are terrible translators. Yet God chooses to translate God's own self in human form and calls us to do the same. If human lives—even holy ones—make for garbled translations of God's grace and power, the Holy Spirit wipes away the smudges long enough to briefly but surely shine through us, so the church can reflect Christ in the world. And incredibly, that is enough. One glimpse of Christ's dazzling presence, one flash of God's radical acceptance, one instance of unconditional love can change us, seed a missional imagination, and become a starting point for consequential faith.

2. The best translators are bilingual

Vernacular speech consists of words and idioms that we learn locally (say "pop" instead of "soda" in New Jersey and people immediately know you're not from around here). But words are not the only vernacular we have. Vernacular architecture is a building style that responds to local climate, land, and traditions, like igloos or adobe huts. Vernacular religions are local expressions of religious traditions, ranging from voodoo to "punk monk" to emerging church communities.[25] So reframing the Word of God in the vernacular of adolescents does not mean dumbing down the gospel or punctuating Scripture with cyberslang (lol). It means building a hospitable space for the gospel using local materials that let newcomers immediately participate in Christian tradition, as they gradually acquire a faith vocabulary.

There is firm theological warrant for this approach. While the religious self-help industry has earned millions by capitalizing on the human desire to "get spiritual," God chose the vernacular: God "got carnal." The central divine act celebrated by Christianity is God's movement towards us, not the other way around. In the Incarnation, God accommodates divine grandeur to our puny capacities to understand. God's self-translation in Jesus Christ, the *missio dei*, is a vernacularizing move, designed to make the inaccessible accessible, the inaudible audible, the invisible visible to ordinary human beings.

Catechesis cannot only engage in conversations behind-the-wall. If Christianity is to negotiate the dominant culture's vision of reality—which, after all, is the one most teenagers share—then we must become fluent in the language of empire while articulating and enacting Christian desires. In the United States, the imperial language spoken on the wall is very close to the vernacular most teenagers speak at home, thanks to omnipresence of global media. Media scholar Henry Jenkins calls the early twenty-first century's global vernacular *participatory culture*, which forms the dominant vision of reality presented to young people through channels like open-source technology, Wikipedia, reality television, YouTube, and so on. These technologies, states the 2006 MacArthur Foundation Report on Digital Learning and Media, have reframed young Americans' expectations for social relationships, educational, and cultural understandings, and have even altered their neurological functioning.[26] Teenagers no longer view themselves primarily as consumers of culture, but as creators of it. While most teenagers do actively create cultural content, what seems to matter more is their sense that their participation is welcome and, when offered, appreciated.[27]

Participatory culture is more than a new venue for adolescent self-expression. The MacArthur report identifies five key characteristics of this culture that reflect its emphasis on direct engagement (see box).[28]

CHARACTERISTICS OF PARTICIPATORY CULTURE

- Low barriers to artistic and civic engagement
- Strong support for creative collaboration
- Informal mentorships that pass experience on to newcomers
- Confidence on the part of members that their contributions matter
- Members feel social connection to each other, if only through appreciation of contributions

Since incentives for creative expression and active participation originate in communities, churches that utilize the arts, media and technology for on-the-wall conversations with teenagers send a strong

TABLE 6.1. Cultural Literacy Skills for Participatory Culture

Play	capacity to experiment with one's surroundings as a form of problem-solving
Performance	ability to adopt alternative identities for the purpose of improvisation and discovery
Simulation	ability to interpret and construct dynamic models of real-world processes
Appropriation	ability to meaningfully sample and remix media content
Multitasking	ability to scan one's environment and shift focus as needed to salient details
Distributed cognition	ability to interact meaningfully with tools that expand mental capacities
Collective intelligence	ability to pool knowledge and compare notes with others toward a common goal
Judgment	ability to evaluate the reliability and credibility of different information sources
Transmedia navigation	ability to follow the flow of stories and information across multiple modalities
Networking	ability to search for, synthesize, and disseminate information
Negotiation	ability to travel across diverse communities, discerning and respecting multiple perspectives, and grasping and following alternative norms

signal of welcome.[29] Furthermore, as parents and other Christian adults become literate in this cultural milieu (see table 6.1), the church becomes more conversant with the imperial view of reality, and more able to credibly introduce alternative worldviews that have been nurtured behind the wall.

3. The best translators invoke imagination

Catechetical conversations behind-the-wall develop what Brueggemann calls a language of "transformative imagination."[30] The conversation on the wall shouts conditions for acceptance, but the discussion behind the wall refuses to foreclose on God's creativity, and in fact supplies young people with the imaginative tools necessary—metaphors and poetry, stories and songs—to resist the Assyrian view of reality. Without religion's language of transformative imagination, young people have only the dominant conversations language to describe the world, a worldview in which Jesus Christ could not possibly make any difference. On the wall where this language is spoken, Moralistic Therapeutic Deism makes perfect sense.

In her elegant little book *The God-Hungry Imagination*, Sarah Arthur blames young people's easy adherence to Moralistic Therapeutic Deism on "*a colossal failure of the imagination regarding both the claims and demands of the gospel.* The failure isn't primarily on the part of youth or even their parents; it's on the part of the church."[31] Her plea for the church to reclaim a role for imagination in handing on Christian tradition is as urgent as it is poetic:

> As Christian teachers and preachers . . . we must always remember that we're not meant to be journalists, merely relaying the facts; we're meant to be bards, speech-weavers, spinning a spell that captures the imagination. Yes, the gospel is the "good news" . . . [but] it is just as importantly the "good spell," a Word that has the power to capture and transform the human imagination.[32]

Arthur views metaphors as critical cultural tools for religious thinking. Even Aristotle considered metaphors "a sign of genius, since a good metaphor implies an intuitive perception of the similarity in dissimilars."[33] Metaphors activate what creativity theorists call "lateral thinking," a co-activation of two parts of the brain that are not normally strongly connected. Lateral thinking is precisely the kind of creative association that links behind-the-wall with on-the-wall conversations.[34]

The use of metaphors to spur lateral thinking is second nature for many youth ministers, accustomed to creating connections between the language of the dominant culture and the language of the church. The practical theologian Pete Ward believes that, in so doing, youth ministers have unwittingly pioneered the kind of transformative imagination Brueggeman advocates for the church as a whole. Echoing Walls's insistence that every translation renews the church, Ward observes that whenever a new connection between church and culture emerges, "the church reinvents itself."[35] Ward believes that people engaged in Christian youth work, thanks to their intuitive ability to translate the gospel for teenagers, have created unforeseen bridges between the conversation of the church and the conversation of our dominant culture. These efforts have yielded "millions of small innovations" in congregations—enough to begin to dissolve the church's ecclesial cholesterol and restore blood flow to those parts of the church where young people participate.

4. Translation is dangerous

This is where we need to stop traffic and hold up a flashing sign that says: DANGER: PROCEED AT YOUR OWN RISK. Our fourth guideline for translation is cautionary: Whenever we participate in the transmission of faith, across cultures or generations, we are putting the gospel into the hands of people new to it, which is a little like giving plutonium to a kindergartner. The sociologist Talcott Parsons once described every generation of teenagers as a "barbarian invasion"; we must either domesticate them or be overtaken by them.[36] Congregations somehow intuit that the young people they love also threaten their very way of life; what would happen if these beloved barbarians got their hands on the church as we know it? Most churches do not really want to risk finding out.

Translation often threatens the people in charge. A central theme in Sanneh's research demonstrates that translating the gospel into indigenous languages allowed local cultures to reflect on the Bible themselves, without importing theology from churches in other parts of the world. Inevitably, this development energizes grassroots Christianity (leading to the explosive expansion of Christianity in these areas),[37] and worries the "established" church. Translation in all its forms—cultural, symbolic, linguistic, human—gives voice to the mute who now can (and who, as they respond to Christ, do) contribute different readings of the gospel to the Christian conversation. Youth ministry is no exception.

The purpose of translating the gospel is access; it makes institutional culture available to those who have been excluded from it. Anna Carter Florence illustrates the point with reading the Bible. The issue is not whether young people can read the Bible (they can). The real issue is . . . well, really, why would they *want* to? What have they seen in the church that would suggest that the Bible is a source of power and wonder? When have they seen their parents derive life and joy from reading scripture? "We have been duped into thinking that the issue is Bible drills instead of instilling a *love of reading the Bible*," Florence claims. "We have been scared into sharing information about the text instead of our passion for it."[38]

Florence is not making a sentimental case for exciting Bible studies. A longtime youth minister, she quickly gets to the heart of things: To communicate to people that reading the Bible is something wonderful and liberating means we have to *share power with them*: the Word's power.[39] That is what translation does: it makes the power of the community, the Word of God, available to young people who assume a different kind of world, and who therefore may employ this power for unforeseen purposes.

WE'VE BEEN HERE BEFORE

In case this all sounds like a new problem, read Acts 15. At the Council of Jerusalem, the Jews confront a problem: Gentiles, outsiders to Jewish faith and tradition, have caught wind of Jesus. Who knew what would happen to the first-century Jewish gospel if uncircumcised Gentiles got their hands on it? So some of the Jews argued for safeguards: "If we circumcise the Gentile Christians, and make them follow the Mosaic law, then we will have some assurances. Then they will follow Jesus as we do. Then they will be like us."

Peter and Paul made an astonishing counterproposal. Let the gospel flourish where it will, they said. As Christ accepted us in our culture, the church should accept the Gentiles in theirs. Jesus did not require us to stop being Jewish in order to follow him, they argued; how can we ask Gentiles to stop being Gentile? No one group of Christians should dictate what faith in Jesus Christ must look like in another culture. Ritual washings, circumcision, and pork prohibitions might make sense to Jewish Christians, but Gentile Christians have a different way of life and consequently, a different way of following Jesus.[40] With that, Peter and

Paul set the missional church in motion. God's self-translation, Jesus Christ, was intended for all people, so the church flung open its doors to outsiders and said, "The gospel is for you, too."

A missional imagination alters the power dynamics of the church. Translating the gospel for young people amounts to entrusting them with matches, for it gives them access to holy fire, which puts the church at risk: what if young people ignite the church? Then where would we be? Indeed. Translating the gospel with teenagers in mind throws open the doors of the church to young people whose perspective on Jesus, if less informed, is also less jaded than our own. Newcomers to Christian faith are prone to believing that Jesus is who he says he is, and they are apt to negotiate risks on the wall that the more seasoned among us would like to avoid.

If we say we want to translate the gospel with young people, this is what we are saying: we are willing to put the very power of the gospel itself—the very power of the Word of God—into the hands of teenagers, people who do not view culture the way we view culture, who do not hear God the way we hear God, who will not worship the way we worship, who will not "do church" the way we want them to simply because they will be listening to Jesus and not to us. Catechesis behind the wall is a mixed bag. Yes, young people fortified by these conversations quickly puncture flimsy spiritualities like Moralistic Therapeutic Deism as the on-the-wall conversation with culture begins to include them. But what if they trust us? What if they love the God we say we love? What if they imitate Christ, share his wasteful grace, and embody his self-giving love in the world? In short, what if they get their hands on the gospel? Then where will we be?

7

Going Viral for Jesus

The Art of Testimony

Pervasive teen inarticulacy [about faith] contributes to our larger
impression that religion is either de facto not that important for most
teens or that teens are getting very little help from their religious
communities in knowing how to express the faith that may be
important to them.
—*Christian Smith with Melinda Denton*

If I have achieved anything in my life, it has been because I have not
been embarrassed to talk about God.
—*Dorothy Day*

She is twelve, and it was Bobby Dunn's idea: writing personal testimonies for other campers to give during evening worship services. Now that she has made a small fortune—she has $300 folded over John 3:16 in her white Bible—church camp is about over, and guilt has gotten to her. But Bobby Dunn, who is dreamy and inarticulate, says he doesn't know how to "make it sound good" in front of the congregation. For this problem, and about twenty dollars, her ghostwriting service has an answer.[1]

Reading Lynna Williams's short story "Personal Testimony" made me wonder why nobody thought of a ghostwriting service for Jesus sooner. Church camps and youth conferences typically encourage "conversational Christianity"—meaning they offer teenagers opportunities to describe their faith, out loud, to fellow tribespeople, which helps explain why camps are so successful in solidifying religious identity in campers. Mission requires testimony, so Christians have learned to approach it from many angles: evangelicals "have personal testimonies," stories about how Jesus entered/transformed/is transforming their lives; Catholics "give testimonies" about how and why they are Catholic; and mainline Protestants—who in the NSYR were skittish about talking about Jesus—nonetheless testify to God's power from the pulpit. With some exceptions (for instance, the Quaker testimony of simplicity, which uses symbolic action to bear witness to God's sufficiency), most churches use the word "testimony" to mean talking about our experience of God, out loud and with others.

Yet apart from Mormons and some conservative Protestants, the NSYR suggests that most American teenagers are like Bobby Dunn: they have enormous difficulty putting religious faith into words. Even for teenagers from churches where testimony is a regular practice, testimony is a learned art that bypasses many young people. As she remembered sharing her experience of God with her youth group, Jill, a highly devoted conservative Protestant from the Midwest, admitted, "I just kept praying that God would ease my nerves, speak through me, and allow people to hear what they needed to hear." Yet despite her anxiety, she felt compelled to state her beliefs outloud: "I felt like it would be selfish to keep my testimony to myself. God has done awesome things in my life, and I don't feel like it's just for me."[2]

Of course, even at camp the language we use to describe faith varies wildly. I blanched when I watched the documentary *Jesus Camp*.[3] The camp director's militant rhetoric, the imposed feel of the children's religious vocabularies, the awkward evangelistic practices designed to win adult approval as much as eternal salvation left me squirming. Watching elementary school children in *Jesus Camp* echo the language, practices, and theological outlooks of their leaders reminded me of watching children play dress up: the clothes didn't fit, but wearing them encouraged children to practice dialogue for roles prized by their church and praised by their elders. In fact, trying out religious language is one of the explicit purposes of the camp profiled in the movie, where children go bowling so they can practice witnessing to bowlers in the next lane.

Our youth pastor showed *Jesus Camp* to a group of mainline Protestant high school students and asked them what they recognized from their own camp experiences. Sixteen-year-old Elizabeth remembered a confirmation retreat in ninth grade that had involved an extensive "faith interview" in which each teenager described how his or her relationship with God had changed through the years. "Just putting faith into words was huge," Elizabeth recalled. "At youth group we talk about everything else, but no one ever asks us to talk about our faith." Reflecting on a segment of *Jesus Camp* where a young girl describes what she called "dead churches" ("where people just sit there"), Elizabeth admitted: "Some parts of the movie were kind of scary. But I have to admit, I really envied the passion those kids had when they talked about their faith."

HIGHLY DEVOTED—OR JUST VERBAL?

If I am honest, one of the things that bothered me about *Jesus Camp* was a faint whiff of recognition: just how different is *Jesus Camp* from what I do in youth ministry, from the faith practices I espouse, or from the camps I attend? I hope there is no comparison; by any measure of Christian formation, *Jesus Camp* is extreme. Yet the movie left little question in my mind: if we had profiled the children in *Jesus Camp* for the NSYR, they would have scored very well in terms of the study's definition of highly devoted faith, if only because they were remarkably verbal about their church's teachings and well-rehearsed in practices that lay claim to a faith vocabulary.

I left *Jesus Camp* with as many questions about what we may have actually measured in the NSYR as I did about fundamentalist camping programs. Did the NSYR really measure highly devoted faith—or did we actually measure a way of talking about faith that adults approve? Can teenagers develop a religious identity using cultural tools like a creed, a community, a sense of purpose, and an attitude of hope that reflect Christianity's peculiar God-story without retreating to the standard lingo of popular piety? Where is the line between faith formation and religious indoctrination when it comes to forming a missional imagination? Can teenagers develop articulate faith without being threatened with theological boot camp?

There is a necessary, but slightly circular, argument inherent in interview research on this point. Highly devoted teenagers in the NSYR were able to verbalize their understandings of God, the church, and religious teachings that influence their sense of purpose and approach to the future; and the fact that they articulated these aspects of their faith is part of the reason we considered them highly devoted in the first place. One of the findings of the NSYR that most exasperates church leaders is the discovery of pervasive religious inarticulacy among teenagers. Even among youth who call themselves Christians, language about Jesus and the particularity of Christian faith seems overwhelmingly foreign, or perhaps simply irrelevant. Smith and Denton write: "The language, and therefore experience, of Trinity, holiness, sin, grace, justification, sanctification, church, Eucharist, and heaven and hell appear, among most Christian teenagers in the United States at the very least, to be supplanted by the language of happiness, niceness, and an earned heavenly reward."[4]

If teenagers are barometers of a larger theological shift taking place in American culture, we can be sure that adolescents are not alone in their religious inarticulacy. Across the board, American Christians turn to categories like "a personal relationship with Jesus Christ," "being saved," "serving Christ" or even "reading the Bible" to express popular forms of Christian devotion. For the most part, these categories are borrowed from the most visible form of American Christianity, conservative evangelical Protestantism—and they accurately describe the way millions of Americans perceive God. Yet the effect of such a prominent evangelical vocabulary in the United States is that religious people of all kinds must either shoehorn their experience of God into this evangelical vocabulary (one committed Muslim in the NSYR's longitudinal interviews talked enthusiastically about her "personal relationship with God")[5] or risk looking religiously immature or disinterested. As a result, American evangelical piety becomes the glass slipper into which all faith experience must fit—or be labeled not religious.

Yet these categories do not begin to exhaust the forms of experience Americans have called "religious" at least since William James.[6] The transformation many Catholics experience through repeated participation in sacraments, the silent witness of the Spirit for Quakers, the prayers of the Orthodox through icons and song are just a few of the ways Americans routinely encounter the Holy and that cry out for an alternative grammar of faith. Since most of the young people we talked to were unaware of the doctrinal distinctions between Christian traditions, it stands to reason that some Christian teenagers, sensing that these common religious phrases do not describe them, opt out of religious discussion altogether to avoid being miscategorized.

What we can say with some certainty is that American young people have enormous trouble putting faith into words. It was unclear whether the young people we interviewed in the NSYR were unfamiliar with religious language or just uncomfortable using it in public (a number of youth we talked to thought talking about religion at school was illegal). The difficulty escalated when the conversation turned to particulars (the name "Jesus" was especially absent from our interviews). Predictably, the exceptions were highly devoted teenagers, who *could* talk about what they believed, and who *did* share stories about religion's impact on their lives—stories in which God had agency and was not merely a distant bystander. Whether these teenagers' faith led them to develop a religious vocabulary, or whether a theological vocabulary opened the door for claiming consequential faith, remains a chicken-and-egg question debated by theologians. The point is that words and faith seem to go together. Christian teenagers who referred to their faith frequently, interpreted their lives in religious terms, or grasped their faith traditions' primary teachings also had a ready religious vocabulary at their disposal.

THE IMPORTANCE OF CONVERSATIONAL FAITH

It comes as no surprise that families and communities that encourage practices in which teenagers must put religious convictions and experiences into words are more likely to have highly devoted teenagers. Latter-day Saints and black Protestant families (74% and 56%, respectively) were overwhelmingly more likely than families from other traditions to "talk about God, the scriptures, prayer, or other religious or spiritual things together" every day or a few times a week. Fewer than one in four mainline Protestant or Catholic families (and fewer than one in ten Jewish families) did the same.[7] Not surprisingly, the Exemplary Youth Ministry Study also identified parents who "engage youth and family in conversations, prayer, Bible reading, and service that nurture faith and life" as a key asset in helping young people develop mature faith (see appendix D).

Faith communities that encourage public conversation about faith also help teenagers develop religious articulacy. Mormons (72%) and conservative Protestants (56%) are especially apt to share their religious beliefs with people not from their faith, compared to only 37% of Catholic youth. Latter-day Saints in the NSYR were more than twice as likely as mainline Protestants, and more than four times more likely than Catholics, to openly express their faith at school. Likewise, nearly two-thirds (65%) of Mormon youth "spoke publicly about [their] own faith in a religious service or meeting" in the last year, and were nearly twice as likely to teach Sunday School or religious education classes than their non-Mormon friends. Singing and teaching Sunday School offer additional training in conversational faith among American

TABLE 7.1. Practices Promoting Religious Articulacy in American Teenagers

	Families talk about religious things every few days or weeks	Sing in a church choir or musical group	Openly express their faith at school some-times or a lot	Spoke publicly about their faith in a religious service or meeting in the past year
Mormon teenagers	74%	49%	88%	65%
Conservative Protestant teenagers	46%	37%	56%	42%
Black Protestant teenagers	56%	52%	56%	34%
Mainline Protestant teenagers	23%	35%	43%	33%
Roman Catholic teenagers	24%	18%	36%	20%

adolescents. More than half (52%) of black Protestant teenagers in the NSYR were involved in a religious music group or choir, followed by 49% of Mormon youth and 37% of conservative Protestants (see table 7.1).[8]

DID WE GET IT RIGHT?

There is a long-standing theological debate over which comes first: religious consciousness, or religious culture and language?[9] Do families with strong patterns of religious devotion create practices that articulate their convictions, or do practices of religious articulacy open the door for developing these convictions? Do practices that help young people articulate faith lead to conversational Christianity, or are other factors—religious families, Christian education opportunities, an existential experience of God, perhaps—really the source of expressed religious devotion? And (don't forget): where does divine revelation fit, if at all? These questions remain untouched by the NSYR. What we do know is that giving young people opportunities to talk about faith in families and congregations is positively correlated with holding religious convictions that they can articulate, critically examine, and confess.

Of course, some will say that teenagers are naturally inarticulate; it has always been thus, so surely it is unreasonable to expect young people to verbalize deeply held religious beliefs in an interview with a stranger. Social scientists debate the reliability of interview methods for unearthing what really matters to people, pointing out that the depth of our convictions may not correspond to the ardor with which we talk about them, and that our deepest beliefs may be so internalized that words do not do them justice. Our most fundamental values are far more likely to surface in stories and practices than in decontextualized interviews.[10]

While the reliability of self-reports must always be carefully scrutinized, it would be a mistake to dismiss teenage inarticulacy about religion as a mere quirk of adolescent development ("teenagers are naturally inarticulate") or as a methodological failing ("teenagers are not saying what they really think"). To overstate either of these concerns would invalidate talking to teenagers at all, about anything. Youth in the NSYR had remarkably nuanced vocabularies about nonreligious subjects, especially those they had studied at school (i.e., sex, drugs, drunk driving, parents, friends, media), and were both articulate and eager to share their opinions on these subjects.[11]

A more likely explanation of the absence of theological vocabularies in teenagers is simply the absence of robust theological conversation in the worlds teenagers inhabit—certainly the worlds of the media and public education, but also the worlds of families and congregations. Since youth do not hear a language of faith, they do not speak one. The "God-talk" young people do absorb from the surrounding culture is much closer to what the homiletician Thomas G. Long calls "God chatter," rather than a usable vocabulary of faith.[12] Without a narrative to give such chatter coherence and meaning, teenagers are left to cobble together a patchwork religious system, borrowed—not from deeply anchored faith traditions or a growing recognition of God's activity in the world—but from appealing parts of a number of myths Americans live by.[13] Americans are schooled in a culture that tells stories about its stories (think Disney) and makes facsimiles of facsimiles (again, any sequel to *High School Musical*).[14] No wonder we do not think twice about revising Christianity for our own needs, or re-envisioning Christian faith through the lenses we prefer. When meaningful religious resources are in short supply, the cultural tools of popular culture, family tradition, civil religion, democratic tolerance, and other cultural narratives must suffice.

Obviously missing from this spectrum of cultural tools is the church. As we saw in chapter 6, unless the church offers an alternative behind-the-wall story of God in Jesus Christ, teenagers naturally assume that the self-serving caricatures of Christianity they see offered by the media are accurate—meaning that Christianity has no apparent purpose except to benefit the believer, and no missional imagination to challenge the scripts supplied by the dominant culture. Even among the 40% of teenagers who said religion was important to them, faith tends to operate as an adolescent's second or third language, not as the language associated with their primary identities. Unless we have a reason to use alternative languages, we always draw upon our mother tongue first as our most accessible cultural tool. As we have seen, youth from Mormon, conservative Protestant, and African American communities are the most frequent exceptions to this rule, in part because religious language is also part of the cultural vernacular of these communities, which allows teenagers to hear it spoken. Furthermore, Mormon, conservative Protestant, and black Protestant communities offer teenagers frequent opportunities to speak about faith publicly, if only to prepare them for their expected vocations as missionaries, evangelists, advocates of God's justice, or all three.

KEEPING IT REAL: THE NECESSITY OF CONVERSATION ABOUT JESUS

Obviously, consequential faith involves more than facile God talk; Christian spirituality embodies as well as espouses beliefs. Yet cultures survive by giving voice to the values, images, and stories by which people "tell themselves" to the next generation. If the indigenizing principle helps us recognize Jesus Christ on Easter morning, the pilgrim principle sends us running from the tomb *to tell*: He is risen, and risen indeed! Even when the pilgrim principle does not send us out from our homes, it sends us out from ourselves; divine grace is a gift, but not one we get to keep. Christ sends us into the world as he was sent: to embody God's good news as we tell it, to enact the divine plan of salvation in word and deed.

That means that Christian spirituality requires conversation to both claim and confess our religious identities for ourselves and others, and to critically examine the role of faith in our lives. But Christian spirituality also requires a particular *kind* of conversation that reinforces the church's unique understanding of who God is in Jesus Christ. To state it bluntly: conversational Christianity requires Jesus-talk, not just God-talk. If talking about faith is something Christian teenagers seldom do, talking about Jesus is something they almost never do—which has crippling effects on Christian identity. Christians point to the life, death, and resurrection of Jesus Christ as evidence of God's love and power (creed); we know the faith community as the Body of Christ (community); we understand our purpose as following Jesus as his disciples (call); and we live in confidence that Christ's will ultimately overcome the world's suffering (hope). Thus, Jesus is simply not an optional category for Christians. So, among Christian teenagers, the absence of a vocabulary indicating a robust Christology (or any Christology, for that matter) has very troubling implications for the church.

Peter Berger and Thomas Luckmann maintain that conversation is the most important vehicle we have for maintaining a reality. "Everyday conversation maintains subjective reality," they write, pointing out that frequency or intensity of conversation "enhances its reality-generating potency."[15] Witness the news-creating power of the media. If no one talked about wealthy celebrities with small dogs, they would cease to be meaningful variables in our lives. The fact that tabloids, talk shows, and news outlets incessantly cover such stories creates reality-generating conversation about them. These stories perpetuate themselves by becoming taken-for-granted realities of our lives simply because people talk about them.

But there is more. Conversation not only maintains reality,

> it ongoingly modifies it. Items are dropped and added, weakening some sectors of what is still being taken for granted and reinforcing others. *Thus the subjective reality of something that is never talked about comes to be shaky.* . . . Conversation gives firm contours to items previously apprehended in a fleeting and unclear manner.[16]

To say it another way, realities that remain at the somatic level last only so long before they disappear into the mist. If Jesus (the Holy Spirit, sin, redemption, or a variety of other Christian non-negotiables) does not get talked about, he soon fades from teenagers' awareness, and therefore vanishes from their structures of meaning. This does not stop Christ from being present in teenagers' lives, of course, but it does significantly lessen their ability to recognize or acknowledge his presence. To a significant degree, we take our cues from Genesis and speak our worlds into being. Doubts (about one's faith, one's talent, one's spouse) can be dismissed until they are verbalized—but once voiced, we must be reckon with them. The converse is also true; if words conjure up subjective reality, silence can make this reality fade away (at least until therapy digs it out of our subconscious).

No wonder Christianity is smitten with words, and with the Word. The key term here is "smitten." Words matter to Christians not primarily because they spread our ideas or accomplish our goals, but because they proclaim our love. For both God and humans, love is a self-communicating impulse. Love goes out from itself toward the beloved; love cannot be contained. God reaches for us in the act of creation, in deliverance, in the gift of the Holy Spirit, but above all in the Incarnation, the life, death, and resurrection of Jesus Christ. So we preach, pray, dance, and sing because—like the ebullient leper who ignores Jesus' instructions to stay mum about his miraculous healing—we tell anyway (Mark 1:40–45). We cannot sit still, and we cannot keep quiet about someone who loves us this much. Once we realize that Jesus is on the move, and that our house is on his list, we cannot go on living as if Jesus doesn't matter.

So the importance the church attaches to words stems from the Word, the God-story of Jesus Christ, to whom all Christian words point. Christianity is not only a translated tradition; it is a living encounter with the Word of God, Jesus Christ. Behind the words of Scripture is the Word, Jesus Christ; behind the story of Jesus' life, death, and resurrection is the reality of God's Incarnation; behind the church's missional imagination stands the *missio dei*, the sending of God, who addresses and lays claim to us. As Paul asked the Romans,

> But how are they to call on one in whom they have not believed? And how are they to believe in one of whom they have never heard? And how are they to hear without someone to proclaim him? And how are they to proclaim him unless they are sent? . . . So faith comes from what is heard, and what is heard comes through the word of Christ. (Rom. 10:14–15a, 17)

Like Judaism and Islam, Christianity is a religion shaped by sacred texts—but until recently, people maintained an oral relationship to these texts: they *spoke them aloud*. The Word of God was an event; thanks to the Holy Spirit's presence, speaking stories about this event aloud makes the God-event present again—in translation to be sure, but truly present nonetheless. Both the Hebrew and Christian Scriptures bear witness to God's partiality to speech and words, not because God is a divine bibliophile, but because God's creativity is oral: God *speaks* the world into being, Jesus is the *Word* of God, and salvation comes in the *name* of Christ. No speech, no creation; no word, no salvation; no language, no faith; no name, no identity—or at least not one that we recognize as Christian, or that we can hand on to our children.

ORAL ARGUMENTS: TALKING OURSELVES INTO BEING CHRISTIAN

Smith and Denton cite the philosopher Charles Taylor who believes that "inarticulacy undermines the possibilities of reality" and warn that "religious faith, practice, and commitment can be no more than vaguely real when people cannot talk much about them."[17] The grammars, vocabularies, dictions, and accents of particular languages shape us into people with particular identities and imaginations.[18] Northrup Frye observes a world-creating role of language, an insight the Roman Empire took quite literally by imposing Latin on conquered subjects in order to confer upon them the identity of Roman citizens.[19] Many immigrant congregations in the United States worship God in their native language, hoping to preserve their primary cultural identity even as their children become socialized into mainstream American culture. Meanwhile, their American-born children—native English speakers—often have difficulty integrating into a church that speaks a "foreign" language. These teenagers not only have a different native tongue from their parents, they imagine the world differently as a result.

If language has world-creating power, a theological vocabulary that helps us talk about God also helps us imagine what a God-shaped world looks like. The Holy Spirit reveals divine truth in the gospel not only to tell us what God has done in Jesus Christ, but to help the church envision a way of life in which the life, death, and resurrection of Christ become the "grammar" of human existence. Teenagers who have trouble articulating what they believe *about* God also seem to have trouble forging a significant connection *to* God—and youth who do not have a language *for* Christ are unlikely to imagine an identity *in* Christ. The practical theologian Thomas G. Long points out,

> We don't just say things we already believe. To the contrary, saying things
> out loud is part of how we come to believe. We talk our way *toward* belief,
> talk our way from tentative belief through doubt to firmer belief, talk our

way toward believing more fully, more clearly, and more deeply. Putting things into words is one of the ways we acquire knowledge, passion, and conviction.[20]

Long contends that we "talk ourselves into being Christian," which means that talking about Jesus Christ actually deepens our identity as people who follow him, while simultaneously extending Christ's call to others. In Hebrew tradition, uttering God's name is the same as invoking God's power. Proclaiming the name of the Triune God, therefore, is a formative act. It changes things—changes us—by widening the cracks in creation where God enters the world.

AS WE SPEAK

Both Smith and Long remind us of the primal connection between language and identity, basic to the human species and fundamental to religious faith. As the primary tool in our cultural toolkits, language does more than express thought; it is our social global positioning system. Language situates us relationally, determines how we group ourselves socially, negotiates how we divide power between ourselves and others.[21] While the impulse to acquire language between the ages of three and seven seems to be innate, linguistic variation is a tool that we use to "construct ourselves as social beings, to signal who we are and who we are not and could not be."[22] As a result, to be able to actually say what God has done in Jesus Christ, for the world and for us—and to confess what this means—is critical for Christian formation, whether "telling on Jesus" takes the form of reciting a creed, singing a song, preaching a sermon, offering personal testimony, dramatizing Jesus' life, death, and resurrection in liturgy, or simply confessing faith. All of these forms of proclamation have been practiced by Christians since the earliest days of the church.

Until relatively recently, churches could assume proficiency in the practices of oral cultures. Prayer involved speaking (*oratio*). Reading (*lectio*) was an oral event, intended to benefit the community as precious letters and books were publicly shared ("mental reading" was virtually unheard of until the printing press made books accessible to individuals; Augustine admired Ambrose for his ability to read while "his voice and tongue were silent").[23] The first catechetical schools borrowed from the rhetorical tradition of the Greek *paideia*, where rhetoric constituted the backbone of the curriculum because participating in public life was impossible without it.[24] As a result, every student studied the art of speaking well, memorized and recited Homer, and participated in debates and discourses that were every citizen's responsibility.

Steeped in this oral tradition, the early Christians adopted a rhetorical model of discipleship formation as well. Following the pedagogical practices of the *paideia*, Christian seekers recounted Scripture orally, offered testimony within the faith community, learned creeds, the Bible, and teachings like the *Didache* by rote. Memorization constituted formation; to know Scripture "by heart" meant the Word of God dwelled within the believer, and shaped and instructed her from within, moving her to acknowledge Christ's truth in her own life. Borrowing a word from the Greek law courts, the new believer sought to be a *martyr* ("witness") for Christ, someone who testified to the truth of Jesus Christ, and who confessed what God's action in Jesus Christ meant for the present.[25]

A CASE FOR CONVERSATIONAL CHRISTIANITY

Conversational Christianity, like conversational French, requires immersion in a culture where the language is spoken, as well as first-hand practice using the language with native speakers. When my daughter's eighth-grade French class traveled to Quebec, students stayed with French-speaking families so they could hear and utilize spoken French. Shannon didn't come home fluent in French, but she came home a lot more comfortable trying to speak it out loud. It should not have surprised me, then, a few summers ago when we picked her up after a church camp she attended with a Baptist friend, that she talked about the "blood of Jesus" all the way home. In our church, the "blood of Jesus" is a phrase reserved for old hymns and visiting great-aunts; I've never heard a teenager utter the phrase. But Shannon was fresh off a week with the Baptists, who had immersed her in a language about Jesus that was relevant to her experience of God in the camp context.[26]

Conversational Christianity requires what situated learning theory calls *legitimate peripheral participation*, which refers to the way newcomers become integrated into communities—namely, by participating in them.[27] Shannon's eighth grade French class did not have the skills to fully engage Montreal's French-speaking culture, but sharing a week with a French-speaking family did not marginalize them either. It gave them real, if tentative, opportunities to participate at the periphery of conversations until they gained sufficient fluency to join in fully. Likewise, while teenagers are still learning the ways of faith, their participation in the Christian community is peripheral, in need of guidance from the community's fully integrated members. But it is also legitimate, valued by God and needed by the church. Learning the community's language is key to teenagers' full participation in the Christian community; newcomers must learn how to talk (and how to be silent) in ways that identify them as members of this community, or that signal their desire not to belong.[28]

You might already see where some churches go awry in ministry with youth. Often, the activities we assign to young people do not prepare them for full participation in Christian life; youth ministry winds up being peripheral but *not* legitimate because it fails to contribute to the church's missional purpose. In truth, much of what passes for Christian formation in American congregations—and a great deal of what passes for youth ministry—is *fake* peripheral participation. We invite teenagers to set up chairs for the ice cream social and call it "mission." We assign teenagers one Youth Sunday a year and call it "worship." We play games in youth group and call it "Christian fellowship." None of these activities are inherently misguided, of course. But they do not necessarily offer teenagers real participation in the Body of Christ, where every limb is just as important as every hair follicle. Setting up chairs can be an act of sacrificial love—or it can just a way to get a job done with strong backs and young people who have no idea where the money is going to go. Youth Sunday can be an offering of exuberant praise and thanksgiving, or it can be an entertaining change of pace for adoring parents. Youth groups can be vehicles for Christian fellowship, but unless teenagers learn to share one another's suffering (not to mention the suffering of people outside the group), Christian youth groups can devolve into gatherings of like-minded friends.

The fact that outreach, worship, and Christian fellowship in most churches can carry on very well without youth at all is a tell-tale sign that their participation in the community is not legitimate peripheral participation. It is indeed just peripheral, and it does nothing to usher teenagers into full membership in the Body of Christ. Legitimate peripheral participation means that adolescents make real contributions to our shared life in God, even while they are still figuring out how to be part of the community of faith. As teenagers become more proficient in the church's language and practices, they become more central to the life of the congregation, and contribute more fully to Christ's mission—until they suddenly discover that they are in a position to help lead in that mission, to bring newcomers on board, and to create the community anew.

THE POWER OF TESTIMONY: RUNNING FROM THE TOMB TO TELL

If conversational Christianity is necessary for "talking ourselves into being Christian"—if telling the story of God in Jesus Christ is necessary for confessing Christian identity to God and others—then families and congregations must participate in telling this story to teenagers and must help teenagers tell it for themselves. Anna Carter Florence offers a way to begin: reclaim the power of testimony for young people, and for churches, who have forgotten how to say what they believe.[29]

Testimony means to give witness. The verb "to witness" has two meanings—to see, and to tell.[30] Testifying means telling what you have seen, the truth from your point of view. It is an interpretation of what happened, not a record of events; a proclamation, says Florence, "of what we have seen and believed." For teenagers, this might be as simple as acknowledging to friends confidence that God is at work in the college decision process, or as involved as sharing one's faith journey in a sermon on Youth Sunday. Testimony draws on our experience—not *every* experience ("riveting, no doubt, as it would be," adds Florence) but "what happens when God meets us, right smack in the middle of our lives." Testimony tells about a time when, by the sheer force of grace, God's story and our story collided. Such an encounter, of course, is far beyond what words can describe—but this is the experience of abundant grace God has given us, and such abundance must be shared. "We have to testify to what we have seen and believed in the gift of this encounter," Florence insists. "It won't be perfect; it won't say everything; but we have to try."[31]

Testimony never ultimately points to what the witness says or does; it points to the One who sent the witness in the first place. As Paul Ricoeur reminds us, "It is Yahweh himself [sic] who is witnessed to in the testimony."[32] Testimony does not originate in or belong to the witness; it comes from beyond the witness, from the God whose good news we bear. Of course this means that words are never enough to match the enormity of the message, but since our account is of God's faithfulness, not ours, testimony actually provides a fairly "safe" way to begin to talk about faith. Granted, it seldom feels that way at first. When one congregation I know introduced testimony into its weekly worship services, volunteers vanished. Nobody could think of a thing to offer, despite the pastor's pleading. Then one Sunday, instead of listing "testimony" in the bulletin, the pastor opened a space in the service for "God-Sightings." You guessed it: people readily shared—teenagers included—as story after story tumbled out about God's faithfulness to the community amidst the fears and foibles of daily life.

To my mind, the provisional, interpretive nature of testimony gives the practice a kind of humility—and a gut-level honesty—that sometimes evades other forms of Christian speech. We never have the absolute truth about God; we have only the corner of the truth God has revealed to us, and we must rely on the Holy Spirit to help the hearer fill in the rest. Like translation, testimony is a hermeneutical practice, not a definitive one. And yet: we are the authorities on the moment our human experience has collided with God's faithfulness, and we can speak to it as God's partners.[33] We are free to tell the story as best we can, and the hearer is free to believe or disbelieve. Florence likes Leif Enger's description:

Is there a single person on whom I can press belief?
No sir.
All I can do is say, Here's how it went. Here's what I saw.
I've been there and am going back.
Make of it what you will.[34]

As a rhetorical form, the "take it or leave it" quality of testimony makes it seem undomesticated and a little reckless. Its authority comes from the God-encounter it describes, not from the credentials or the skill of the person giving witness. This, in fact, is why history often shows testimony being practiced by people barred from religious leadership—women and youth, for example.[35] Drawing on the authority of the divine made testimony prophetic and daring, and even today it has a kind of unprocessed authenticity that appeals to teenagers, who view testimony's inclusion of personal experience and interpretive chutzpah as a postmodern seal of approval.

Consequently, testimony tells the story of God in Jesus Christ using speech that is passionate, subjective, and invested. Testimony neither dissects an argument, nor makes one; it is more inclined to sing. Nor is testimony merely autobiographical; it always points to God, to what God has done, and to what we believe this means for us and for the church. In testimony we throw ourselves on a text the way Jacob tackled the angel, demanding that it bless us (Gen. 32:22–32)—or perhaps the way Mary Magdalene flung herself at Jesus on Easter morning before he stopped her (John 20:17). But *then* testimony runs from the tomb to *tell*: "Here's how it went. Here's what I saw. I've been there and am going back."

So you could say, rhetorically, testimony is opportunistic; it has an endless array of forms, an inexhaustible number of occasions for which it is appropriate. In the panoply of faith practices that have captured the imagination of contemporary practical theologians, testimony is one of the most versatile, available to anyone who seeks God, useful for all of us who need to talk ourselves into being Christian. While testimony is helpful for preachers, youth ministry claims it for a range of contexts, from worship to small groups and family conversations. Like translation, testimony plays a part in both behind-the-wall and on-the-wall conversations, but unlike catechesis, its emphasis is less on handing on a prior tradition than on naming and claiming God's activity in the world *right now*.

LEARNING TO "SPEAK CHRISTIAN": TOOLS FOR TEACHING TESTIMONY

A missional imagination requires theological language that points to the sending nature of God. Such a language is not acquired by fiat but by participation. We prepare young people for the art of testimony through practices that plunge them into the waters of a baptismal community. There is an art to learning the rhetorical form of testimony, as homileticians like Florence can attest. But if youth ministry is to confront Moralistic Therapeutic Deism, we must back the cart up a little further, for before they can learn the art of testimony, teenagers need to become comfortable speaking Christian conversationally. Learning language is not only an intellectual exercise; it is, above all, a social exercise, a way to locate ourselves in a skein of relationships beside people who love and follow Jesus Christ, while distinguishing ourselves from people who do not. Indigenizing practices reinforce our identities as participants in a baptismal community, but the pilgrim principle prohibits us from staying there. Christ sends us out of our churches to confess who we love and to say what we have seen.

Though often overlooked—mostly because they are informal educational methods that are hard to include in printed curriculum—churches have long used practices like *spiritual apprenticeships* and *faith immersions* to plunge young people into Christian "language communities" that give them the language necessary to testify to God's faithfulness. These limited experiences of Christian community provide young people with both a faith vocabulary and with opportunities to practice using that vocabulary, without requiring immediate proficiency in religious speech. Educational theorists would categorize both approaches as exercises in *situated learning*, or "learning from the middle" of community whose practices are already established. Yet the early church pioneered these methodologies in the ancient catechumenate, as seekers entered the Christian community for a long period of preparation and communal formation.

Spiritual Apprenticeships: The Practice of Sacred Eavesdropping

In the Middle Ages, young people were apprenticed to a master in order to learn a trade or an art. We think of this relationship as a pragmatic one: the purpose of an apprenticeship is to gain knowledge and learn necessary skills. But in the Middle Ages, to be an apprentice meant more than this. To have a trade meant having an identity, a language, an eye for the art and not just technical expertise. In the master-apprentice relationship, the master hands on a way of being in the world, a sacred outlook, and a toolbox stocked with stories, habits, and virtues intended to help the apprentice carry the master's work forward. A master carver does not carve stone because he has the skills for it; he carves stone because he is a *stone carver*, and has therefore acquired the tools and dispositions necessary for carving. This is who he is: someone who carves. He speaks the language of carving. He takes part in practices associated with those who bring into view life hidden in a rock.[36]

Of course, historically apprenticeship was a mixed bag; not all apprentices signed on willingly, and sometimes masters were abusive or passed on deformative as well as transformative practices. Contemporary educators underscore the need for mutual regard between a so-called master and the learner. Most cultures have a version of the master-student relationship, a sacred trust in which a group's distinctive use of a cultural toolkit is passed along from expert to novice. Coaches, basket weavers, parents all use apprenticeship models as they engage, as the ethicist Stanley Hauerwas puts it, in the "hard work of teaching the language of a task"—which for Hauerwas is as physical as learning to carve stone.[37] The first task of a stonecarver's apprentice, he observes, is to engage in the art of eavesdropping in order to imitate the *speech*—not the skills—of the master. "Note the order," commands Hauerwas. "Speech precedes practice, which precedes virtues . . . . You adjust to being a stone carver by talking."[38]

The Irish sculptor Seamus Murphy recalls his apprenticeship at O'Connor's stoneyard in Ireland's County Cork. At fourteen, he was plunged into the oral culture of carving. He relays how advice flowed freely in the stoneyard, as each carver shared his accumulated experience. Murphy recalls the wisdom imparted by a lifelong carver who never stayed at any one job very long. The itinerant carver warned him:

> There are three important things to consider if you want to stay in a place: the men, the work, and the stone. If the men are good I'm inclined to stay, and if the work is interesting I forget the men, but if the stone is bad, nothing could keep me! Because, dammit, nothing torments a man more than nursing a treacherous . . . stone only to find after all your trouble

that it was only blackguarding you. Just as you are about to say, "I'm a thunderin' bit of flesh to handle that cantankerous lump," and feel you've begun to master it, out you'll blow a corner. It happened to me with a block of the [highway] Aherla. I had the stone worked and was just square-chiselling the margin when off came about four inches of the end. ... I packed up on the spot.[39]

This is testimony. A master carver testifies to the truth of carving: the stone's vices (for instance, how easily it can break), the carver's virtues (patience, for one, since soapstone scratches and alabaster bruises), standards of the trade (using sandbags to absorb vibrations from hits to the stone), habits of the artist (hold your thumb on the outside of the chisel to protect it from the hammer). Inherent in the practice of apprenticeship is a tension between conserving the tradition and presenting a prophetic new voice—a tension inherent in handing on faith as well. Artists are regularly counseled to "learn the rules so you can break them," advice the church also takes to heart, with different communions favoring more traditional or more prophetic approaches. But no faith community survives without evolution.[40] Imitating the master carver does not mean slavishly copying him; rather, imitation creates a secure foundation that new carvers may trust and build upon.

The earliest form of discipleship education (and, as Paul's relationship with young Timothy reveals, the earliest form of youth ministry) was apprenticeship. Talking about Jesus is no substitute for following him, for Timothy or for us; yet talking about Jesus is necessary to claim and confess our identity in Christ, and to discern through the community of faith the footprints we should follow. People who "speak Christian," as Hauerwas puts it, speak the truth in love; it is this speech, not doctrinal sophistication or facile God-talk, that marks the mature follower of Jesus. Young people who learn to speak Christian learn it from experienced Christians. Youth are apprentices in a community that talks about Jesus, where people testify to what it costs to love him and to love others because of him.

Most teenagers have few structured opportunities to eavesdrop on the grammar, vocabularies, habits, virtues, or practices of mature Christian adults. As I found out the hard way, mentoring models of Christian formation are difficult to pull off primarily because so few adults are willing—not because they lack the interest, but because they lack spiritual vocabularies, and therefore confidence, to convey their religious convictions to another person. But we should not give up too soon. Spiritual apprenticeships offer effective venues for introducing young people to a language of faith, as families and congregations become safe zones where people speak Christian as their native tongue. The first step toward spiritual apprenticeship is shedding the misconception that teenagers want adults to leave them alone. Most teenagers are quite positive about their relationship with their parents,[41] and four out of five teenagers who attend church or synagogue willingly name adults in their congregations whom they enjoy talking to, and who give them lots of encouragement. In the NSYR, three out of five youth named one or more adults in their congregations, other than their parents, to whom they can turn for support, advice, and help. In fact, the number of adults available for such support (in churches and elsewhere) rose proportionally to teenagers' religious devotion.[42]

So what does this tell us? First, we can expect most teenagers to respond positively to adults (including parents) who take them under their wing to practice meaningful discipleship. Apprenticeships intentionally pair integrated community members with newcomers. Peer groups have their place in ministry, but when churches mimic the age-stratification created by a market-driven culture, discipleship-formation suffers. Second, apprenticeships benefit more than the apprentice. To return to Hauerwas's example of stone carving: an apprentice is not just learning how to become a master carver. She is also actually doing the work of carving, along with the master, and in that way contributes to the work of the studio. As young people contribute to the faith community, their competence as members of that community grows; it is in doing the work of ministry that Christ shapes us into ministers.

Finally (and this is a deal breaker), teenagers learn to articulate faith by hearing adults articulate theirs. This brings us back to our familiar problem: American adults may be no more religiously articulate than their children—suggesting that master carvers in the Christian community are in very short supply. Even if teenagers respond positively to adults who take an interest in them, even if youth engage in meaningful discipleship practices with adults, if adults cannot speak Christian any better than young people can, spiritual apprenticeship fails.

The solution is not to abandon apprenticeships but to engage the pilgrim principle: look for places where adults can move beyond their comfort zones and talk about their faith in teenagers' presence. Adults commonly long for the quality of ministry churches offer young people, and there is *no* reason that the informal practices of formation that we have come to expect in youth ministry should not characterize all ministry. Adults need spiritual apprenticeships as much as their children do—and adults need them first. Group spiritual direction, covenant groups, practice in oral prayer, lay leadership in worship, singing hymns and praise songs—and of course, the formal practice of testimony itself—are congregational practices that give adults, and not just teenagers, opportunities to put faith into words. Not only do such practices cultivate theologically articulate adults fully capable of mentoring teenagers, they make the congregation itself an environment where young people learn the language of Christian faith because they are immersed in a community that speaks it.

Faith Immersions: The God-Story as Decoder Ring

If apprenticeships allow young people to learn the language of discipleship through the stories, habits, and virtues passed on by a mature disciple to a newcomer in the faith community, Christian immersion experiences or "faith plunges" offer laboratories where teenagers can practice these language skills in a protected environment—namely, a space in which articulate faith is encouraged. All language training utilizes immersion experiences at some point, but these experiences are only as good as the guidance before and the debriefing after. Real or simulated, these laboratories dramatize a key element of the Christian story: the idea that baptism is only the first of many immersions in Christian life, that Christian growth proceeds by "going under" with Christ, and joining him in resurrection. The British theologian David Ford points out that Jesus' own life was the "embodiment of multiple overwhelmings": immersion in the Jordan River, temptation in the desert, agony at Gethsemane, betrayal, torture, and crucifixion. Then came resurrection, "the most disorienting and transformative overwhelming of all."[43] No wonder the Christian life begins by "going under." Baptism (the Greek word *baptizein* means to swamp or submerge) dramatizes the dying-and-rising grammar of Christian liturgy, seeding a Christian vocabulary in the church.[44]

The most common faith immersions in youth ministry are camps, retreats, mission trips, youth conferences, and other temporary Christian subcultures that plunge teenagers into communities that are structured to emphasize God's immediacy and activity. In the Christian camp or retreat subculture, daily rhythms may be patterned on gospel narratives, and religious language may be used without censure. Ideally, participating in a congregation offers a similar plunge into Christian community, but except for highly sectarian groups that operate almost exclusively behind the wall, most American congregations have difficulty separating themselves from the dominant culture. Most teenagers find it easier to make out the Christian community's distinctiveness in the wilderness, at a conference, or in some other demarcated zone where young people themselves help construct idealized versions of the world they think God intends.

Religious camps have impressive records of helping young people become more intentional about devotion, more secure in their faith identities, and therefore more confident and explicit in telling the God-story of their tradition. There are many reasons for this, including the fact that the parents of teenagers who attend such programs tend to be religious enough to think sending their children to a faith-based camp is a good idea. Longitudinal studies found that (compared to their peers) college students who had attended a Jewish camp as teens were more observant of Jewish ritual, more positive about Jewish and Zionist identity, more inclined to date and marry Jews, and more active in Jewish life on their campuses.[45] It comes as no surprise that religious communities with the largest numbers of highly devoted teenagers in the NSYR were the ones most likely to send their young people to camp. Even controlling for family income, teenagers whose parents were Mormon (78%) or conservative Protestant (54%) were more likely to attend religious camps than youth from other religious traditions.[46]

Like travel abroad programs that give teenagers a live-in view of another culture, faith immersions surround teenagers with temporary (but authentic) communities of discipleship in a focused, 24/7 context.

Since language is such an important factor in community member-ship, participants quickly develop insider vocabularies, making camps, conferences, retreats, mission trips, and other short-term Christian communities ideal places to inculcate language that points to Christi-anity's peculiar God-story. Furthermore, these experiences typically function as oral cultures where an intimate, and personally relevant language of faith can be spoken. The God-language used at camp is seldom a tool for retrieving history or casting a vision for the future; rather, it is the decoder ring for teenagers' *immediate experience* of God during the event itself and for interpreting one's life in relationship to this experience.

To be sure, short-term immersions foster cultural familiarity, not fluency. What faith immersions like camps, conferences, and other short-term Christian communities offer young people is concentrated practice in the words and deeds that testimony involves. Faith immer-sions help teenagers rehearse long-term commitments that call for real acts of sacrificial love. As a matter of course, teenagers in temporary discipleship communities practice the dying-and-rising pattern (gram-mar) of Christian life. The condensed curricula and focused environ-ments of these events dramatize and reinforce rudimentary theological concepts (vocabulary) in ways that are difficult for weekly church edu-cation programs. Teenagers gain practice and clarity (diction) as they discuss their lives in religious terms with others. Finally, faith immer-sion experiences typically help young people consider ways to keep the distinctive Christian accent in their lives once they return home (a feat normally accomplished by regular returns to a community where youth hear this accent spoken).

Of course, temporary communities like camps and conferences—important as they are to get a taste of Christian community and identity—do not replace the long journey of accompaniment offered by families and congregations. Unless a language is reinforced by daily experience, we lose our vocabulary; language requires both direct teach-ing and opportunities to use it to be serviceable. So while Christians frequently cite St. Francis's dictum, "Preach the gospel; when necessary, use words," sometimes words *are* necessary to the gospel. Allusions only communicate to an inside crowd, and as the NSYR points out, teenagers are very unlikely to be in it.

THE GOSPEL AS TELL-ALL

Without a story to tell, there is no faith; without a language to tell our story, Christianity remains on mute—and the church's missional imagination atrophies. The gospel is unambiguous: good news is meant to be shared. The pilgrim principle inherent in Christianity—the gospel's boundary-crossing imperative, the good news "gone viral"—insists that God's message of good news is not just for us. Enacting the pilgrim principle in youth ministry means that families and congregations hand on the story of faith, not as a generic tale of niceness but as the revelation that God loves us too much to lose us, a story that comes to us through the messy particularity of the life, death, and resurrection of Jesus Christ. This is the God-story that the church confesses, and that families and faith communities must articulate for teenagers called to run from the tomb to tell: "Here's how it went, here's what I saw. I've been there and I'm going back."

8

Hanging Loose

The Art of Detachment

Religious congregations and other religious organizations are
uniquely positioned in the array of social institutions operating in
the United States to embrace youth, to connect with adolescents, to
strengthen ties between adults and teenagers. This could only be good
for all involved. But it will not happen automatically. It will require
intentionality and investment.

—*Christian Smith with Melinda Denton*

The soul needs amazement, the repeated liberation from customs,
viewpoints, and convictions, which, like layers of fat that make us
untouchable and insensitive, accumulate around us. What appears
obvious is that we need to be touched by the spirit of life and that
without amazement and enthusiasm nothing new can begin.

—*Dorothy Soelle*

July 3, 2009, 6:30 p.m.

*I'm home. I guess I had expected, prior to the trip, that my arrival home
would be accompanied by an immediate return to all the things I had missed:
familiar food, (clean!) hot water, my cherished iPod, and my laptop addic-
tion. Well, I have showered. But I haven't touched my computer; I've barely
glanced at my iPod. To be honest, I don't even want to see them. One of the
first things I did when I got home was give away half of the jewelry I had
intended to keep for myself, and then throw away some assorted crap that
had accumulated, just for good measure. I've spent as much time outside
today as possible, writing in our hammock and insisting on eating dinner*

on the deck. I'm not ready to live indoors yet. Deep down, I'm afraid of
this return to luxury. Or perhaps afraid is not the right word—more like
reluctant, or wary. I don't want to slip into my pre-Mexico self like a
hermit crab returning to an abandoned shell, and I know how easy it
could be.[1]

That is how Gabrielle Hovendon remembers coming home after her
youth group's mission trip to Mexico last summer. Like thousands of
teenagers every summer, Gabrielle and the youth from First Presbyterian Church of Watertown headed for Mexico to build homes, in this
case with a project called Amor. "Any faith element with Amor is BYOB
(bring your own Bible)," explained Gabrielle's youth pastor Matt, when
he sent me Gabrielle's journal from the trip. "Gabes" had been class
valedictorian a month earlier, and she came to the mission trip with a
short history in the congregation and virtually no experience away from
home. Still, she had no illusions about what the trip was about. She
wondered: What would be different? What would be the same? Is the
moon different in Mexico than in Watertown, New York? *What do I*
know? she wrote in her first journal entry. *Certainly not how to build a*
house, and only that things will be different. Different is good. Two different
moons are okay. But a different person, a better person, is what I think
we're all aiming for.

AIMING FOR TRANSFORMATION

Of course, Gabrielle was exactly right. Short-term mission trips serve a
number of purposes in Christian formation, many of them debatable.
One in three American teenagers takes part in a cross-cultural service
project before finishing high school, and so-called volun-tourism is on
the rise. No book that calls the church to reclaim a missional imagination can ignore the role of these often-transformative, often-abused
programs in youth ministry.[2] Some studies suggest that more than a
million and a half Christians from the United States travel abroad on
short-term mission trips each year.[3] As the missiologist Karla Koll points
out, "The material aid and economic resources brought by short-term
mission groups to local churches and communities far exceed whatever

help may be flowing through centralized denominational channels"—a phenomenon that recipients do not always experience as positive.[4] Research on the impact of short-term missions on both participants and recipients is mixed; lasting changes are difficult to substantiate on either side. At the very least, this research raises enough questions that youth pastors should approach mission trips with teenagers with caution and intentionality.

Yet while mission trips offer much to criticize (we can start with the expense, the tourist connotations, mixing up service-learning with Christian servanthood, and the nomenclature—i.e., mission is not a trip),[5] mission trips nonetheless open many teenagers to the Holy Spirit's transformation and often provide appreciated, if limited, assistance to people in need.[6] When we approach mission trips as opportunities for cross-cultural encounter, when middle-class teenagers sign on as learners instead of "fixers," and when servant opportunities are shared with and directed by the local community, these cross-cultural experiences can become important ministries—to *teenagers*. The real gift of the church mission trip is seldom the porch that was built or the gutters that were replaced, though these are often graciously received. The gift of these decentering encounters with "otherness"—the human other and the Divine Other—is faithful *reflexivity*, a kind of self awareness that allows us to momentarily view ourselves and others from a new vantage point as we watch God work.

Reflexivity is the process, to co-opt Andrew Walls's metaphor, of choosing to change seats in the human auditorium. Spiritually, it refers to the discipline that some medieval theologians called *detachment*.[7] Modern psychological theory uses this word to designate damaged relational bonds, but in the Middle Ages detachment was a term used by the church. It simply meant disentangling ourselves from whatever distracts us from Jesus Christ, so all of our attention—and all of our lives—may be fixed upon him. The effect of spiritual detachment is liberation, freeing us from lesser allegiances so we can entertain new possibilities that Christ presents for us and for the world.

Spiritual disentanglement is a necessary and ongoing practice of discipleship, especially for those of us who live in a culture where every desire finds its balm in a flashy but fleeting solution or amusement, usually available for purchase. Yet these remedies only distract us from our true longings, acute during adolescence, that reveal our hunger for God. Writers like C. S. Lewis observed that even religion can become a distraction from faith. In *The Screwtape Letters*, Screwtape—a harried undersecretary from the Department of Temptation in Hell—advises "junior tempter" Wormwood to keep Christians focused on reflection *about* Jesus so they will not reflect *on* him: "We thus distract [people]'s minds from Who He is, and what He did."[8] Screwtape muses, "It is funny how mortals always picture us [demons] as putting things into their minds: in reality our best work is done by keeping things out."[9]

"Decentering" is an educational approach designed to shake loose old assumptions to make room for new possibilities that can be considered from a posture of creative displacement. In the church, decentering practices eject us from our existential comfort zones and bring us to a new place (often symbolized by physical relocation) from which we can reconsider God's action in the world and in us. It is safe to assume that the disciples' recognition of Christ behind the locked doors of the Upper Room threw them into an existential tailspin: the Jesus they knew was dead, and yet here he is, talking to them, rendering their identity as mourners obsolete. In this momentary displacement, suspended between who they thought they were and who God calls them to become, the disciples loosen their grip on their old assumptions and entertain a reality that just moments ago seemed unfathomable. Jesus is alive. The Lord is risen. Salvation has come.

Spiritual detachment enacts the liminal principle of the gospel that we discussed in chapter 5. In youth ministry, liminal practices leverage dissonance for the sake of divine transformation. Thrust into spaces where none of our usual cultural tools work, we are forced to step back and scan for new ones. In so doing, we observe ourselves and our situations anew, rethinking our former understandings of God, self, and others. Such reflexivity indicates a maturing consciousness, according to the cognitive psychologist Robert Kegan, who views the capacity to intentionally and self-critically observe ourselves as the central factor enabling personality growth.[10] A century of research across disciplines reveals a consistent pattern in the creative process: after a stage of preparation, a period of incubation or gestation is necessary before insight emerges. Reflexivity both prepares us for, and helps us lay claim to, personal change and growth. Experience shapes us whether we are reflective about it or not; but mature discipleship depends on faithful reflexivity to integrate into our emerging identities those experiences in which God grasps us and lets us see ourselves and others differently.

REFLEXIVITY AND THE ENCOUNTER WITH "OTHERNESS"

Tim Clydesdale's research on college freshmen revealed that young people entering college tend to stash the identities they have formed in their families, communities, and churches in an "identity lockbox," effectively hitting the pause button on ego formation. Yet three groups of students—"future intelligentsia," "religious skeptics and atheists," and "religious emissaries"—consistently buck this trend. Because they do not compartmentalize their previous self-understandings, these students' identities continue to mature in continuity with their prior identifications. What unites these diverse students is a shared capacity for reflexivity, or the ability to observe themselves and their society from alternative points of view, which allows for a critical perspective on popular American moral culture:

> These teens grow up doubting core elements of popular American moral culture and thus reflecting upon their deeper identities and broader perspectives on the world regularly. When they enter college, this does not change. They become highly-desirable students, because they genuinely engage with class materials and because they demonstrate intellectual curiosity, creative engagement, social awareness, or all three.[11]

Clydesdale found that only about one in seven college freshman actually possessed the intellectual curiosity, creative engagement, and social awareness necessary to avoid the identity lockbox phenomenon, and most of these (more than 85%) fell into the category of "religious emissaries," young people nurtured in behind-the-wall conversations that gave them the cultural tools that challenged society's dominant narratives.[12] What this tells us is that faithful reflexivity does not come naturally. A capacity for critical self-awareness must be cultivated.

Typically, it goes hand-in-hand with a growing awareness of others—and in the church, with a growing awareness of God. Most of the church's signature practices aim for these forms of awareness. The goal of prayer, scripture reading, worship, and works of mercy all invite an encounters with the Other—human or divine—and make us aware of God, others, and ourselves in a new way.

Encounters with others de-center us, precipitating a momentary suspension of self in which we dangle precariously outside our comfort zones, uncommitted. We feel vulnerable and unattached. We frequently experience the Holy Other intensely in such spaces. Social scientists parse such holy encounters in terms of their emotional, cognitive, sensate, and neurological effects, but these experiences can never be adequately understood by taking them apart. We do not analyze such transformative moments as much as we allow them to engulf us; we do not grasp them as much as they grasp us. As the physicist Fritjof Capra writes:

> The great shock of twentieth-century science has been that systems cannot be understood by analysis. The properties of the parts are not intrinsic properties but can be understood only within the context of the larger whole.... Ultimately—as quantum physics showed so dramatically—*there are no parts at all.* What we call a part is merely a pattern in an inseparable web of relationships.[13]

The importance of such "experiences of the whole" has not been lost on educators. Instead of focusing on analysis and deconstruction, experiences of faithful reflexivity sharpen skills of self-awareness and alert us to the webs of interconnection that bind us to the universe. Donald A. Schon points out that these are artists' insights, not technicians.' Schon maintains that artistry is learnable and coachable, but not teachable. In design, for example, "one must grasp [the design] as a whole in order to grasp it at all."[14] This is not to say there are not component parts of reflexive faith that can and should be practiced, but until young people (and the rest of us) have experienced the coherence of the whole design—*until we have experienced God's engulfing presence with us*—the relationship between faith and other aspects of our lives will seem opaque and meaningless.

DEISM UNPLUGGED: RELIGIOUS EXPERIENCE
AND AMERICAN TEENAGERS

Religious experience matters to American teenagers. Gabrielle described it as "beginner's luck":

> *Beginner's luck . . . is not only something that I believe exists, but also something that I think helped make this trip perfect in so many ways. . . . When I say beginner's luck, don't think I'm neglecting God. If you read [Paulo Coelho's] definition of beginner's luck,[15] you'll find that I really mean more of a divine will, the universe's conspiracy to hook a neophyte onto something worthwhile.*

The National Study of Youth and Religion defined spiritual experience operationally (and narrowly) as a commitment to live one's life for God, an experience of powerful worship, an answered prayer or sense of divine guidance, or the experience or witnessing of a miracle.[16] Only Jewish and nonreligious teenagers in the study were very unlikely to have "made a personal commitment to live life for God," and more than one in five nonreligious teenagers said they had witnessed "a miracle from God." Seventy-five percent of Mormon and conservative Protestant teenagers, and almost as many mainline Protestant youth, say they have worshipped in moving and powerful ways (only Catholic teenagers had trouble thinking of a meaningful experience of worship). More than half of Christian teenagers interviewed said that they had witnessed a divine miracle, that God answered their prayers, or gave them specific guidance. All told, four out of five American teenagers reported having had a religious experience—and 40% named three or more.[17]

A complicated portrait of teenagers' deism emerges from this research.[18] The NSYR face-to-face interviews revealed a lack of confidence in God's activity in the world—yet in the phone interviews, most teens (65%) said they thought God was a "personal being involved in the lives of people today." Only about one in four (27%) thought God created the world but was not involved in it (the definition of classical deism), or that God was an impersonal cosmic life force.[19] In fact, more than one in five *deist* teenagers said they felt "very or extremely close" to God—the same God they do not believe is active in the world (Smith and Denton's comment on the finding: "Go figure").[20]

As Gabrielle's example suggests, however, having a spiritual experience or a sense of personal closeness to God—and choosing to relate to society as someone changed by this experience—are two different things. Picture a triadic, relational view of the self, with God at the apex, and "self" and "other" located at the other points (see fig. 8.1).[21]

In a triangle, a change in one angle alters every angle. When the other confronts us—whether God, our neighbor, or even the other within ourselves described by Carl Jung[22]—every part of our consciousness is affected. At whatever point the other-encounter dislocates our previous assumptions—whether at the juncture of self, other, or Other—our new awareness of one relationship changes our awareness of all three. The Greek word for this dramatic change of perspective was *metanoia*, or "turning around." Christians translate *metanoia* as "repentance" (a more accurate translation is "to change one's mind"), and the experience of Christ's presence in these turning moments is the stuff of countless spiritual memoirs. Saul's blinding encounter on the road to Damascus offers one commonly cited paradigm: after three days of spiritual reflexivity, when Saul is literally and metaphorically in the dark, dangling between

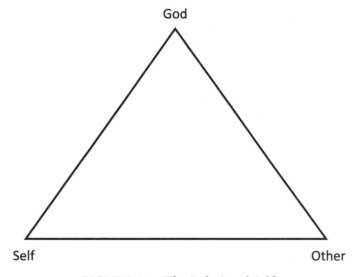

FIGURE 8.1. The Relational Self.

his old life and the one Christ calls him to live, Saul emerges with a new relationship with Christ, and a new identity as a result. Renamed Paul, he is baptized and becomes the church's best example of missional faith.

What such spiritual experiences have in common is their effect: they catapult us into liminal spaces where we find ourselves briefly balanced on the edge of a void—what the practical theologian James Loder called "the potential for non-existence"—where it dawns on us that we are not the center of the universe.[23] This realization fills us with awe and terror; many of the teenagers we interviewed for the NSYR described their first reflexive moment as an encounter with suffering, a response to a death or a cataclysmic loss. At the same time, teenagers recognized these spiritual experiences as creative spaces filled with wonder, turning points where new futures seemed possible in light of new spiritual understandings. Because dangling near the void decenters us, we momentarily move out of our own way, allowing for a mysterious but clearer glimpse of the sacred.

LOOKING FOR THIN PLACES: THE LIMINAL PRINCIPLE OF THE GOSPEL

The ancient Celts believed that the world is perforated with thin places, locations where God seems near enough to touch, where the membrane separating heaven and earth is so thin that humans and angels can almost hear each other sing. A passive, distant God was impossible for a Celt to imagine. The holy pervaded all of Celtic life; in Ireland you could stumble into a thin place in a sheep pasture or a burial tomb. Like Jacob marking the spot of his angelic dream (Gen. 28:10–18), and like teenagers who keep journals and take pictures to remember a site of divine encounter, Celts littered their landscape with rocks and monuments proclaiming *this* to be a thin place, or *that* to be holy ground, places where God reached through heaven's floorboards and grabbed humans' attention.[24]

If you detect sacramental overtones in this description, you are right. A thin place "is a sacrament," says the biblical scholar Marcus Borg, "a means whereby the sacred becomes present to us. It is a means of grace."[25] The decentering encounter—a recognition of the void, human finitude, that comes from being confronted with otherness—leaves us moved, sometimes literally, to a place where the Holy is palpable and we can only respond with awe. Whether teenagers step into a thin place through a traditional rite like the Eucharist or fall into one on a cross-cultural mission trip, thin places act as holy reminders of Christ's presence, and we return from them slightly askew. To be clear: there is no magic that comes from standing in a thin place. Confronting the void or taking part in a liminal practice is closer to plunging teenagers into a baptismal pool, or offering them bread and wine during communion.[26] Liminal practices like prayer, pilgrimage, outreach, Sabbath, and worship simply pull us momentarily out of *chronos* time and suspend us in *chairos* time, long enough to briefly grasp our limited humanity, and gasp at God's power and mercy.

Like the Celts, youth ministers have learned to capitalize on thin places. Commenting on the paradigm-shifting importance of mission trips for many college students, Susquehanna University chaplain Mark Radecke describes the role reflexive practices play in helping his students connect the dots between faith and action:

> When reflection on practices of faith is minimal or missing, when those involved in service projects do not . . . ponder the situation of those served and relate these to the sacred scriptures and practice of their own community, then precious opportunities to make explicit the connections between faith and life are forfeited. Mushy and indistinct god-talk substitutes for engagement with the "master stories" of students' faith.[27]

Karla Koll also stresses the essential role of critical reflection before, during, and after such liminal experiences: "Without reflection," she writes, "action becomes simply activism."[28] Spiritual experience without faithful reflexivity—for example, a reflection process that frames the liminal experience with the gospel—is like a vivid dream that dissolves the moment we return to consciousness, or the moment the youth group returns to Watertown. The emotional imprint of the experience may linger, but the dream's content is lost forever.

We do not control spiritual experience in our children nor do we teach them how to have one. Anyone who has ever planned a middle high retreat knows that God freely moves in, around, through, and often in spite of our most carefully designed staging areas for divine activity. It should not surprise us that, compared to other findings of the NSYR, the role religious experience played in teenagers' lives received scant attention. What is significant about the NSYR is that religious experience received *any* attention—and Smith and Denton explicitly lift up "spiritual experience" a causal factor contributing to moral identity, helping distinguish religious teenagers from their nonreligious peers—even when they do not recognize those differences themselves.[29] Claiming causality is a bold move in social scientific research, yet the NSYR found the variable of spiritual experience too important to ignore.[30] If such liminal experiences are acknowledged by social scientists, what might they mean for the church?

LEAVING IN ORDER TO FIND OURSELVES

For Christians, the best guides for faithful reflexivity are not scholars, but mystics—contemplatives who understand the necessity of temporary apartness from society in order to become detached (decentered) from self interest, in the service of perceiving God more clearly. Throughout Christian mystical tradition, detachment serves as a precondition for spiritual insight. Gabrielle recognizes the essential role apartness plays in her own transformation:

Back in the pharmacy where I work, when I was telling some of the people I work with about the trip, they joked that I could have just stayed at home and done the same thing. But they were wrong. We did have to leave, and I'll tell you why. In order to view our surroundings in such sharp juxtaposition to our homes in Watertown, we had to be somewhere very different. To be truly affected by this difference, I at least had to make a clean break to a place that was, both literally and figuratively, worlds away. In other words, actually going to Mexico was a necessity for this trip to affect us all in the way it did, to change our lives and our thoughts, our hearts and (can these be changed?) our souls. We had to leave in order to find ourselves. We just can't get lost along the way.

Church history is dotted with colorful contemplatives who cultivated a liminal existence as a more or less permanent way of life; most developed a rhythm of tacking back and forth between assimilation into society, separation, and re-assimilation. Many scholars describe adolescence itself is a kind of liminal space, although the inescapability of a participatory media culture has complicated this position. The anthropologist Victor Turner suggested a kind of middle-ground liminality for complex, postmodern societies, where participation in social ritual is more voluntary and individualized than in pre-modern cultures. Turner believed that in complex societies, institutions (like churches) create *liminoid* experiences—practices that temporarily suspend participants in a "marginal zone" of nonintegration, reflection and experimentation for the sake of education and growth.[31]

Christian detachment and the reflexive practices that cultivate it— sacraments, prayer, pilgrimage, for instance—fall into this category. While sacraments and prayer represent the church's most countercultural (and arguably most liminoid) practices, the practice most commonly associated with liminality is pilgrimage. Christian pilgrimages physically disembed us from our point of origin so that we can follow Jesus to Jerusalem, spiritually (e.g., through the liturgical calendar during Lent and Holy Week) and sometimes literally (e.g., through a trip to a holy site).[32] In the transfiguration story, the disciples blithely follow Jesus to a mountaintop—a thin place—and literally see him in a new light. From their flabbergasted glimpse of Jesus' messianic identity, they get an inkling of what following him will cost, though they lack a vocabulary to describe it. Peter blathers on about building shelters. In Matthew's account, Jesus tells the disciples to keep the event under wraps until after his resurrection (an aside that must have been equally astonishing). In Luke, the disciples ponder the revelation in stunned silence.[33]

Youth ministers see similar reactions to sacred experience in young people, and we long for their powerful effects on adolescent faith. We are prone to spring immediately from ideas into action, knowing that our time with teenagers is short—but in so doing, we sacrifice contemplative space necessary for prayer, repentance, reflection, or simply the awe or delight of discerning Christ's presence. Mark Yaconelli attributes youth ministry's obsession with action to a deep anxiety that pervades American churches. He illustrates the difference between ministry rooted in anxiety and ministry rooted in love (see Table 8.1),[34] and points out:

TABLE 8.1. Anxiety versus Love in Youth Ministry Mark Yaconelli

Youth ministry rooted in ANXIETY...	Youth ministry rooted in LOVE...
...*seeks control* (How do I make kids into Christians?)	...*seeks contemplation* (How can I be present to kids and God?)
...*seeks professionals* (Who is the expert that can solve the youth problem?)	...*seeks processes* (What can we do together to uncover Jesus' way of life?)
...*wants products* (What book, video, curriculum will teach kids faith?)	...*desires presence* (Who will bear the life of God among teenagers?)
...*lifts up gurus* (Who has the charisma to draw kids?)	...*relies on guides* (Who has the gifts for living alongside kids?)
...*rests in results* (How many kids have committed to the faith?)	...*rests in relationships* (Who are the kids we've befriended?)
...*seeks conformity* (Are the young people meeting our expectations?)	...*brings out creativity* (What's the fresh way in which God is challenging us through our youth?)
...*wants activity* (What will keep the kids busy?)	...*brings awareness* (What are the real needs of youth?)
...*seeks answers* (Here's what we think. Here's who God is.)	...*seeks questions* (What do you think? Or as Jesus said, "Who do you say that I am?")

We cannot undergo this transformation by the sheer strength of our own will or intellect. It is only by yielding that we can even begin to embody the freedom of God. . . . We have to allow God to "de-program" us from habitually relating to kids as projects that need managing rather than persons who need God's love and trust.[35]

In other words, when churches focus on keeping young people active *for* Jesus, we may forget to teach them how to be present *with* Jesus. Without decentering encounters and the reflexive space they make possible, we shield young people—and ourselves--from God's re-creation, and we dismiss the importance of detachment in helping young people see themselves, the church, and the world from Christ's point of view instead of ours.

"THINGS FALL APART": THE BLESSINGS OF BEING OFF-KILTER

Proponents of transformative learning theory note the importance of clash, conflict, and creative disequilibrium as precipitating factors in change and growth. Right away Gabrielle notices the tension between her middle-class comfort and the task before her in Mexico. Crossing into Tijuana, she discovers, is "not at all what I expected":

> *Mexico has billboards and highways. It has campaign signs, flowers and grass (where it's watered), baseball fields, and soccer games to the hundredth power. It even has ritzy hotels and a Nexium building. But there is a difference between Mexico and America. Though perhaps not different planets, they are certainly different countries. The houses—can they be called houses?—that crowd the dusty cliffs seem held together more by hope than by the laws of physics and gravity. And that's what we're here to bring— more hope, and better houses. . . . We are giving what we have—maybe not all of it, but hopefully the best we can do—and following Jesus. . . . I think we all wish that we could temporarily cast off the culture that raised us and build whole towns, whole villages.*

Every mission trip alumnus recognizes those words—yet disequilibrium is why we come. We are most open to divine reconstruction when we lose our balance, when the Legos® of our carefully constructed selves fall apart so that God can rebuild us in new ways. Christians often experience this disequilibrium as a divine courtship, comparing holy transformation to falling in love, which is exactly what happened to Gabrielle in Rosarito. After the key-giving ceremony that celebrated the building project's completion, Gabrielle wrote:

> *Nothing could capture the tears in Hermilla's eyes as she stood in her new house. . . . I told her as we were leaving, "Espero que su casa nueva sea*

maravillosa." I hope that your new house is marvelous. I should have said, I hope you remember us the way we will remember you. Thank you for changing our lives, even though it was us who were supposed to be changing you.

Though we think of liminal experiences as being mystical and evanescent, most of the time they encompass more tangible or even troubling encounters. This is the void Loder talks about: the recognition that a lifetime is not enough, that the world's suffering—and God's suffering—exceeds our puny imaginations. Gabrielle found her void in the poverty of Rosarito, Mexico, but in this decentering encounter, she is also overcome by a "sweet shame" that convicts her through the villagers she had ostensibly come to help.[36] The extent of these people's witness to her stopped Gabrielle in her tracks. Her diary of the trip (all 138 pages of it) reads like a love story, a familiar one to people like Dean Brackley, one of the Jesuits who replaced the martyred priests in San Salvador in 1989. Brackley describes the experience of visitors to San Salvador:

A sweet shame comes over them, not a bitter remorse but more like the shame one feels when falling in love. The visitors feel themselves losing their grip; or better, they feel the world losing its grip on them. What world? The world made up of important people like them and unimportant poor people like their hosts. As the poet Yeats says, "things fall apart"; the visitors' world is coming unhinged. They feel resistance, naturally, to a current that threatens to sweep them out of control. They feel a little confused—again—like the disorientation of falling in love. In fact, that is what is happening, a kind of falling in love. The earth trembles. My horizon is opening up. I'm on unfamiliar ground, entering a richer, more real world.[37]

Gabrielle comes unhinged in Mexico, and her horizons expand. Things do indeed fall apart, and she stands on unfamiliar ground, unguarded against new ideas, new relationships, new roles, and new sources of hope. This unguardedness, writes the theologian Sang Hyun Lee, is the creative blessing of liminality, which gives the marginalized two advantages over those fully incorporated to society: an openness to new ideas and relationships, and a critical distance from which to evaluate society, including the church.[38] In Mexico, doing new work with new people under new circumstances, Gabrielle begins to reconsider the person she was in Watertown. Her defenses melt, making her pliable to Holy Spirit's prompting to think about God, herself, and others in new ways. In the reflection times throughout the week, Matt reframes his youth group's sense of cultural and existential clash with the gospel of Matthew, sharing the story of the rich young man who sneaks out one night to ask Jesus what he must do to be saved. As Matt describes Jesus' challenge to this young man to give away his most cherished possessions—to leave his comfort zone and follow Jesus—Gabrielle recognizes herself in the story for the first time.

TEACHING TOWARD TRANSFORMATION: TOOLS FOR FAITHFUL REFLEXIVITY

"Logical consciousness"—our awareness of *how* the world works according to rational processes like theories, laws, and concepts—lies at the heart of most Western education.[39] "Mythical consciousness," on the other hand—our understanding of *why* the world works as it does—operates symbolically, and encompasses "our deepest beliefs, myth, faith, spirituality, the unsaid, the unthought, and so forth."[40] Proponents of transformative learning argue for pedagogies that expand both the logical and mythical dimensions of consciousness. Teaching toward transformation typically involves four distinct moments: (1) a disorienting dilemma; (2) critical self-reflection on our prior assumptions; (3) discourse that puts into words the insights derived from our critical reflection; and (4) action (see fig. 8.2).[41]

Christian teaching tends to tap into transformative learning theory somewhat intuitively. Like transformative learning, Christian teaching aims to enlarge consciousness—though the church credits expanded consciousness to the work of the Holy Spirit, not to teaching methodologies. Like the Greek *paideia*, the prototype for the church's earliest educational efforts, Christian teaching seeks *morphosis*, an epistemological transformation so profound that it changes not just what the learner knows, it also changes the learner. Transformative learning

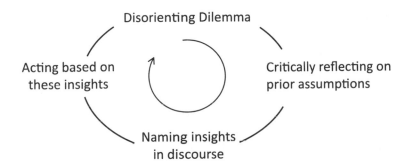

FIGURE 8.2. Teaching Reflexivity.

reflects the *paideia*'s emphasis on wisdom and wonder more than modern education's insistence on data and deconstruction. In Christian formation, knowing more is never the point; knowing God is the point.

Educational theorists consider transformative learning an adult learning strategy, based on the premise that young people whose egos are not yet fully formed cannot truly experience ego transformation.[42] Happily, most parents and youth ministers missed that memo. People invested in the formation of young people utilize many elements of transformative learning theory with effective regularity. Adolescent egos have not yet hardened, and teenagers are not well rehearsed in rationalism's dark art of separating body, mind, and spirit. So thoughtful youth ministers like Matt instinctively address young people's hunger for soul-penetrating, consciousness-expanding experiences by launching processes of transformative learning.[43] Every year, youth ministers immerse teenagers in cross-cultural encounters, cajole them into unasked for leadership roles, and confront them with Bible studies on cultural and theological sticking points. In doing the daily work of ministry, these church leaders eject young people from their comfort zones and catapult them into disorienting dilemmas—thereby introducing them to a larger story in which God has given them a part to play.

That is what happened to Gabrielle.

I have an illegible note on my last page of notes. I can still read one of the words... and it says "transcends." Transcends what? Boundaries. Boundaries

between a million things: boundaries between rich and poor, between com-
fort zones and courage, between old knowledge and new realizations,
between Spanish and English, between Mexico and the United States.
Boundaries between who you were and who you have become. These bound-
aries were challenged, and, I like to think, broken—or, since broken is a
negative-sounding word, how about transformed?

Boundaries, of course, are challenged by liminality. There are a number of ways to understand why the boundaries challenged by Gabrielle's
experience in Mexico made such a deep impression. Clearly, her remarkable capacity for self-reflection contributed immeasurably to her growth
on the trip. We also must acknowledge the catalytic role played by Matt,
who lassoed the trip's liminal potential by constructing frequent opportunities for reflection and provided biblical resources to help youth
evaluate government policies in Rosarito, life in Watertown, Mexican
culture, and Scripture itself. Having prepared the teenagers with cultural briefings beforehand, Matt also created multiple occasions during
the trip for students to put their insights into words, and he challenged
them to specific actions that would help transfer their learning to situations back home.[44]

Gabrielle could have gone to Mexico and had a good week; instead,
she came back converted, not by a come-to-the-altar, existential promise to live for Jesus (though these have their place), but by a reflexive
encounter with sacred texts in which something she was willing to call
God nudged her, repeatedly, to make joyful decisions that were unimaginable before Mexico. Two reflexive practices from the trip are especially noteworthy for their role in Gabrielle's changing spiritual
awareness: a disorienting dilemma, and contemplation.

EXAMINING PRIOR ASSUMPTIONS: THE
DISORIENTING DILEMMA

During the trip, in one of the many discussions about the young ruler who
must give up his possessions to follow Jesus, Matt issued a challenge to all of
us. He challenged us to each give away our most prized possession—not

necessarily our most expensive, but the one with the most sentimental value. He also set a deadline on it, telling us to give it away to someone for whom it would have significant meaning by the end of the summer. Now, there were a lot of sharp inhalations and an outbreak of mutterings when Matt announced this. Everyone instantly began racking their brains to see what that would be. Some people knew right away that they couldn't—people for whom their most treasured possession was a wedding ring or something they wanted to pass down to their daughter in time. But I was intrigued, and I really wanted to do it. I only had one problem: I couldn't think of what my most precious possession actually is. For the rest of the trip, and for about three weeks afterward, I racked my brain for ideas.

The challenge Matt issued to the youth during the mission trip came from Matt. 19:16–30, the only version of the story to call the rich man who came to Jesus "young." The story launches a disorienting dilemma for Gabrielle, unmasking her identity as a consumer and an achiever. Disorienting dilemmas are events, natural or constructed, that pull the rug out from under us far enough to make our existing cultural toolkits inoperable.[45] Disorienting dilemmas can be as ordinary as adjusting to a Mac after years of owning a PC, or as profound as traversing a ropes course, adopting a child, changing jobs, or going into therapy. In each case, the uncertainty of the new situation launches a period of self-reflection and scanning for new options as we examine our prior assumptions, figure out what tools are missing or no longer operable, and look for new resources that can resolve the dissonance.

Of course, not every disorienting dilemma is positive. A parent's death or divorce, a friend's drug use or suicide attempt disorient us as well. So do manipulative teaching tactics, which means that ethical vigilance is required on the part of anyone who attempts such decentering practices (i.e., constructing an event solely to elicit tears, or scaring teenagers into confessions before God, are clearly out-of-bounds). Yet disorienting dilemmas go hand-in-hand with spiritual transformation. A burning bush, an angel in the living room, Saul's three days in the dark: all of these decentering experiences could be considered disorienting dilemmas that shifted recipients' attention away from themselves and riveted their attention on God. This radical change of focus causes us, as it caused Moses, Mary, and Paul, to re-examine our assumptions about who we are, to reflect on our current habits, and to scan for new options. Transformative learning does not just yield new information; it incites a paradigm shift.

Any optical illusion will prove the point, but let's use one that, thanks to the Internet, now has an international following. Take a look at this photo of snow melting on a mountain (see below).[46] A number of stories circulate about the origins of this photo; the most common one attributes it to a Chinese photographer who was struggling religiously. Since the Japanese invasion of China in 1937, he had seen a great movement toward Christianity, but he was unsure what to make of this new faith. One day, riding home on his horse, he felt compelled to photograph the melting snow. When he developed the film, he was shocked to see Jesus' face in the picture—and was so

convicted by the tenderness of Christ's gaze that he became a Christian.[47]

If it sounds a little like seeing Jesus' face on a tortilla, it is; in one (probably apocryphal) version of the story, illegal Chinese house churches used this photograph as a litmus test to distinguish true believers from government spies. When I show this photo to my class, panic sets in. Those who cannot make out Jesus' face in the photograph will not rest until they do (if you are one of them, look at the adapted picture below).[48] The unseeing students turn to their classmates who *can* see the image—the already converted—and ask them to point out the face of Christ. Once students see Jesus' image for themselves, they crow with joy and relief. They are not spies after all.

There is a point to all this hullaballoo, which has to do with the power of a reframing experience. Once we have given the picture meaning, it can never just be a set of black and white blotches again.

Once we assign the photograph spiritual significance–once we make out Jesus' face–we can never *un*-see him in the photograph. A paradigm shift of sorts has occurred. Logically and emotionally, an expectation has been established; a path has been laid that our senses will follow until challenged. Just because some people do not see Jesus in the picture does not change the fact that the image can be discerned by those who recognize Jesus' face; but once we see the image for ourselves, we are changed. From that point on, we can ignore the image, deny it, or even forget the picture exists—but we can no longer look at the photograph without seeing the face of Jesus there.

The picture offers a compelling metaphor for the many ways teenagers come to faith. Some youth recognize Jesus easily while others find him only after much teaching, pointing and reflection. Some are eager to solve the mystery right away; others grow frustrated and even angry if they cannot resolve it, which leaves them out of the "game." And some never recognize Jesus in the picture at all—which does not change the fact that others insist that he is there. The exercise demonstrates the disorienting dilemma's power to motivate learning. When the photograph first confronts us, our usual apparatus for making meaning often fails, leading to unsettling cognitive dissonance. We have to find new ways to make sense of the picture (even if it means dismissing it altogether); we must employ new skills, and scan for new information to decode it. I have learned that students who cannot see Jesus in the picture check out of the rest of the discussion, immune to anything else I have to say until they can resolve the disorienting dilemma by making meaning out of—and peace with—the photograph.

The resolution of a disorienting dilemma is not simply a matter of satisfying our curiosity. In the process of reflecting on the photo, or any other unsettling situation that we must resolve, something concrete happens in our brains. Our neurons literally line up in new ways, creating a neural pathway, laying a track that our nerve impulses travel the next time we see this picture. To use Piaget's terminology, we are creating a cognitive "schema," or category of understanding. That is why we cannot un-see the image of Jesus once we have decoded it. Transformative learning is not just a matter of learning more; it changes us. The disorienting dilemma alters our perspective, allowing us to see the picture in a new way.

DISCOVERING NEW INSIGHTS:
CONTEMPLATION

Transformative learning helps young people move toward the paradigm shift necessary for Christian identity. Yet it is not the church's primary resource for faithful reflexivity. Christian tradition has another word for the process of reflexive transformation that occurs in a liminal space: prayer. Although Gabrielle did not realize it, her journal represents an extended exercise in contemplation, very close to what Ignatius called a prayer of *examen*, as she opens her heart as far as she can to engage in searing self-examination. The purpose of the Ignatian *examen*, or "examination of consciousness," is to become self-aware before God. Prayer is the church's primary form of reflexivity, and therefore the primary catalyst for Christian identity formation, integration and maturity.

I have called Gabrielle's journal an exercise in contemplation instead of prayer only because her gaze is on her own reactions to Mexico rather than on Christ (the classic posture of contemplative prayer focuses on God alone). But she is not far from the conviction of faith either, which begins with such reflexive practice. As John Calvin observed, "Without knowledge of self there is no knowledge of God. . . . But as these are connected together by many ties, it is not easy to determine which of the two precedes and gives birth to the other. For . . . no [one] can survey himself without forthwith turning his thoughts towards the God in whom he lives and moves."[49] While Ignatius's examination of consciousness was intended for the mundane traffic of daily life, most of us engage in such examination when we find ourselves in life's boundary waters. Gabrielle examines her consciousness in this setting, exploring her pre-Mexico self, and discovering and experimenting with the new person God is calling her to become in the course of the mission trip.

Gabrielle is probably unaware of the Ignatian *examen*, a prayer that is typically is divided into five parts. I've given the parts contemporary names to make them easier to remember:[50]

THE IGNATIAN EXAMINATION OF CONSCIOUSNESS (PRAYER OF EXAMEN)

1. *Recall* that you are in God's presence.
2. *Return* thanks to God for the gifts of the day.
3. Ask God to *reveal* the truth as you look at your actions and attitudes with honesty and patience.
4. *Review* the day, looking especially for *spiritual consolations* (places of increased love for God, hope and charity towards others, sorrow for sin, interior joy, peace, movements toward God, etc.) and *spiritual desolations* (places of unrest, darkness of the soul, self-focused desire, lack of confidence, sadness, thoughts that lead away from God, separation from God).
5. *React and respond* to Jesus personally, putting into words your heart's desire, asking forgiveness, strength, and hope to confront desolations, and giving thanks for consolations.[51]

Though lacking the Ignatian form, Gabrielle's journal reveals a moving examination of consciousness as she earnestly tries to put her own life in conversation with the gospel text about the rich young ruler. She struggles especially with her own selfishness. Recalling a day she spent at the market, she reflects:

> *One of the saddest things I saw all day was an old woman sitting on a blanket. She was trying to sell these unappetizing little pellets of gum, gross little turds of chicle, and I felt so bad for her that I was going to stop and pull out some money for her. But my group didn't stop, and neither did I. How much would I have given her? Certainly, if I could go back, I would have stopped and pulled out some change. Would I have given her my lunch of rice cakes and peanut butter? Probably, because I wasn't too hungry that day. But would I have given away my dinner at the campsite after the first day? Would I have given up my sun shower had she needed it, and as a result been filthy overnight? I don't know.*

In the end, Gabrielle thinks that one of the ways the trip changed her most is in her attitude toward material possessions. She writes in retrospect:

> [The trip] didn't so much make me hate opulence as it made me realize how I don't need material goods to be happy. It's funny, that's what Matt has been trying to tell us with his Bible passage about the young ruler all week . . . but it really took this trip to make it real. I don't feel repulsed by what I have. I feel sickened by how little it does, how long it took me to learn how to share.

It is hard not to compare Gabrielle's desire for generosity with a prayer attributed to Ignatius himself: "Lord, teach me to be generous. Teach me to serve you as you deserve; to give and not to count the cost, to fight and not to heed the wounds, to toil and not to seek for rest, to labor and not to ask for reward, save that of knowing that I do your will."[52] As Gabrielle's journal unfolds, her grip loosens on her possessions, especially the jewelry she loves to buy—just as her grip loosens on her old self, until by the journal's end she is openhanded, having given away most of her souvenirs, along with her heart, in Rosarito.

What happened to Gabrielle was *metanoia*, a changing of heart and mind. Most Christians use the shorthand term: conversion. The problem is that we forget that conversion is an ongoing process more often than a one-shot deal—and that *we* don't turn young people around, God does. By the standards of the NSYR, you could view Gabrielle's journal as a disappointment: we know nothing of her parents' faith, she makes few references to Jesus Christ, she offers little in the way of doctrinal awareness. She refers to discussions that Matt instigates about Scripture, and she wrestles with these passages explicitly. In the end, Gabrielle is won by the mission trip, by Mexico, and by all that these symbolize (including the church). But one wonders if she is as thoroughly won by Christ.

Perhaps not yet. But Gabrielle (like the rest of us) is a work in progress, and in the process of faithful reflexivity launched by the trip to Mexico, Christ invites her to reconsider her identity in relationship with God and others. She recognizes Christ's encounter as she grapples with sacred texts that suddenly seem to lay claim to her. As Gabrielle herself points out, God is not absent from this grappling process. For many teenagers, Christ indwells thin places (which explains the jokes about Jesus "living at Ghost Ranch"—or Lakeside, or Lake Junaluska, or Mount Hermon, or Saranac—fill in your favorite Christian camp or summer experience here). Developmentally, teenagers tend to conflate the symbol with the sacred thing it represents, until the symbol *is* the sacred, which explains why they loyally return to the same youth conference year after year, replicate meaningful rituals without variation, and frequently practice a kind of spiritual transference that projects onto Christ the qualities of a youth leader, and projecting onto the youth leader the qualities of Christ.[53]

The liminal principle of the gospel reminds us that God works through disorienting human experiences—not just on the mountaintop but in the reflexive processes these experiences engender. Reflexivity requires more than critical reflection; it requires a language and a community to confirm new insights.[54] Ultimately, the Watertown congregation will prove more crucial to Gabrielle's emerging faith than the trip to Mexico. The new insights that she gained on the mission trip will need plausibility structures and social relationships to give credence to her new view of reality.[55] During a mission trip, the prospect of living our entire life within a spiritual framework may seem very appealing and entirely possible. But then we come home—and unless we come home to faith communities and families who imagine the world in ways that reinforce our decentered perspectives and our newly discovered loves and worldviews, the experience of God on the mission trip will soon evaporate. Gabrielle may begin to doubt whether the community, the relationships, and the faith she found in Mexico were real after all. The liminal moment, in which the rich young ruler's decision seemed so relevant to Gabrielle's own life, could become an event remembered, perhaps a significant one, but not a life lived.

SACRAMENTAL IDENTITY: GOD'S ECHO

Authentic experiences of Christian community and the significant experience of being claimed by a holy text serve as transforming moments in the ongoing, lifelong process of conversion. Gabrielle, for one, does not let them go easily:

Did I mention why I waited almost a week to get my things from the church?
Have I told you why I haven't unpacked my sleeping bag or sleeping mat yet?
It's for the same reason that I keep delaying on this journal. As soon as I pick
up the bags, another part of the journey is over. The minute I shake out the
Mexican dust from my belongings, I feel like I've lost another tangible link to
the past. And the instant I finish this journal . . . I'll—what?

Something important is preserved in the etymology of catechesis, which means "to echo back." An echo distorts, but preserves, the original utterance, and indeed must be connected to its source to exist at all. An echo does not copy the original sound; it transports the original sound across space and time. When God chooses to encounter us using frankly distorted human forms, these forms do not just bear information about God. God actually enters the world through human beings, decisively in the Incarnation but also in flawed human practices like baptism and the Eucharist, pilgrimage and prayer—practices God chooses to indwell and employ to give us missional imaginations, and transform us into followers of Jesus.[56]

But these practices are, by definition, ambiguous. Echoes can be faint, and sometimes we must step away from the din to hear clearly. Decentering practices like disorienting dilemmas and contemplation cultivate detachment by aiming for honest, uncluttered encounters with Otherness, both human and divine, so we can focus on the self-giving love of Jesus Christ instead of on ourselves. Instead of making it easier for young people to fit into the surrounding culture, decentering practices *deform* adolescents for success in the dominant culture, which asks our allegiance to lesser gods. Decentering practices like mission trips and prayer pave the way for epiphanies, conversions, and other threshold experiences where youth glimpse who Christ really is, and what loving him really costs. Faithful reflexivity reveals our reluctance to distinguish Moralistic Therapeutic Deism from Christian teaching, since it means we must untangle God's mission from our own. In fact, our refusal to distinguish Moralistic Therapeutic Deism from the governing goals of global capitalism or therapeutic individualism is how the church's governing god story got to be about *us* rather than about God in the first place.

Meanwhile, I have intentionally left you with a disorienting dilemma. Remember Matt's challenge to the Watertown group, to give away their most cherished possession by the end of the summer, in order to more fully follow Christ? At the end of her journal, Gabrielle is still wrestling with which item to give away:

My iPod? No. While special to me, I could certainly recover if I had to replace it. My class ring? I debated on this one for a long time, ultimately rejecting [it]. I could only give it away to my sister. Plus, my parents bought it for me, and I'm sure they wouldn't be thrilled if I announced one day at dinner that I was giving it away. . . . Finally, I forced myself to examine what I owned that I couldn't replace. [My] photos from countless performances would be meaningless to anyone else. Still, I had not hit on it.

Then, one night, it hit me as suddenly as a summer storm. My stories. Whenever there is a chance of losing them on my computer or in my countless files of paper, I experience true moments of panic. My writing is my greatest treasure, for it is truly irreplaceable. You only really get one chance with writing something, I've found, and so I try to make every word count.

Suddenly I knew. And I knew it was right the moment I thought of it, mainly because of my immediate "oh God no" reaction. "I can't give that away," I told myself. "I'll want to look back on it and remember when I'm old and forgetful." But it all fit; it all made perfect sense. And, as soon as I figured out what, I was just as quickly able to figure out who I am to give it to. It's you, Matt. It is my way of saying Thank You for Everything. You gave me the chance not only to go to Mexico and write this journal, but you also made the environment we worked in conducive to the kinds of changes I needed to have happen. [You] will know what best to do with it. After I've typed it all, I plan to give it away. And then I will delete it all.

And she did.

9

Make No Small Plans

A Case for Hope

Since the seventeenth century more and more people have discovered,
originally to their surprise, they could ignore God and the church
and yet be none the worse for it.
—*David Bosch*

Christianity has died many times and risen again; for it had a God
who knew the way out of the grave.
—*G. K. Chesterton*

I came close to calling this chapter "A Case for Doubt"—which described
all too well the way I felt on many days during the five years I participated in and wrestled with the National Study of Youth and Religion. I
have addressed hundreds of people on this subject during that time.
Some have defended Moralistic Therapeutic Deism as a reasonable
Christian outlook. Few have denied either the fact or the power of its
existence, with young people or with the adults who love them.

Here is what usually happened when I spoke about the study's findings: a pall of recognition would settle over the room. Not many doubted
the description of those churches overcome by Moralistic Therapeutic
Deism, but nobody knew what to do about it. I couldn't stop thinking
about the rich young man that Matt taught about on the mission trip,
the one who came to Christ in the middle of the night asking what good
thing he must do to get eternal life (Matt. 19:16). Those of us grappling with the study's conclusions—pastors, parents, youth ministers,
volunteers—were full of knowledge and good intentions; most of us
were doing ministry in a country with more resources for Christian

youth work than anywhere else in the world. We came to conferences to ask what good things we must do so that the adolescents we love can get the life God has promised. But when we heard that having a highly devoted faith, by the definition of the study, meant relinquishing our comfortable, generic Christianity, we—like the rich young man who came to Jesus—went away sad. Scripture doesn't tell us the rich young man's next move. Nor does it tell us ours.

Although this story is sometimes read as an injunction against wealth, it is really about goals and priorities—and in the Gospel of Matthew it is about the goals and priorities of a young person. His question to Jesus (not unlike American teenagers' approach to religion in general) is about what he himself can get out of religion: "What good thing must I do to get eternal life?" For him, religion is useful; it helps him get what he wants (in this case, a prepaid ticket to eternity). Many young people can identify with his eager desire to please; the success narrative of American culture is writ large in American teenagers, thanks largely to well-meaning adults who have taught them that church is valuable insofar as they get something out of it. God will help you if you're in trouble. Church will make you a better person. Youth group will look good on your college resume. Step right up.

Jesus does not indict our teenagers (or us) any more than he indicted the rich young man. He wasn't putting the young man to a test; he was describing the reality of the situation. Here was a kid who had his hands full—too full, apparently, to receive all the grace God wanted to give him. So Jesus tells the young man: "Go, sell your possessions and give the money to the poor, and you will have treasure in heaven; then come, follow me." But, we are told, the young man went away sad, for he had great wealth (Matt. 19:21–22).

And then there is the effect this research had on me personally. For the past five years, I have spoken with both critics and champions of the research in this book, with students in my classes and with pastors at conferences, trying to make peace with the data I helped to collect. I stayed up way too late on too many nights trying to realign my own sense of call with the youth we interviewed, trying to make sense of the fact that a lot of people, youth and adults alike, have trouble seeing Christ in church. For the first time in twenty years of ministry, I had to admit that *I* often have trouble seeing Christ in church. And yet—the church is where Christ found me, and it is where Christ continues to call me to serve. Where is the problem? In church? Or (the likely answer) in me?

One night, after spending too many days alone with these questions, I hit "send" on an email to most of the youth ministers in my address book—people whose ministries I admire, who already knew something about the National Study of Youth and Religion, and who (I was pretty sure) would help me out in a jam. I explained the book I was writing and admitted that I didn't know how to solve Moralistic Therapeutic Deism without turning the church on its head—which was such an overwhelming proposition that it made me want to throw up my hands and go to the beach. I begged for help:

> You've been in youth ministry long enough to see faith "take" and you've seen it wash over people like a wave that goes back out to sea. You've seen congregations grow and you've seen them go through the motions. You've seen some kids walk away from faith but more kids faking it or getting by on a thimble-full of grace, and you've seen a few actually catch fire, usually not because of us.
>
> *What keeps you in ministry with young people—really? What gives you enough hope to stay in this business?*

What I got in return was a deluge. People sat down at their computers and pounded out pages, not paragraphs—some pastoral, some cynical, all of them brimming with the age-old pastoral tension between frustration and hope.

POSTCARDS FROM THE FRONT

There were far too many responses, far too passionately rendered, to share with you, though they are in a folder on my desk that I will keep, oh, maybe forever. People at all levels of youth ministry seem to share a rock-solid (some might say foolhardy) sense of call to ministry with young people, matched only by an equally abundant (some might say foolhardy) faith in teenagers themselves. Jenny, a seminarian, wrote: "Everything rational in me tells me to run while I still can. But everything that truly feels real and life-giving tells me to keep with it. To watch youth grow up in life and faith is an honor I do not have words for. I guess I am still holding tight to the promise that God is working regardless of whether I am or not." Mike, after a blistering year of pastoral ministry, agreed: "I stay because kids who were going into the Marine Corps work with the poor in DC and four years later go into the Peace Corps instead. I like that it's messy. I like that it's hard. I get to help people cross over into a new world. Although it's pricey, it's the best seat in the kingdom."

If anything besides an irrational sense of call and an irrational confidence in teenagers keeps us in ministry, it seems to be joy. Sarah, a volunteer, said: "I have no clear reason why I bother with any of it, other than the urge to exercise the spiritual gift of teaching with the only demographic in the church that seems open to learn anything. Plus, I have an unaccountable love for these kids. Where else in the life of the church do you get questions like: 'What if God came to earth in the form of a duck and was shot and killed?' *Well*?" Matt, a pastor, admitted: "The older I get, the more I feel that I didn't choose faith, ministry, or youth ministry. They chose me. I don't do this because I feel like it. I do it because everything else I've done has felt like a lie. (Especially retail. I *really* suck at retail.)" Andrew, who teaches youth ministry, summed up dozens of sentiments when he said, "Measuring faith is about as elusive as measuring a quark. Direct measurement is nearly impossible; we have to look for the secondary signs. I don't lose hope because, while the NSYR can give me the *numbers*, I know the *names* of the kids who have found faith, and who have found it on my watch. That is why I can't give up hope . . . Matt, Lex, Kevin, Kirk, Kira, William, Clover—they won't let me."

WHERE DOES THIS LEAVE US?

The National Study of Youth and Religion is a study that I mostly admire, but it also deeply disturbs me. The origin of the word "doubt" is "two": it describes being drawn to two opposite feelings at the same time and having to choose between them. While I leave this project haunted by a strange combination of defeat and hope, my own experience as a pastor and a teacher—refreshed by the testimony of others who sense God's call to love young people for Christ—reminds me that what separates hope from doubt is hope's ability to stand in the known and look expectantly into the unknown. Since Christians believe that God is responsible for the future, and that Jesus Christ has already redeemed it, this expectancy fills us with joy instead of dread. Some etymologists trace the word "hope" to "hop," which suggests "springing and dancing" or "leaping in expectation."[1] In fact, the joyful "leap to faith" that Kierkegaard described is what we seek for young people—not because our ministries are faithful, but because God is.

So at the end of this project, I find that I have arrived at only two conclusions with any confidence. Here is the first: When it comes to vapid Christianity, teenagers are not the problem—the church is the problem. And the second: the church also has the solution.

Moralistic Therapeutic Deism serves an adaptive purpose in American society, which means it is probably here to stay. One person told me that Moralistic Therapeutic Deism is the way the church survives in American society by equipping people to be happy enough. Approaching God instrumentally, as an invisible tool that empowers us do good and feel good, makes sense in a pluralistic consumer culture. Social survival in this culture requires turning down the heat on Jesus and other confessional particularities while highlighting personal and communal benefits that make anxious people feel safe and valued. While I know this is an emaciated version of the gospel, I am also generally in favor of people feeling safe and valued, and I have devoted a large part of my life trying to make the world a hospitable place for those who do—and who do not—agree with me. In ways that I both do and do not recognize, I too have invited the Moralistic Therapeutic Deism symbiote into my home and church. I feel defeated because I am convinced that this compromises the gospel, which calls us to share the good news of God's grace and salvation for all people in Jesus Christ. Yet I sympathize with Christians who default to Moralistic Therapeutic Deism because they deem it better than religious bigotry that can make the gospel seem like anything but good news.

THE FALLACIES OF DISCOURAGEMENT

Moralistic Therapeutic Deism would probably be less insidious if we did not go around calling it Christian. If it we recognized it as another faith altogether, we could step outside it, if we wished, to examine it—or, as a couple of emails suggested, employ all the church's missional imagination to address it. No such luck. Several contributors to my email deluge thought it was nearly impossible for teenagers (or adults) to grasp, in the words of a college chaplain, "the pervasiveness of the American Gospel of Consumerism" while living in it.

It's easy to fall prey to one of two fallacies in the face of the church's complicity in Moralistic Therapeutic Deism. The first is to think that the only alternative to Moralistic Therapeutic Deism is religious bigotry, and that the only alternative to religious bigotry is diluted faith. A good deal of philosophical writing suggests just the opposite—that situating ourselves within a deeply held tradition makes us less rigid. Having an existential home base gives us the confidence to reach out toward others without feeling threatened by them, and without needing to make them become like us.[2] The gospel "makes strange" the society we live in; the Christian story provides an alternative way to make sense of our lives, a behind-the-wall conversation that offers possibilities beyond the entropic political or economic scripts handed to us by the culture at large. The fact that Christians believe that God, in Jesus Christ, was one of us and therefore engaged with culture does not diminish the fact that Christ is utterly more than this, as the Easter story dramatically demonstrates.

An equally vexing fallacy—and one that could be read into the National Study of Youth and Religion itself—is the assumption that there is only one way to interpret Christianity's core beliefs, and that this interpretation that must be taught if teenagers are to adopt a consequential Christian faith of their own. In fact, the texts and practices of Christian tradition have broad parameters that have been interpreted and reinterpreted endlessly; one of the true miracles of Christianity may simply be the fact that we still recognize it after two thousand years of innovation, renovation, and adaptation. This is not to say that all interpretations are equal, and I will go to the mat for a Trinitarian theology in which Jesus serves as the plumb line for divine love.

Yet while I am passionately in favor of teaching Christian doctrine to teenagers—just as I am in favor of teaching our family's history to our children—neither set of stories is immune to corruption. I take that as a given, and I think the rabbis and early church mothers and fathers did too. After all, they did not excise contradictions from the canon. Instead, they saw a multitextured truth emerge from multiple tellings of the faith community's stories, and left the problem of harmonizing the details to modernists. I side with these early teachers, for whom a story's susceptibility to revision was offset by a general principle of inclusiveness. Unless teenagers hear the gospel, harbored in sacred texts in all their problematic wonder, they have no basis for either accepting or rejecting the gospel in the first place. Scholars solve the problem of multiple texts in many ways, including the postmodern deconstructivist's solution of making all texts equally questionable. This just means that scholars have stopped squabbling with God in order to squabble with each other. So be it; but it's squabbling with God that interests teenagers.

Young people looking to us for meaning and hope do not need us to protect God (and God certainly does not need our protection); they need us to model a theology marked by patience, determination, and above all, humility as postmodern Christians honestly confront historical, biological, cultural, and sociological research that may challenge who we thought we were.[3] If we take this research seriously, we will recognize what Christianity's critics see all too well: The contemporary church has strayed, often badly, from the course set before us by the earliest followers of Jesus, who believed in his messianic mission and that God raised him from the dead—and who understood themselves to be sent, as Christ was sent, into the world as instruments of divine love. We are the inheritors of this tradition, and there is no escaping the church's call to participate in the messianic, redemptive purpose of God's love in Jesus Christ, empowered by the Holy Spirit, whose grace is what makes ministry possible in the first place.

THE STRANGE HOPE IN THE NATIONAL STUDY OF YOUTH AND RELIGION

Oddly, I leave this project strangely hopeful. The best news about Moralistic Therapeutic Deism is that teenagers do not buy it as faith. They buy *into* it—it shapes them nicely for fitting into American society, since it conforms so neatly to America's dominant cultural ethos. Youth and parents are correct if they think that Moralistic Therapeutic Deism will outfit them better for success in American society than Christianity will.

Those who want to succeed in American life, and attain high levels of visibility in it, will find that being theologically bland helps immeasurably. Yet the gospel is very clear: God wants to liberate us from being defined by these circumstances, so that we are free follow Jesus regardless of the culture we call home.[4]

But is Moralistic Therapeutic Deism to be taken seriously as a religion, a tradition of life-giving truth and life-orienting power? Teenagers seem dubious. Afraid of being branded as religious zealots (while being gladly zealous for almost anything else), many American churches have overcompensated, setting the bar low for religious commitment of any kind, tending God's garden with forks and spoons when tractors and backhoes are in order. Speaking of mainline Protestant churches, the ethicist L. Gregory Jones warns: "Churches seem trapped in a narrative of decline. . . . We reassure ourselves that God calls us to faithfulness, not success, which is true. But . . . too often we turn 'faithfulness' into a misguided justification for aiming low, settling for mediocrity, and remaining content with decline." Jones wonders if the dreams of American Christianity have become too small, and he offers the words of the nineteenth-century architect Daniel Burnham:

> Make no small plans. They have no magic to stir humanity's blood and probably themselves will not be realized. Make big plans; aim high in hope and work. . . . Remember that our sons and daughters are going to do things that will stagger us. Let your watchword be order and your beacon, beauty. Think big.[5]

If American churches are thinking small, there is a reason: Moralistic Therapeutic Deism sets our sights on ourselves, not the stars. Yet a missional imagination inspired by the gospel requires the church, above all, to think big: to lash our ambitions to the cross, and set our hopes on Jesus Christ, who established the church for the world, nothing less . . . which means that we are not here, any of us, for ourselves.

One of religion's by-products is its capacity to enlarge the human imagination. Religious passion can be as dangerous as a box of TNT, or as powerful as unrequited love. Faith can topple towers or governments, it can manipulate millions or set millions free, it can cause death or overcome death. The church, at various times, has been on every side of the passion equation, but when we get it right Christian discipleship means following a God who loved us enough to die for us, and who calls us to love others just as deeply. While Moralistic Therapeutic Deism shapes teenagers' bland expectations of the church, most American young people participate in Moralistic Therapeutic Deism without surrendering to it. When compared to young people in other parts of the English-speaking world, American teenagers (like American adults) appear positively besotted with religion—but even those who say religion matters to them seem to consider Moralistic Therapeutic Deism worthy of little more than compliance, and hardly worth radical commitment.

WHAT HAVE WE LEARNED?

It may be that young people are not the religious relativists we make them out to be. It may simply be that Christianity—or what passes for Christianity, as teenagers see us practice it—does not merit a primary commitment. It may be that the only time young people see churches point to Christ's exclusive claims is when we raise the flag on Jesus to claim him for ourselves, like Antarctica for the queen. Teenagers are right to give little credence to such distortions of the gospel: whenever "Christianity" suggests that some people are more welcome before God than others, this pseudo-gospel must be rejected. The historic teachings of the church side with teenagers over and against the religious claims and practices of many American congregations. The particularity of Christ is exactly what prevents the church from being an exclusive club, and the life, death, and resurrection of Christ is precisely the act of God that makes it possible for every human being to stand before God.

In these pages we have identified two resources that can help us understand how to counter Moralistic Therapeutic Deism with consequential faith: (1) highly devoted teenagers themselves, and (2) highly devoted congregations, in which youth and adults alike teach, tell, and take part in the Christian God-story to cultivate missional imaginations for the church and for the world. Some teenagers do possess consequential faith, a phenomenon that seems linked to highly devoted parents who participate in religious traditions that emphasize a particular set of cultural tools. Some congregations, like those identified by the Exemplary Youth

Ministry study, do encourage adolescents' desire to live their lives for God. By attending to the arts of translation, testimony, and detachment, we inch toward recovering the church's missional imagination, a way of envisioning a world that embodies Christ's self-giving love.

What can we learn from those faith communities in which young people consistently demonstrate consequential faith? *First,* we learn that it can be done. If Mormons, and to a lesser extent, conservative and black Protestants, can foster such faith in teenagers, so can the rest of us. As one youth pastor pointed out in his email, Moralistic Therapeutic Deism does not colonize churches—people do. And to a large extent, we can determine the degree to which our congregations choose to imitate Christ and participate in the divine ethic of giving, or practice a risk-averse gospel of self-fulfillment.

Second, religious formation is not an accident. Teenagers reporting high degrees of religious devotion did not get that way on their own; their faith is the legacy of communities that have invested time, energy, and love in them, and where the religious faith of adults (especially parents) inspires the faith of their children. Smith and Denton write, "How religiously serious and involved American teenagers are is not merely randomly or individually determined, but reflects the influence of particular social locations and especially key social relationships and organizations. Parents, friends, youth organizations, religious congregations, and youth group leaders all appear to have significant influence on the shape and extent of American teenagers' religious and spiritual lives."[6]

Third, the cultural tools associated with consequential faith are available in every Christian faith community, although these tools are more obvious in communities where the governing theology ("peculiar God-story") highlights, in word and deed, those aspects of the Christian story that speak to God's personal and powerful nature, the interpersonal and spiritual significance of the faith community, the centrality of Christian vocation, and the hope that the world is ultimately in good hands. At the same time, the mere presence of these cultural tools does not ensure consequential faith in young people or anyone else. The power of the Holy Spirit activates missional imaginations and thus empowers the church to resist and overwhelm self-focused spiritualities with the self-giving love of Jesus Christ.

Fourth, consequential faith has risks. The love of Christ is love that is worth dying for. Congregations are far more reluctant to ask this kind of faith of teenagers than teenagers are to respond to it. Churches differ in the kinds of faith identities they are willing to tolerate in young people. In some congregations, a foreclosed Christian identity—one that is imposed on teenagers rather than freely chosen by them—is preferable to risking youth with no Christian identity at all, especially if the congregation's governing theology holds that teenagers' souls are in eternal peril without a personal profession of faith. Other Christian communities think a diffused religious consciousness is preferable to an imposed one that might prevent teenagers from thinking about faith freely and critically, and stunt their future growth in the church. Both of these alternatives shy away from the primary claim of the gospel—that God loved young people enough to die for them, which is what makes the love of Christ so compelling. Consequential faith is the result of responding to Christ's call to follow him into the world as bearers of the gospel, and neither rigid nor diffuse religious identities can survive a mission where love is the primary cargo. Churches help young people develop consequential faith best when they focus, not on who *they* are—or on who they want young people to be in order to perpetuate their theological brand—but by focusing on who Christ is calling young people to become as he sends them into the world on his behalf.

Fifth, we are called to participate in the imagination of a sending God, which is different from reinventing the church through our own creativity. The arts of translation, testimony, and detachment are just a few of the ways in which Christian tradition participates in God's missional creativity. A God-shaped imagination is bent on the redemption of the world and not just the church—which places self-serving spiritualities like Moralistic Therapeutic Deism on notice. The single most important thing the church can do to cultivate missional imagination in young people is to develop one as a church, reclaiming our call to follow Christ into the world as envoys of God's self-giving love.

HOPE ON THE PHONE

What gives me hope? Lizzie.

The phone just rang and Lizzie sang out her hello. Lizzie is on the leadership team for a large denominational youth conference in Montreat,

North Carolina. She called to tell me she has arrived, and that it is "awesome." Lizzie and I attend the same church, which is as full of Moralistic Therapeutic Deists as any I know; yet Lizzie's faith, at sixteen, has a buoyant intensity that lights her up from the inside, thanks to—well, to what, exactly? That's precisely what this book has tried to discern. I got to eavesdrop on Lizzie's life briefly during the year I spent as her confirmation mentor. Without question, her faith is shaped by her devout family, by encouraging adults in our congregation, by the deep investment of her youth pastor, and by unusually large doses of existential intelligence and reflexive skills that help Lizzie gravitate toward things of the spirit.[7]

But I know dozens of teenagers with similar tools in their toolkits who do not have Lizzie's robust faith. Lizzie is on familiar terms with God (a name she uses more easily than "Jesus"). Her creed is undeniably personal but also holds fast to a God whose suffering love is for everyone. She adores her home congregation but often considers it a barrier to vibrant faith; she prefers the galvanizing, pulsating energy of the Montreat youth conference as a way to experience the Holy Spirit. "I think churches where you can experience God are better for teenagers. That's what we do at Montreat—here I can *feel* God," Lizzie tells me. Like most denominational events, the Montreat youth conferences are bastions of theological branding, and her denomination's recognition of her creativity and leadership, combined with substantial opportunities to use both, have forged in Lizzie a powerful sense of call. She believes that her life has a purpose, and a divinely created one at that. This purposefulness gives her hope; she believes God will use her for something good—"to change the world," as she puts it—and in doing so she is certain that she is following Christ, helping to bring God's will to fruition.

A creed, a community, a call, a hope—all cast in a particular story through which Jesus confronts Lizzie at home and at school and sends her out to love the world on his behalf.

Thinking about Lizzie at Montreat stirs up a memory. At fifteen, I headed to Lake Erie for a United Methodist youth missions conference, with no suspicion that Lakeside—a tiny town notable mostly for the number of retired clergy and youth gatherings it attracts each summer—would forever become holy ground for me. My primary objective was to get a tan, but instead I came home with a sense of purpose that, more than three decades later, I have not been able to shake. My own story echoes that of Zach, a freshly minted youth pastor who answered my email: "What keeps me in youth ministry, despite evidence that Moralistic Therapeutic Deism is predominant and growing? The knowledge that *I* was once that kid who faked faith, and *I* was once that kid who got by on a thimble-full of grace."

What I get to do—and I get to do this for a *living*, which after all these years still humbles and astonishes me—is to walk young people like Zach and Lizzie into God's plans for them. In Zach's case, nobody saw ministry coming; in Lizzie's case, nobody will be surprised. My role in the faith journeys of young people like Zach and Lizzie is embarrassingly small: naming a God-sighting here, inviting them to pray or serve there. Mostly what I do is show up, and get to know them, and respond to them as the incredible creatures God made them to be, while trying to be a faithful Christian adult alongside them.

As a Christian adult, I have an advantage that Zach and Lizzie do not have: mileage. I know they are more than the scripts society has given them. I know God has made them to be more than consumers, more than airbrushed images in an ad, more than victims of their economic or family circumstances, more than applicants to the college or grad school or job of their choice. What Christian adults know that teenagers are still discovering is that every one of them is an amazing child of God. Their humanity is embedded in their souls as well as their DNA. Their family is the church, their vocation is a grateful response for the chance to participate in the divine plan of salvation, their hope lies in the fact Christ has claimed them, and secured the future for them. If we, the church, lived alongside young people as though this were true—if we lived alongside *anybody* as though this were true—we would be the community Christ calls us to be.

That would be more than enough.

Religious Affiliations of U.S. Adolescents, Ages 13–17

Teen religious affiliation	Percentages
Protestant	52
Catholic	23
Mormon	2.5
Jewish	1.5
Jehovah's Witness	0.6
Muslim	0.5
Eastern Orthodox	0.3
Buddhist	0.3
Pagan or Wiccan	0.3
Hindu	0.1
Christian Science	0.1
Native American	0.1
Unitarian Universalist	0.1
Miscellaneous other	0.2
Don't know/refused	1.8
Teen not religious	16
Teen affiliates with two different faiths	2.8

Source: National Survey of Youth and Religion, 2002–2003. Christian Smith with Melinda Denton, *Soul Searching: The Spiritual and Religious Lives of American Teenagers* (New York: Oxford University Press, 2005), 31.

Note: Percentages may not add up to 100 due to rounding.

The National Study of Youth and Religion: Summary of Findings

Finding #1: Most U.S. teenagers embrace some religious identity and are affiliated with a religious organization.

More than 75% of U.S. teens between the ages of thirteen and seventeen call themselves as Christians, and nearly three in five youth say they attend religious services at least monthly. Most youth practice their faith sporadically, but a large minority—about 40%—go to church at least weekly, pray at least daily, and are currently involved in a religious youth group.[1] Slightly more than half (55%) say they have made "a personal commitment to live life for God."[2] In total, about half (49–51%) of U.S. teens say religion is important in their lives.[3]

Finding #2: Most U.S. teenagers follow in their parents' footsteps when it comes to religion.

Contrary to popular opinion, teenagers tend to go along with the religious beliefs and level of commitment of their parents, not necessarily because they buy into it, but because they don't consider religion worth arguing about. Religion is seldom a source of conflict for teenagers. As Smith points out, the conventional nature of young people's faith lends itself to routine and inertia. While the study did not interview parents about their own faith beyond demographic identification, the evidence suggests that religious commitment, understanding, and practice among teenagers reflects—to an astonishing degree—that of their parents.

Finding #3: While most U.S. teenagers feel generally positive toward religion, religion is not a big deal to them.

The authors of the NSYR expressed surprise that teenagers overwhelmingly lacked hostility toward religion. According to the NSYR, "the vast majority of U.S. teens view religion in a benignly positive light."[4] Most youth (even nonreligious youth) believe religion has much to offer, and those who attend church tend to feel positively about their congregations. Almost all young people point to advantages and benefits religion offers individuals and/or society.

Yet the spiritual seeking we hear so much about in the media seems to be a phenomenon left to older adolescents; it was almost invisible among the youth in this study. Teenagers gladly grant people the right to explore other religions, or to cobble together their own eclectic, alternative spirituality—but they are not doing this themselves. While religion is seldom a source of conflict for teenagers (the good news), it is also seldom a source of identity (the bad news). Most American teenagers, observes Smith, "tend to view religion as a Very Nice Thing," but it does not claim them, or even concern them greatly, and they have a very limited understanding of its influence in their lives.[5] While sociologists have long demonstrated known religious beliefs and practices do, in fact, shape the values and lifestyles of U.S. adolescents, teens themselves tend to think of religion as wallpaper: it's an accepted part of their lives that stays in the background, and therefore doesn't merit much thought.

Finding #4: The vast majority of teenagers in the U.S. say they're Christians.

Popular assumptions about religious pluralism among American adolescents seem to be overstated. Three out of four U.S. teenagers say they are Christian (about half are Protestant and one-quarter are Catholic). The next largest group is young people who say they are "not religious" (16%), although follow-up interviews found that some of these youth were nominal Christians (and some interpreted "nonreligious" to mean belonging to a "nondenominational" Christian church). The third largest group is Mormon (2.5%) followed by Jews (1.5%).[6] Denominational distribution among teenagers mirrored that of American adults.

Finding #5: Mormon teenagers are faring best.

In nearly every area, using a variety of measures, Mormon teenagers were consistently the most positive, the most healthy, the most hopeful, and the most self-aware teenagers in the study. Mormon young people also showed the highest degree of religious vitality and salience, the greatest degree of understanding of church teaching, and the highest degree of congruence between belief and action. After Mormon youth, the greatest degrees of religious vitality and salience were found among conservative Protestant and black Protestant teenagers, followed by (in order) mainline Protestant, Roman Catholic, Jewish, and nonreligious teenagers.

Finding #6: The single most important influence on the religious and spiritual lives of adolescents is their parents.

The best social predictor of what a teenager's religious life will look like is to ask what her parents' religious lives look like. By and large, notes the study, parents "will get what they are." While grandparents, other relatives, mentors, and youth ministers may be very influential, parents are most important in forming their children's spirituality. The study states: "Teenagers do not seem very reflective about or appreciative of this fact."[7]

Finding #7: Supply and demand matters to the spiritual lives of teenagers.

The more available religiously grounded relationships, activities, programs, opportunities, and challenges are for teenagers, the more likely they will be religiously engaged and invested. In other words, "congregations that prioritize youth ministry and support for their parents, invest in trained and skilled youth group leaders, and make serious efforts to engage and teach adolescents seem much more likely to draw youth into their religious lives and to foster religious and spiritual maturity in their young members. This appears to be true of local congregations, regional organizations such as diocese and state conventions, and entire religious traditions."[8] Stated negatively, churches that do not invest in their youth find that youth are unlikely to invest in them.

Finding #8: Spiritual and religious understanding are very weak among American teenagers.

The vast majority of U.S. teenagers are, to quote the NSYR, *"incredibly inarticulate* about their faith, their religious beliefs and practices, and its meaning or place in their lives."[9] When asked, many youth defaulted and just said they had no religious beliefs, or unknowingly described beliefs that their own churches consider heretical. This was even true for teenagers who regularly attended church, with mainline Protestants being "among the least religiously articulate of all teens," and with Catholics close behind.[10]

Smith makes a pointed observation here. "We do not believe that teenage inarticulacy about religious matters reflects any general teen incapacity to think and speak well," since many youth interviewed were impressively articulate about other subjects. Rather, Smith hypothesizes that youth were inarticulate in matters of faith because no one had taught them how to talk about their faith, or provided opportunities to practice talking about it. For a striking number of teenagers, the NSYR interview seemed to be the first time any adult had asked these young people what they believed, and how it mattered in their life.[11] Smith concludes, "Our distinct impression is that very many religious congregations and communities of faith in the United States are failing rather badly in religiously engaging and educating youth."[12]

Finding #9: Teenagers tend to espouse a religious outlook that is distinct from the traditional faith commitments of most U.S. religious traditions—an outlook we might call "Moralistic Therapeutic Deism."

Moralistic Therapeutic Deism serves as a "default position" for adolescent religiosity when religious communities' engagement and education of youth is weak. But there is more to the story, for young people seem to be barometers of a larger theological shift taking place in the United States. The study concludes: "Moralistic Therapeutic Deism is, in the context of their own congregations and denominations, actively displacing the substantive traditional faiths of conservative, black, and mainline Protestantism, Catholicism, and Judaism in the U.S. . . . It may be the new mainstream American religious faith for our culturally post-Christian, individualistic, mass-consumer capitalist society."[13]

Finding #10: Religion doesn't claim teenagers' time or attention, compared to other social institutions, activities and organizations.

A number of institutions are so built into adolescents' lives—school, the media, peer groups—that teenagers don't even think of them as holding sway over their schedules or decisions. They simply *are*, and teenagers participate in them because they are insidious and pervasive. Teenagers typically view religion, on the other hand, as optional; it is not, for many of them, just there in the same way that media, school, and families are ever present. Rather, religion functions as an "add-on," an extracurricular activity, something you do if you feel like it or if you have time. Social and cultural forces (therapeutic individualism, mass-consumer capitalism, the digital communications revolution, to name a few) co-opt teenagers' participation, giving competing worldviews very little room to shape our thinking or our decisions about how to use our time.

Finding #11: Highly religious teenagers appear to be doing much better in life than less religious teenagers.[14]

The NSYR observed "sizable and significant differences in a variety of important life outcomes between more and less religious teenagers in the United States." This supports the assumption that religious identities, organizations, and practices shape people's lives in important ways, despite the fact that most teenagers are only dimly aware that this is happening.

What does not help is the persistent tendency of adults to frame adolescent life as "other," "a tribe apart," as Patricia Hersch has put it.[15] According to the NSYR, generational continuity far outweighs any generation gap we might observe, causing Smith to plead for adults "to stop thinking about teenagers as aliens."[16] Most problems that we associate with teenagers are in fact inextricably linked to adult-world problems; furthermore, most teens want and seek strong relationships with adults. Smith views churches as uniquely positioned, among the array of social institutions in the United States, "to embrace youth, to connect with adolescents, to strengthen ties between adults and teenagers."[17]

Characteristics of Teenage Faith, Summarized from NSYR data

	LDS	Conserv. Prot.	Black Prot.	Mainline Prot.	Roman Cath.	Non-religious
Religious service attendance						
*Once or more a week	**71%**	55%	41%	44%	40%	–
*Would attend once or more/week if up to teen	**69%**	63%	48%	47%	40%	12%
*Attends with one/both parents	**85%**	78%	82%	77%	73%	–
Characteristics of faith						
*Faith shaping daily life is very/ extremely important	68%	67%	**73%**	50%	41%	14%
*Faith shaping major life decisions is very/extremely important	**66%**	65%	**66%**	53%	41%	19%
*Teen feels very/ extremely close to God	44%	48%	**49%**	40%	31%	9%

	LDS	Conserv. Prot.	Black Prot.	Mainline Prot.	Roman Cath.	Non-religious
*Few /no doubts about faith in past year	**91%**	81%	78%	51%	44%	–
Religious beliefs						
*Believes in God	84%	94%	**97%**	86%	85%	49%
*God is personal/ involved in lives of people today	76%	**77%**	74%	69%	64%	30%
*Believes in judgment day when God will reward or punish	85%	88%	**91%**	63%	67%	33%
Religious experiences						
*Has made personal commitment to live life for God	69%	79%	74%	60%	41%	13%
*Has had spiritual experience in worship that is moving/powerful	76%	70%	59%	64%	37%	11%
*Has experienced definite answer to prayer or specific guidance from God	67%	65%	61%	53%	42%	18%
Personal religious practices in past year						
*Public profession of faith	**79%**	54%	53%	59%	41%	–
*Has been involved in a religious youth group	**87%**	86%	76%	86%	59%	31%

	LDS	Conserv. Prot.	Black Prot.	Mainline Prot.	Roman Cath.	Non-religious
*Teen is leader in youth group	**36%**	19%	15%	19%	5%	–
*Attends religious education or Sunday School weekly/more	**35%**	12%	9%	7%	2%	1%
*Attended religious camp, retreat, or conference	**86%**	55%	42%	60%	36%	15%
*Attended mission trip	**70%**	33%	28%	42%	23%	6%
Family religious practice						
*Family talks about God/spiritual things once a week or more	**80%**	60%	68%	34%	34%	14%
*Family gives thanks before/after meals	**84%**	67%	79%	54%	45%	18%
*Teen prays with parents other than meals or formal religious services	**79%**	53%	56%	35%	36%	11%

NOTE: Some categories have been combined for readability. For complete figures, see Christian Smith with Melinda Denton, *Soul Searching: The Religious and Spiritual Lives of American Teenagers* (New York: Oxford University Press, 2004).

The 2004 Study of Exemplary Congregations in Youth Ministry: Assets for Developing Spiritually Mature Youth

(www.exemplarym.com)

CONGREGATIONAL ASSETS

1. Faith maturity

God's living presence—Congregation members possess collective sense of God's living presence in community, at worship, through study, and in service

Centrality of faith—Congregation members recognize/take part in God's sustaining/transforming life and work

Emphasizes prayer—Congregation members practice the presence of God as individuals and as a community through prayer and worship

Focus on discipleship—Congregation members are committed to knowing/following Jesus Christ

Emphasizes Scripture—Congregation members value Scripture's authority for their life mission

Centrality of mission—Congregation members witness, seek justice, serve, and promote moral responsibility

2. Pastoral leadership strength

Spiritual influence—Pastor(s) know and model the transforming presence of God in life/ministry

Interpersonal competence—Pastor(s) build sense of community and relate well to adults/youth

Supports youth ministry—Pastor(s) understand, guide, and advocate for youth ministry

Supports leaders—Pastor(s) affirm and mentor youth and adults leading youth ministry

3. Congregational qualities

Supports youth ministry—Congregation makes ministry with young people a high priority

Demonstrates hospitality—Congregation values and welcomes all people, especially youth

Strives for excellence—Congregation sets high standards, evaluates, engages in continuous improvement

Encourages thinking—Congregation welcomes questions and reflection on faith and life

Creates community—Congregation reflects high quality personal and group relationships

Encourages support groups—Congregation engages members in study, prayer, conversation about daily faith

Promotes worship–Congregation expands and renews spirit-filled, uplifting worship in the congregation's life

Fosters ethical responsibility—Congregation encourages individual and social moral responsibility

Promotes service—Congregation sponsors outreach, service projects, and cultural immersions both locally and globally

Demonstrates effective practices—Congregation does variety of ministry practices/activities

4. Youth involvement

Participate in the congregation—Youth engaged in wide spectrum of congregational relationships/practices

Assume ministry leadership—Youth are invited, equipped, and affirmed for leadership in congregational activities

YOUTH MINISTRY ASSETS

1. Youth minister strength

Provides competent leadership—Youth minister reflects superior
theological, theoretical, and practical skill and knowledge in
leadership
Models faith—Youth minister is a role model for youth and
adults, reflecting a living faith
Mentors faith life—Youth minister assists adult leaders and youth
in faith, one-on-one, and in groups
Develops teams—Youth minister reflects clear vision, attracts
gifted youth and adults into leadership
Knows youth—Youth minister knows youth and changes in
youth culture,
utilizes these understandings in ministry
Establishes effective relationships—Youth minister enjoys effective
relationships with youth, parents, volunteers, and staff

2 . Youth and adult leadership

Equip for peer ministry—Youth practice friendship, caregiving,
outreach supported through training and caring adults
Establish adult-youth mentoring—Adults engage youth in faith
and life, supported by informed leadership
Participate in training—Youth/adult leaders evaluate/equip youth
and adults for ministry in atmosphere of high expectations
Possess vibrant faith—Youth and adult leaders possess and
practice a vital and informed faith
Competent adult volunteers—Youth and adult volunteers foster
authentic relationships and effective practices with youth
within a clear vision strengthened by training and support

3. Youth ministry effectiveness

Establishes a caring environment—Youth ministry provides
multiple nurturing relationships and activities, resulting

in a welcoming atmosphere of respect, growth, and belonging

Develops quality relationships—Youth ministry develops authentic relationships among youth and adults, establishing an environment of presence and life engagement

Focus on Jesus Christ—Jesus' life/ministry inspires the church's mission, practices, relationships

Considers life issues—Youth ministry values/addresses the full range of young people's lives

Uses many approaches—Youth ministry intentionally and creatively employs multiple activities appropriate to its mission and context

4. Parental involvement

Possess strong parental faith—Parent(s) possess and practice a vital and informed faith

Promotes family faith practices—Parent(s) engage youth and family in conversations, prayer, Bible reading, and service that nurture faith and life

Reflects family harmony—Families express respect and love, create faith-promoting atmosphere

Fosters parent-youth relationships—The congregation offers parent/youth activities that strengthen parent/youth relationships

Religious vs. Therapeutic Terms and Phrases Used by Teenagers in Face-to-Face Interviews

(number of teenagers who explicitly mentioned these terms or phrases in the National Study of Youth and Religion. *Note*: these are not total numbers of times that teenagers used a word or phrase, but simply the number of teens who used them)

Theological concepts	Therapeutic concepts
Personally sinning/being a sinner (47)	Personally feeling, being, getting, or being made happy (112)
Obeying God or the church (13)	Feeling good about oneself or life (99)
Repenting from wrongdoing (12)	Feeling better about oneself or life (92)
Expressing love for God (9)	Being/feeling personally satisfied or enjoying life (26)
Righteousness (human or divine) (8)	Being/feeling personally fulfilled (21)
Resurrection/rising again of Jesus (7)	
Giving glory/glorifying God (6)	
Salvation (6)	
Resurrection of the dead/Last Day (5)	
Kingdom of God (5; 2 Christian, 3 Mormon)	
Discipleship/being a disciple (4)	
God as Trinity (4)	

Theological concepts	*Therapeutic concepts*
Keeping Kosher (4; of 18 Jewish interviews)	
Grace of God (3)	
Bible as holy (3)	
Honoring God in life (3)	
Loving one's neighbor (3)	
Observing high holy days (3; of 18 Jewish interviews)	
God as holy/reflecting holiness (2)	
Justice of God (2)	
Self-discipline (0)	
Working for social justice (0)	
Justification/being justified (0)	
Sanctification/being sanctified (0)	

Reported by Christian Smith, "On Moralistic Therapeutic Deism as Teenagers' Actual, Tacit, De Facto Religious Faith," Princeton Lectures on Youth, Church and Culture, St. Simon's Island, Georgia (January 7, 2005). Available online at http://www.scribd.com/doc/7699752/Moralistic-Therapudic-Deism-by-Christian-Smith (accessed January 22, 2010).

Notes

Epigraphs

George Whitefield, "The Almost Christian," Sermon 43, The Anglican Library (2001), www.anglicanlibrary.org/whitefield/sermons/43.htm; also see http://catalogue. nla.gov.au/Record/3377624.

John Wesley, "The Almost Christian," Sermon 2, Thomas Jackson, ed. (1872), http://new.gbgm-umc.org/umhistory/wesley/sermons/2/. Thanks to Andrew Zirschky for pointing me to this sermon.

Part 1, Chapter 1

The epigraphs in this chapter are drawn from:

Ralph Waldo Emerson, adapted by Chaim Stern, *Gates of Understanding*, vol. 1 (New York: Central Conference of American Rabbis, 1977), 216.

Christian Smith with Melissa Lundquist Denton, *Soul-Searching: The Religious and Spiritual Lives of American Teenagers* (New York: Oxford University Press, 2005), 171. By historical Christian tradition, Smith indicates that he means Christianity as specified by numerous, defining historical creeds and confessions, including the Apostle's Creed, the Nicene Creed, the Chalcedonian Creed, the Athanasian Creed, Canons of the Council of Orange, the Belgic Confession, the Westminster Confessions, the Heidelberg Catechism, the Augsburg Confession, the Canons of Dort, the Scots Confession, the Thirty-Nine Articles of the Church of England, the First London Confession of Faith, the Schleitheim Articles, the Articles of Religion of the Methodist Church, Documents of the Second Vatican Council, and the Catechism of the Catholic Church. See Smith and Denton, *Soul-Searching*, 322.

Douglas John Hall, "Christian Ministry in a Post Christian Social Context" (occasional paper, Knox College, Toronto, ON, May 11, 2005), www.utoronto.ca/ knox/pages/News%20and%20 Events/Douglas%20Hall%20Address.pdf (accessed June 27, 2006).

1. Robert Wuthnow, *After the Baby Boomers: How Twenty- and Thirty-somethings Are Shaping the Future of American Religion* (Princeton, NJ: Princeton University Press, 2007).

2. The phrase "youth ministry" is an increasingly inadequate name for the church's ministry with young people, thanks to the vagueness of the culturally determined term "youth," the expansion of adolescence, the demarcation of emerging adulthood as its own lifestage, and the technical connotations of the term "ministry," which obscure the theoretical dimensions of the field. I retain the phrase "youth ministry" in this book to acknowledge its common usage, but I intend the term to cover late childhood through emerging adulthood, and to include a broad range of congregational, parachurch, and familial youth ministry forms.

3. Sara Savage, Bob Mayo, Sylvia Collins-Mayo, and Graham Cray, *Making Sense of Generation Y* (London: Church House Publishing, 2006), 154.

4. John Wesley, "The Almost Christian" (July 25, 1741), Sermon 2, Thomas Jackson, ed. (1872), new.gbgm-umc.org/umhistory/Wesley/sermons/2/, Thomas Jackson, ed. (accessed August 20, 2009). Young people were no more immune to this semi-religious outlook during the Great Awakening than in our day; Whitefield himself was only twenty-five when he preached this sermon in 1739, and Wesley delivered his version "before the University" at St. Mary's in Oxford on July 25, 1741.

5. Ibid.

6. James K. A. Smith, *Desiring the Kingdom: Worship, Worldview, and Cultural Formation* (Grand Rapids, MI: Baker Academic, 2009), 171.

7. See Tim Clydesdale, *The First Year Out: Understanding American Teens after High School* (Chicago: University of Chicago Press, 2007) and Sara Savage et al., *Making Sense of Generation Y* (London: Church House Publishing, 2006) for two similar descriptions of adolescent faith; the longitudinal data from the NSYR itself also reinforces these findings. See Lisa Pearce and Melinda Denton, *A Faith of Their Own: Stability and Change in the Religiosity of America's Adolescents* (Oxford University Press, forthcoming) and Christian Smith with Patricia Snell, *Souls in Transition: The Religious and Spiritual Lives of Emerging Adults* (New York: Oxford University Press, 2009).

8. Wuthnow, *After the Baby Boomers*, 62–63.

9. Smith and Denton, *Soul-Searching*, 124.

10. Hall expounds on this theme in many of his writings; for a concise statement, see his unpublished lecture, "Stewards of the Mysteries of God," Lutheran Theological Seminary at Gettysburg (October 27, 2005), Stewardship of Life Institute and Arthur Larson Stewardship Council, www.stewardsoflife.org (accessed May 19, 2009).

11. Hall credits a number of theologians with his thinking on this point, including Tillich's "Protestant principle," Bonhoeffer's "religionless Christianity," as well as Karl Barth and the Niebuhr brothers. Douglas John Hall, untitled lecture (2009 Princeton Forum on Youth Ministry, Princeton Theological Seminary, Princeton, NJ, April 28, 2009).

12. Smith and Denton, *Soul-Searching*, 171.

13. Robert Wuthnow describes the turn from a "dwelling" spirituality to a "seeking" spirituality among Americans in *After Heaven: Spirituality in American since the 1950s* (Berkeley: University of California Press, 1998); he sees another turn toward "practice-based" spiritualities taking place in the early twenty-first century. Also see

Wade Clark Roof's analysis of Americans as "seekers" in the midst of a "quest culture" in Roof, *Spiritual Marketplace: Baby Boomers and the Remaking of American Religion* (Princeton, NJ: Princeton University Press, 1999), 46.

14. Jeffrey Arnett, *Emerging Adulthood: The Winding Road from the Late Teens through the Twenties* (New York: Oxford University Press, 2004), 165.

15. Cf. Richard A. Settersten Jr., "Becoming Adult: Meanings and Markers for Young Americans" (working paper for the Network on Transitions to Adulthood, March 2006), MacArthur Foundation. Also see Richard A. Settersten Jr., Frank F. Furstenberg Jr., and Rubén G. Rumbaut, eds., *On the Frontier of Adulthood: Theory, Research, and Public Policy* (Chicago: University of Chicago Press, 2005).

16. Friedrich Schweitzer, *The Postmodern Lifecycle* (St. Louis, MO: Chalice Press, 2004), 40–63.

17. In its concern for moral fairness, Moralistic Therapeutic Deism resembles what sociologist Nancy Ammerman calls "Golden Rule Christianity"—a theologically fuzzy form of Christianity that honors moral practices more than specific beliefs, as churches approach the Bible pragmatically rather than dogmatically. Ammerman suggests that Golden Rule Christianity may be the dominant form of religiosity among middle-class suburban Americans. See Nancy Ammerman, "Golden Rule Christianity: Lived Religion in the American Mainstream," in *Lived Religion in America*, ed. David Hall (Princeton, NJ: Princeton University Press, 1997), 196–216.

18. Smith and Denton, *Soul-Searching*, 31.

19. Ibid., 262.

20. The average stay of a youth minister in 2006 was 3.9 years. See Rick Lawrence, "3 Dirty, Rotten Youth Ministry Lies," *Group Magazine* (September-October 2006), 77, cited in Mark DeVries, *Sustainable Youth Ministry* (Downers Grove, IL: InterVarsity Press), 93.

21. For lists of relevant research on family influences on adolescent religiosity see Search Institute (http://www.search-institute.org/research/publications.html#families) and the National Study of Youth and Religion (www.youthandreligion.org). A number of authors have translated this research for youth ministry and Christian formation; cf. Mark DeVries, *Family-Based Youth Ministry* (Downers Grove, IL: Intervarsity Press, 1994); Marjorie Thompson, *Family: The Forming Center* (Nashville. TN: Upper Room, 1997); Merton Strommen and Dick Hardel, *Passing on the Faith* (Winona, MN: St. Mary's Press, 2000); also, Roland Martinson and Wesley Black, "Study of Exemplary Youth Ministries in Congregations" (2004), www.exemplarym.org (accessed January 21, 2010).

22. An extended critique of the theological shortcomings of the American practice of youth ministry in mainline churches appears in Kenda Creasy Dean, *Practicing Passion: Youth and the Quest for a Passionate Church* (Grand Rapids, MI: Eerdmans), 2004.

23. Smith and Denton, *Soul-Searching*, 166, 171.

24. Ibid., 171.

25. Ibid., 262.

26. For a summary of some of the most recent research, see ibid., 330–31.

27. The results of the longitudinal studies are available in two books: Lisa D. Pearce and Melinda Lundquist Denton, *A Faith of Their Own: Stability and Change in the Religiosity of America's Adolescents* (Oxford University Press, forthcoming); and Christian Smith with Patricia Snell, *Souls in Transition: The Religious and Spiritual Lives of Emerging Adults* (New York: Oxford University Press, 2009).

28. Smith and Denton, *Soul-Searching*, 127.

29. Ibid., 165.

30. James Fowler's seminal research on cognitive stages in faith development established "synthetic conventional" faith as the most common stage of faith during adolescence. See Fowler, *Stages of Faith* (San Francisco: Harper and Row, 1981), 151–73.

31. Smith and Denton, *Soul-Searching*, 262.

32. Ibid., 131 (emphasis original).

33. Ibid., 131–32.

34. Ibid., 133.

35. The study is cautious in making interreligious comparisons. While the NSYR oversampled Jewish teenagers, their numbers were insufficient to make judgments about the overall religious behavior of Jewish youth. Ibid., 298–300.

36. Ibid., 263. It is worth quoting Smith and Denton fully on this point: "Despite the fact that religion seems quite weak at the level of adolescent subjective consciousness, that most teens can hardly coherently articulate their own beliefs, that religion seems to operate mostly as an unfocused, invisible dynamic operating in the background of teenagers lives, and that many social and cultural forces exert effects that tend to undermine serious religious faith and practice, we nevertheless observe sizable and significant differences in a variety of important life outcomes between more and less religious teenagers in the United States. Highly religious teenagers appear to be doing much better in life than less religious teenagers."

37. For a review of this literature, see ibid., 330–31. See also J. M. Wallace Jr. and T. A. Forman, "Religion's Role in Promoting Health and Reducing Risk among American Youth," *Health Education and Behavior* 25 (December 1998): 721–41.

38. Smith and Denton, *Soul-Searching*, 218–58. Since high degrees of religiosity correspond positively to a sense of overall well-being, it comes as no surprise that, of all teenagers studied, Mormon youth are faring best (261).

39. Ibid., 262.

40. See Donald Juel, *A Master of Surprise: Mark Interpreted* (Minneapolis, MN: Fortress Press, 1994), 62.

Chapter 2

The epigraphs in this chapter are drawn from:
Christian Smith with Melinda Denton, *Soul Searching: The Religious and Spiritual Lives of American Teenagers* (Oxford: Oxford University Press, 2005), 262.

C. S. Lewis, *Mere Christianity* (New York: Macmillan, 1952), 113.

1. Alicia included the link to the site she was reading: www.christianpost.com/article/20050418/6266.htm (accessed May 4, 2006). Her email is used with permission.

2. Alicia would recognize this as hyperbole (i.e., the research did not involve "some random person coming up" and asking teenagers about their faith). Background information and baseline relationships were established with teenagers and parents by letter and phone, prior to meeting teenagers face to face. For a detailed description of the research method, see Smith and Denton, *Soul-Searching*, appendix B, 292–301.

3. Except in cases where teenagers gave us written permission to use their names, or in cases where I am citing other published literature, I have changed the names of all minors except my own children. Teenagers interviewed by the NSYR were coded by number; I have assigned fictitious names for the purpose of readability.

4. Melinda Denton, "Oral Summary of NSYR Findings" (presentation to United Methodist youth workers, Myrtle Beach, SC, February 2004).

5. Smith and Denton, *Soul Searching*, 266.

6. By historically orthodox church teachings, I am referring to the story of salvation history found in the Hebrew and Christian scriptures, summarized in the Apostles' and Nicene Creeds, and basic doctrinal positions reflecting a Trinitarian view of God. Religious practices include both works of piety (worship, sacraments, prayer, contemplation, fasting, searching Scripture, spiritual discernment, etc.) and works of mercy (compassion, hospitality, justice, almsgiving, stewardship, etc). Christian practices are ongoing constitutive activities of a community that echo and embody the life, death and resurrection of Christ in the context of Christian communities.

7. Smith and Denton, *Soul-Searching*, 150.

8. Because this book is written for those interested in Christian formation, I have not included the data on Jewish teenagers (who comprised 1.5% of the youth in the study) in my analysis.

9. The shift toward deism, particularly in the leadership of liberal churches, has been noted elsewhere; Rodney Stark identifies this deistic leaning as typical of the liberal reaction to "fundamentalism" and revivalism, especially among clergy. See Stark, *One True God: Historical Consequences of Monotheism* (Princeton, NJ: Princeton University Press, 2001), 252.

10. Smith and Denton, *Soul-Searching*, 166.

11. Most nonwhite young people date outside their ethnic groups, and more than a third of white teenagers have dated a nonwhite (72% said people dated people of other races because they cared about the other person, while less than 20% said interdating was a rebellion against parents or as an attempt to "be cool"). About two-thirds (63%) of white students who have not dated interracially would consider dating someone who was not white, while 58% of black students would consider dating a nonblack. Alison Stein Wellner, Population Reference Bureau, "U.S. Attitudes Toward Interracial Dating Are Liberalizing" (June 2005), http://www.prb.org/Articles/2005/USAttitudesTowardInterracialDatingAreLiberalizing.aspx (accessed January 31, 2008).

12. See Robert Bellah, "Civil Religion in America," *Daedalus* (Winter 1967): 1–21.

13. Smith and Denton, *Soul-Searching*, 31.

14. The theologian who has posed this question most pointedly for the contemporary church is Miroslav Volf, *Exclusion and Embrace* (Nashville, TN: Abingdon Press, 1996).

15. See Smith and Denton, *Soul-Searching*, 63, 70.

16. Ibid., 124–26.

17. Dr. Seuss (Theodore Geisel), *Thidwick, the Big-Hearted Moose* (New York: Random House, 1948), 16.

18. G. K. Chesterton, *Heretics* (New York: John Lane: Bodley Head, 1905), 97.

19. A number of researchers note shortcomings of interview methods; cf. Jeffrey Stout, "Liberal Society and the Language of Morals," *Soundings* 69 (Spring/Summer 1986): 32–59. The NSYR used standard mixed method research principles to maximize reliability (i.e., multiple conversations, culturally matched interviewers, alternative phrasing, etc.).

20. Smith and Denton, *Soul-Searching*, 250.

21. Cf. Kenda Creasy Dean, *Practicing Passion: Youth and the Quest for a Passionate Church* (Grand Rapids, MI: Eerdmans, 2004).

Part 2, Chapter 3

The epigraphs in this chapter are drawn from:

C. S. Lewis, "Christian Apologetics," in *God in the Dock: Essays on Theology and Ethics* (Grand Rapids, MI: Eerdmans, 1970), 101.

Christian Smith with Melinda Denton, *Soul-Searching: The Religious and Spiritual Lives of American Teenagers* (New York: Oxford University Press, 2005), 116. I have retained the term "Mormon" instead of "Church of Jesus Christ of Latter-day Saints" because this is the term employed by the NSYR. I distinguish Mormonism from historically orthodox Christianity, which includes Protestant, Catholic, and Orthodox churches that derive their tenets of faith from the Christian Bible and teachings summarized in the Eastern and Western church's historic creeds and confessions.

Joseph Smith Jr., as quoted in John Henry Evans, *Joseph Smith: An American Prophet* (Salt Lake City, UT: Deseret Book Company, 1989), 9.

1. Kate Taylor, "Study Finds LDS Faith Helps Teens Avoid Risks," *Oregonian*, May 19, 2005.

2. Osmond family members carried copies of their family missionary tract with them, signing them when approached for autographs. The family takes credit for initiating 25,000 Mormon baptisms. "Update: Donnie and Marie: Mormon Image Makers," *Sunset Magazine* 10 (May-June, 1978), 6; www.sunstoneonline.com/magazine/searchable/Issue10.asp (accessed September 1, 2006).

3. Smith and Denton, *Soul-Searching*, 220.

4. Ibid., 228–29.

5. Ibid., 228. Despite the fact that some youth are in undeniable peril, the NSYR found that most American teenagers seem basically healthy, reasonably happy, and are well on their way to developing the necessary skills for functioning in a consumer society.

6. Ibid., 108.

7. Ibid., 218–58. Smith and Denton note the difficulty of assigning causal outcomes; these differences are noted while controlling for other variables.

8. Ibid., 70, 108–17, 261.

9. Joseph Smith as quoted in Elaine Jarvik, "LDS Teens Tops in Living Faith," *Deseret Morning News,* March 15, 2005, http://deseretnews.com/dn/view/0,1249,600118667,00.html (accessed August 7, 2008).

10. Tim Clydesdale, "Abandoned, Pursued, or Safely Stowed?" (paper, Social Science Research Council, 2006; published February 6, 2007); available at http://religion.ssrc.org/reforum/Clydesdale.pdf (accessed June 1, 2009).

11. Ann Swidler, "Culture in Action: Symbols and Strategies," *American Sociological Review* 51 (April, 1986): 273.

12. Cited by Cynthia Duncan, *Worlds Apart* (New Haven, CT: Yale University Press, 1999), 189.

13. For Swidler, cultural tools may include an array of resources useful in constructing identity; ideologies, images, experiences, relationships, stories, and practices may all be considered cultural tools. See Ann Swidler, *Talk of Love: How Culture Matters* (Chicago: University of Chicago Press, 2001), 73–75.

14. Western assumptions about the self, which inform most theories of identity formation, presume the presence of some version of these categories of faith to organize our cultural tool kits: a governing ideology, a community of belonging, a sense of life's purpose and direction, and a hopeful outlook on the future as necessary to a young person's successful transition into adulthood. Erik H. Erikson's theory of identity formation, the most influential of these theories, is a case in point; see Erikson, *Identity, Youth and Crisis* (New York: W. W. Norton, 1968).

15. The "peculiar story" takes Swidler's cultural toolkit theory in a different direction from Swidler's own research. Swidler argues that goals, values, and intentions do not factor into our cultural toolkits, simply because they are unreliable predictors of how we actually act; but in Christian theology, being formed in Christ means that theological meaning is relevant and necessary to our use of cultural tools; specifically, it transforms our cultural toolkits by putting Christ in charge of them. See Swidler, "Culture in Action," 274.

16. The NSYR is the latest of numerous studies spanning several disciplines that attest to Mormon well-being; they are readily available in searches of social science abstracts and public health surveys. The National Longitudinal Study of Adolescent Health (2001–02) and UCLA's Spirituality in Higher Education: A National Study of College Students' Search for Meaning and Purpose (2005) are two examples.

17. Jarvik, "LDS Teens Tops in Living Faith."

18. Age of first intercourse data is from the National Longitudinal Study of Adolescent Health; the actual percentages for nonvirginity from the NSYR are 12.6% of Mormon teenagers, compared to 20.5% of all teenagers. The National Longitudinal Study of Adolescent Health reports parallel patterns of nonvirginity in higher percentages—which is intriguing, since the study looked only at adolescent girls. In this study, 21.7% of Mormon girls had had sex, compared to 36.2% of all teenage girls. In both studies, black Protestants were the most likely teenagers to be nonvirgins, followed by nonreligious teens; conservative Protestants were the third most likely to have had sex. See Mark Regnerus's excellent study of adolescent sexual practice and religion, *Forbidden Fruit: Sex and Religion in the Lives of American Teenagers* (New York: Oxford University Press, 2007), 123–27.

19. Smith and Denton, *Soul-Searching*, 35, 37, 54–55.

20. Ibid., 40, 46. The importance placed on Mormon identity is extremely high, which makes questioning faith risky since rejecting Mormon identity results in being "disfellowshipped," a sanction seldom practiced in other churches except in extreme Christian subcultures (e.g., the Amish).

21. Taylor, "Study Finds LDS Faith Helps Teens Avoid Risks."

22. Richard N. Ostling and Joan K. Ostling, *Mormon America: The Power and the Promise* (San Francisco: HarperCollins, 1999), 183. Church sources estimate that between 55–70% of eligible LDS youth are enrolled in seminary at any given time; cf. William E. Berrett, "Church Education System," *Encyclopedia of Mormonism,* vol. 1, *Church Education System* (New York: Macmillan, 1992), www.lightplanet.com/mormons/daily/education/ces_eom.htm (accessed October 30, 2005). Online accounts of "seminary experiences" abound, particularly among ex-Mormons, who point to many of the same problems (shoddy teaching, indoctrination, uninvested teenagers) that characterize the educational programs of many religious communities.

23. Smith and Denton, *Soul-Searching*, 40. Since youth who say religion is important to them are more likely to have friends who share their religious beliefs, the presence of highly devoted Mormon teenagers who live in communities that are mostly Mormon is not surprising. The range of religious doubt among non-Mormon teenagers is fairly small. The number of teenagers who said they had had "few or no doubts" about religious beliefs in the past year were: Jews (75%), Black Protestants (78%), Roman Catholics (79%), conservative Protestants (82%), mainline Protestants (84%), and Mormons (91%). Black Protestants and Roman Catholics expressed the highest level of doubt (21% each said they had "many or some doubts" about religious beliefs in the past year).

24. James Marcia's work, furthering the psychosocial identity theory of Erik H. Erikson, posited four identity statuses: achieved identities (chosen after a period of questioning), foreclosed identities (chosen without a period of questioning or doubt), diffused identities (unwilling and unable to commit to identity or the questioning necessary to achieve one), and moratorium (not yet committed). Identity-achieved individuals have passed through a period of questioning and exploration, achieving a resolution by committing to particular beliefs and life goals. Foreclosed individuals, on

the other hand, have committed to a particular set of attitudes, values, or plans without experiencing a period of identity crisis. James Marcia, "Development and Validation of Ego-Identity Status," *Journal of Personality and Social Psychology* 3 (1966): 551–58.

25. Cf. Blake Ostler, "Revisioning the Mormon Concept of Deity," *Element* 1:1 (Spring 2005), www.smpt.org/member_resource/element/ostler_element1–1.html (accessed August 30, 2006). The theologian Douglas J. Davies sees Mormons as counterbalancing the authority of tradition in Catholicism and the authority of Scripture from the Reformation with "prophetic" authority—charismatic vision invested in human beings—as a means to know God. "Jural and Mystical Authority in Religions: Exploring a Typology," *Diskus* 3 (1995): 2.

26. While Mormon apologists often trace the concept of "progression" to themes of *theosis* found in the writings of Athanasius, orthodox Christians generally interpret this as a misreading; the Holy Spirit's transformation allows humans to participate in the life of God thanks to divine grace and redemption, but there is no human progression toward godhead. Cf. Philip Edgecumbe Hughes, *The True Image* (Grand Rapids, MI: Eerdmans, 1989), 281.

27. Robert Millet, address to the 1998 Church Educational System Fireside, cited in Richard N. and Joan K. Ostling, *Mormon America: The Power and the Promise* (San Francisco: HarperCollins, 1999), 312.

28. Cited in Ostling, *Mormon America*, 304.

29. Smith and Denton, *Soul-Searching*, 60, 64.

30. David Campbell and J. Quin Monson, "Dry Kindling: A Political Profile of American Mormons" (paper, Conference on Religion and American Political Behavior, Dallas, TX, August 2002; updated August 4, 2003), 20.

31. Unique to Mormons is the renowned practice of wearing temple garments (sacred underwear), bestowed at the time of a young adult's endowment ceremony at the temple (Ostling, *Mormon America*, 181). The teenagers interviewed for the NSYR were too young for the endowment ceremony and therefore did not wear or mention temple garments.

32. Smith and Denton, *Soul-Searching*, 55. 74% of Mormon teenagers say that their family talks about God, the scriptures, prayer, or other religious or spiritual things together a few times a week or every day. Black Protestants were next most likely to talk about faith in their families every day (27%) and to pray with their parents (56%).

33. Charles W. Nuckolls, "Mormonism as an Ecclesiology and System of Relatedness," *FARMS Review* 16 (2004): 315. Mormons tend to see the individual as the unit of salvation (accomplished by grace and atonement of Jesus Christ) but the family as the unit of exaltation (ultimate salvation in the celestial kingdom). For a detailed analysis of Mormon soteriology, and for a discussion of the family as the unit of exaltation specifically, see Douglas J. Davies, *The Mormon Culture of Salvation* (Aldershot, Hampshire, UK/Burlington, VT: Ashgate, 2000), 67.

34. Smith and Denton, *Soul-Searching*, 46–53.

35. The Mormon boys we interviewed corroborated Molly's sense that following missionary service, boys are expected to marry.

36. For Mormons, baptism is the condition for entry into the Celestial Kingdom. Mormons do not baptize before a child's eighth birthday, the result of a revelation in 1831 designating age eight as the point at which children become accountable for their sins and bear personal responsibility for their conduct. Children older than eight who cannot discern between right and wrong (perhaps because of mental limitations) are not considered accountable for their sins, and therefore are not required to be baptized; like all children who die before the age of eight, these youth are considered fully saved through the atonement of Jesus Christ. The Book of Mormon views infant baptism as a "solemn mockery before God." (Moroni 8:4–23). See "The Doctrine and Covenants of the Church of Jesus Christ of Latter-day Saints," Section 68:27, http:// scriptures.lds.org/dc/68 (accessed September 30, 2008).

37. Ostling, *Mormon America*, 181.

38. Smith and Denton use the term "subculture" to mean a set of people with distinct behaviors and beliefs within a larger cultural system—which, of course, is clearly true of the Church of Jesus Christ of Latter-day Saints. Cf. Christian Smith, *American Evangelicalism: Embattled and Thriving* (Chicago: University of Chicago Press, 1998). An alternative definition of "subculture" influential in youth studies comes from the "Birmingham school" of anthropology in the 1960s, which equates subculture with acts of resistance, protest, and refusal by which youth seek to differentiate themselves from the mainstream. Cf. Mike Brake, *Comparative Youth Culture: The Sociology of Youth Cultures and Youth Subcultures in America, Britain, and Canada* (London: Routledge and Kegan Paul, 1985). This view was criticized for overlooking subcultures that lack a strong theme of resistance (as anthropologist Grant McCracken puts it, "The Birmingham school never seems to study anyone who is not brave and plucky"). See www.cultureby.com/books/plenit/html/Plenitude2p24 .htm (accessed December 1, 2004).

39. Mormons bear out Smith and Denton's "subcultural identity theory" in most—though not all—ways. Smith and Denton proposed this theory to explain the persistence and strength of American evangelicals. Cf. C. Smith, *American Evangelicalism*, 89–119. The Mormon church's "subcultural identity" something of a paradox. In 2005–06, Mormons made up 3% of the U.S. Congress, compared to 1.9% of the general population—and two (Orrin Hatch and Mitt Romney) have made serious presidential bids. As for American evangelicals, "subculture" must be a relative term for Mormons. For religious affiliation of congressional representatives, see www .adherents.com/adh_congress.html#109 (accessed August 14, 2006).

40. Carol B. Thomas, "Spiritual Power of Our Baptism," *Ensign* (May 1999): 93.

41. Smith and Denton, *Soul-Searching*, 108–17, 290. Most Protestants and Catholics do not view Mormons as Christians, though Mormons almost universally dispute this. Some scholars see a distinct break in the Mormon tradition away from Trinitarian theology after 1835, while others point to "re-Christianizing" trends in Mormonism throughout the twentieth century. Cf. John L. Brooke, *The Refiner's Fire:*

The Making of Mormon Cosmology, 1644–1844 (Cambridge: Cambridge University Press, 1996). The Presbyterian Church (PCUSA), one of the few major Protestant denominations to officially study the question of whether Mormons are Christians, concluded that Latter-day Saints express "allegiance to Jesus Christ in terms used within the Christian tradition" but nonetheless are not regarded as "within the historic apostolic tradition of the Christian Church." The report advised putting Mormon-Presbyterian relations under the rubric of "interfaith," like Jewish-Presbyterian relations. At least one branch of Mormonism (Community of Christ) stresses its continuity with mainstream Christianity and places a high priority on relationships with other communions. See Ostling, *Mormon America,* esp. 315–33.

42. The NSYR corroborated other studies that found demographic propensities toward religious devotion: Blacks and Hispanics tend to be more devoted than whites; girls tend to be more devoted than boys, younger teenagers tend to be more devoted than older youth, and teenagers from the South tend to be more religiously devoted than teenagers from the Northeast (who were the *least* religiously devoted of all groups). Teens with more highly educated parents tend to attend religious services more often, and teens in higher income families are less likely to say that faith is important in their lives. Smith and Denton, *Soul-Searching,* 107, 110, 287–88.

43. Teenagers are more likely to participate in a religious youth group and attend religious services if they also join organized activities at school and in the community; they are also more likely to be highly devoted if their church has youth programs and a full-time youth minister. Mormons are the exception to this rule; full-time youth ministers are rare in Mormon stakes (Smith and Denton, *Soul-Searching,* 113–14). The converse is also true: "When religious communities do not invest in their youth, unsurprisingly, their youth are less likely to invest in their religious faith" (ibid., 262)

44. Ibid., 108. Young people who attend church without their parents—a sign of religious devotion that the NSYR examined specifically—are most likely to be conservative Protestants who are actively involved in a church youth group, attend religious camps or retreats, and attend a church with a full-time youth minister. See ibid., *Soul-Searching,* 113–14; also 57–58.

45. In a global postmodern society, withdrawing into what sociologists call "sheltered enclaves" capable of resisting modernity seems to be almost impossible. Cf. C. Smith, *American Evangelicalism,* 67–69, 118–19.

Chapter 4

The epigraphs in this chapter are drawn from:

Christian Smith with Melinda Denton, *Soul-Searching: The Religious and Spiritual Lives of American Teenagers* (New York: Oxford University Press, 2005), 269.

Walter Brueggemann, "Ecumenism as the Shared Practice of a Peculiar Identity," *Word and World* 28 (Spring 1998): 133.

1. A 1991 study from the Carnegie Council of Adolescent Development, looking at the religious youth programs of the ten largest Protestant denominations in the

United States, the American Catholic Church, and the three largest Jewish religious youth organizations in the United States, found two goals for youth work shared by every denomination: giving young people a faith identity, and offering them safe passage into adulthood. See Kenda Creasy Dean, executive summary, "A Study of, and a Review of the Literature about, Protestant, Catholic, and Jewish Religious Youth Organizations in the United States" (unpublished white paper, Carnegie Council of Adolescent Development, Washington, DC, 1991).

2. Douglas John Hall, *The Cross in Our Context* (Minneapolis, MN: Augsburg Fortress, 2003), 137.

3. Ibid., 40.

4. Emil Brunner, *The Word and the World* (London: Student Christian Movement Press, 1931), 110.

5. Hall, *Cross in Our Context,* 139–43.

6. Ibid., 139.

7. See Kenda Creasy Dean, *Practicing Passion: Youth and the Quest for a Passionate Church* (Grand Rapids, MI: Eerdmans, 2004).

8. The purpose of "reflecting" Christ's love varies according to theological tradition; these theological nuances were not explored by the NSYR.

9. Like many highly devoted teenagers, Kelsey shows early signs of competencies she will need for thriving adulthood: an ability to take responsibility for herself, independent decisions, emotional self-control. These competencies are associated with pro-social behavior (including civic and educational engagement), resilience, relational success, and a sense of purpose. See Peter Benson et al., "Executive Summary: Successful Young Adult Development," (research review, Bill and Melinda Gates Foundation, December 10, 2004), 2, 7, www.gatesfoundation.org/nr/Downloads/PNWG/EarlyLearning/SuccessfulDevelopment.pdf (accessed July 27, 2008).

10. Smith and Denton, *Soul-Searching,* 27.

11. William Placher, "Why Creeds Matter," *Christian Century* (September 20, 2003), 23.

12. In two polls, 29% of Americans say they believe that God controls what happens on earth. George Gallup and Jim Castelli, *The People's Religion* (New York: Scribner, 1989); also Harris Interactive #60, October 16, 2003, http://www.harrisinteractive.com/harris_poll/index.asp?PID=409 (accessed November 30, 2004). Protestants (38%) are also more likely than Catholics (21%) and Jews (9%) to believe that God controls what happens on earth.

13. A feeling of "closeness" to God is a particularly important feature of American evangelical traditions, and one of the few measures in the NSYR in which Mormons scored below other youth, probably because Mormon theology lacks a relational view of conversion. See Smith and Denton, *Soul-Searching,* 46.

14. Many black Protestant youth in the NSYR had trouble articulating doctrine but were quite conversant in the operationalized theologies of their churches, including the coherence between "Sunday" and "Monday" in the black community, the

privileging of biblical narratives over dogmatic theology, and the view that social activism embodies Christ's moral concern.

15. Americans are known for prioritizing pragmatic aspects of religion over doctrine; witness Alexis de Tocqueville's observation (1831): "Go into the churches and you will hear morality preached; of dogma, not a word." Cited in George Wilson Pierson, *Tocqueville in America* (New York: Oxford University Press, 1938), 154.

16. Rodney Stark, *For the Glory of God* (Princeton, NJ: Princeton University Press, 2003), 376. Youth ministry research has also paid more attention to religious practices than to these practices' theological substance. Funding is partially responsible; the Lilly Endowment, which has a particular interest in religious practices, funded the lion's share of youth ministry research in the United States and Canada in the late twentieth and early twenty-first centuries—including the NSYR and some of my own research.

17. Cf. Rodney Stark, *Exploring the Religious Life* (Baltimore: Johns Hopkins University Press, 2004). Stark compared data from religious research in thirty-four nations and concluded, "Images of Gods as conscious, powerful, morally concerned beings function to sustain the moral order." See Stark, *For the Glory of God*, 376.

18. Rodney Stark, *One True God: Historical Consequences of Monotheism* (Princeton, NJ: Princeton University Press, 2001), 20–23, 28.

19. Catherine of Siena, "Letter to Jerome of Siena," *The History of Catherine of Siena and Her Companions*, trans. Augusta Theodosia Drane, 3rd ed., vol. 1 (London: Longmans Green, 1899), 179.

20. Robert Wuthnow, *Growing Up Religious: Christians and Jews and Their Journeys of Faith* (Boston: Beacon Press, 1999), 192. This is a measurable shift in patterns of religious affiliation. In his classic 1955 study, *Protestant, Catholic, Jew,* the sociologist Will Herberg found that many Americans "join churches as a way of naming and locating themselves socially." See Herberg, *Protestant, Catholic, Jew* (Garden City, NY: Anchor Books, 1960, 41). Alan Wolfe notes the contemporary American Christians tend to invert this pattern—adjusting our beliefs to fit where we belong, instead of vice versa. See Alan Wolfe, *The Transformation of American Religion* (Chicago: University of Chicago Press, 2003), 64–65.

21. Connectedness is the healthy, protective relationship between youth and contexts where they have a sense of place, and feel respected and valued. Cf. Janice Whitlock, *Places to Be and Places to Belong: Youth Connectedness in School and Community* (Ithaca, NY: Cornell University/ACT for Youth, September 2004), 9.

22. Smith and Denton, *Soul-Searching*, 58.

23. Ibid., 60.

24. Ibid., 64.

25. Rodney Stark and Roger Finke, *Acts of Faith: Explaining the Human Side of Religion* (Berkeley: University of California Press, 2000), 118.

26. Smith and Denton, *Soul-Searching*, 156.

27. Ibid., 156–57.

28. Ibid., 53. After Mormons, mainline Protestant teenagers were most likely to take part on mission teams (70% of Mormon and 42% of mainline Protestant

teenagers have been part of one or more "religious missions team or service project," compared to 33% of conservative Protestants, 28% of black Protestants, and 23% of Catholic teenagers). These statistics should be considered alongside socioeconomic variables; the middle class status of many American Mormons and mainline Protestants affords financial resources that make possible some forms of outreach that are less common for youth in other traditions.

29. Phil Schwadel and Christian Smith, *Portraits of Protestant Teens: A Report on Teenagers in Major U.S. Denominations* (Chapel Hill, NC: Odom Institute, 2005), 62. Similar patterns surround the practice of talking about one's religious faith with others. Almost three out of four Mormon teenagers (72%), and more than half of conservative (56%) and mainline Protestant (51%) youth say they have shared their religion with someone not of their faith; only 41% of Roman Catholic teenagers say the same. Smith and Denton, *Soul-Searching*, 46. Interestingly, 58% of Jewish teenagers said they shared their faith with someone not of their faith—a significantly higher proportion than other Protestant communities; meanwhile, black Protestants only shared their religious faith with someone not of their faith 41% of the time.

30. Smith and Denton, *Soul-Searching*, 168.

31. Ibid., 164.

32. Ibid., 164.

33. As Jurgen Moltmann puts it, eschatology is "the key in which everything is set." *Theology of Hope* (San Francisco: Harper and Row, 1967), 16.

34. Smith and Denton, *Soul-Searching*, 225.

35. For two interpretations of the ongoing task of negotiating identity throughout the lifecycle, and the importance of religious commitments during this process, see Friederich Schweitzer, *The Postmodern Lifecycle* (St. Louis, MO: Chalice Press, 2004), and Robert Kegan, *In Over Our Heads* (Cambridge, MA: Harvard University Press, 1994).

36. James Marcia nuanced and extended Erikson's notion of identity formation, arguing for a dynamic view of identity, which he viewed as a structure of beliefs, abilities, and past experiences about the self. For Marcia, identity involved adopting a sexual orientation, a set of ideals/values, and a vocational direction. Marcia contended that the content of identity can change throughout the lifecycle, but structure must be in place during adolescence for this to occur. He posited four identity statuses: foreclosure, diffusion, moratorium, and achievement. Cf. James Marcia, "Development and Validation of Ego Identity Statuses," *Journal of Personality and Social Psychology* 3 (1966), 551–58.

37. Roland Martinson, "The Spirit and Culture of Youth Ministry: A Study of Congregations with Youth of Vital Faith" (working paper, Luther Theological Seminary, October 12, 2004), appendix A. This definition is based on the characteristics of committed youth as defined by two previous studies, "Five Cries of Youth" and "Effective Christian Education," both conducted by Search Institute (Minneapolis).

38. Thanks to Church of Scotland youth minister Jonathan Fraser for introducing me to Jean Luc Marion's views on God's excessive giving. Marion's theology of giving

is concisely explained by Stephen Webb, *The Gifting God: A Trinitarian Ethic of Excess* (Oxford: Oxford University Press, 1996), 129ff.

39. Assessing spiritual maturity in terms of fruitfulness is a biblical image that became normative for sixteenth-century Carmelite reformer Teresa of Avila, who famously advised the nuns in her convents to assess their spiritual health the way gardeners discern the health of their gardens: if a gardener wants to know how his garden is faring, he does not look at the soil or the water, he looks at the flowers. If the flowers are beautiful and flourishing, reaching maturity and bearing fruit, the garden is healthy. The water supply (prayer) may therefore be deemed sufficient, guaranteeing more flowers in the future. But if the flowers are withering on the vine, something is wrong—not with the flowers, but with the water supply. See Teresa of Avila, *The Collected Works of St. Teresa of Avila*, vol. 1, trans. Kieren Kavanaugh and Otilio Rodriguez (Washington, DC: ICS Publications, 1987), 137–38.

40. As told by C. S. Lewis, *Mere Christianity* (New York: Walker and Co., 1987), 205.

41. Feminist anthropologists point out that centuries of women have influenced their patriarchal culture by controlling reproduction. Cf. Carole M. Counihan, *The Anthropology of Food and Body: Gender, Meaning and Power* (London: Routledge, 1999).

42. Smith and Denton, *Soul-Searching*, 113–14.

43. Results of the study are available at www.exemplarym.org.

44. Scriptural authority in this case does not refer to literal interpretation; rather, these congregations view Scripture, with the interpretive lens used by given communities, as normative for their practices.

45. Robert Fulghum, *It Was on Fire When I Lay Down on It* (New York: Villard Books, 1989), 175ff. Thanks to Ron Foster for sharing this story with me.

46. Andrew Walls, "The Old Age of the Missionary Movement," *International Review of Mission* 77 (January 1987): 26.

Chapter 5

The epigraphs in this chapter are drawn from:

Christian Smith with Melinda Denton, *Soul-Searching: The Religious and Spiritual Lives of American Teenagers* (New York: Oxford University Press, 2005), 270.

Jonny Baker, "Mission among Young People in 'Secular' Europe," *Lausanne World Pulse* (June 2008), www.lausanneworldpulse.com/947?pg=all (accessed June 9, 2009). Baker is referring to European youth, but his insight is relevant for American teenagers as well.

1. Rick Reilly, "There Are Some Games When Cheering for the Other Side Feels Better than Winning," *ESPN: The Magazine* (December 28, 2008), http://sports.espn .go.com/espnmag/story?section=magazine&id=3789373 (accessed May 1, 2009).

2. Kate Ashford, "Best Places to Live: Top 1000," CNNMoney.com (2007), http:// money.cnn.com/galleries/2007/moneymag/0707/gallery.BPTL_top_100.moneymag/ 97.html (accessed May 3, 2009).

3. Demographic data from http://en.wikipedia.org/wiki/Grapevine_Texas (accessed May 1, 2009).

4. See John Howard Yoder, *Body Politics: Practices of the Christian Community Before the Watching World* (Scottdale, PA: Herald Press, 2001).

5. This exegetical insight comes from the Rev. Dr. Emily Anderson, pastor of First Presbyterian Church in Maryville, Tennessee, who preached this passage at the 2009 Princeton Forums on Youth Ministry at Princeton Theological Seminary, Princeton, NJ (April 28, 2009), where she also shared story of the Faith Lions.

6. Daniel Berrigan, *Steadfastness of the Saints: a Journal of Peace and War in Central and North America* (Maryknoll, NY: Orbis, 1985), 22. Thanks to David White for introducing me to Berrigan's book.

7. Dietrich Bonhoeffer, *The Cost of Discipleship* (New York: Simon & Schuster, 1995), 89.

8. Karl Barth, *Church Dogmatics IV.3b* (Edinburgh: T&T Clark Publishers, 1962), 875; also, *Church Dogmatics IV.3a* (Edinburgh: T&T Clark Publishers, 1962), xi–xii.

9. Alan Hirsch, "Defining Missional," *LeadershipJournal.net* (December 12, 2008), www.christianitytoday.com/le/communitylife/evangelism/17.20.html (accessed 7 June 2009).

10. Lesslie Newbigin, *The Gospel in a Pluralist Society* (London: SPCK, 1989), 141.

11. Tertullian, Robert Dick Sider, ed. "Apology," *Christian and Pagan in the Roman Empire: The Witness of Tertullian* (Washington, DC: CUA Press, 2001), 61.

12. The particular phrase "little Christ" is attributed to Martin Luther, *Address to the Christian Nobility of the German Nation*, cited in James Kittelson, *Luther the Reformer* (Minneapolis, MN: Fortress, 2003), 151. The Online Etymology Dictionary traces the current use of the word "mission" to 1598, when Jesuits sent members abroad, from L. *missionem* (nom. *missio*) "act of sending," from *mittere* "to send." www.etymonline.com/index.php?term=mission (accessed May 31, 2009).

13. See Walter Brueggemann, *Interpretation and Obedience* (Minneapolis, MN: Fortress Press, 1991), especially chap. 3, "The Legitimacy of a Sectarian Hermeneutic," 41–69. Henry Jenkins describes the cultural situation of the digital age in similar terms; Jenkins views the technological developments of our time less as a digital revolution than as a cultural one, less apt to replace earlier technologies than to renegotiate new relationships with them; see Henry Jenkins, *Convergence Culture: Where Old and New Media Collide* (New York: New York University Press, 2006).

14. Lamin O. Sanneh, *Disciples of All Nations: Pillars of World Christianity* (New York: Oxford University Press, 2008), 27–28.

15. Andrew Walls, *The Missionary Movement in Christian History: Studies in the Transmission of Faith* (Maryknoll, NY: T&T Clark, 1996), 258.

16. The Rt. Rev. Graham Cray et al., *Mission-shaped Church: Church Planting and Fresh Expressions of Church in a Changing Context* (London: Church House, 2004), 41.

17. Ibid., 12.

18. This language dominated much of the early writing about youth ministry as a field, beginning with parachurch ministries who viewed schools as mission fields,

continuing through the 1970s and early 1980s, when "youth culture" was viewed as a mission field (by the 1980s, youth culture and popular culture had become virtually indistinguishable, and the language of mission faded somewhat).

19. A penetrating critique of this strategy is found in Andrew Root, *Revisiting Relational Youth Ministry: From a Strategy of Influence to a Theology of Incarnation* (Downers Grove, IL: IVP Books, 2007).

20. See Sandi Carpello, "Outreach Red Bank Program Offers Understanding; Hopes to Engage Area Teens in Bible Study," *Hub* (August 29, 2003), hub.gmnews .com/News/2003/0829/Front_Page/003.html (accessed July 8, 2007).

21. The term "missional church" gained currency through the work of a group of scholars known as "The Gospel in Our Culture Network," which led to several prominent publications advocating a missionary role for the church in North America. See especially Darrell Guder, *The Continuing Conversion of the Church* (Grand Rapids, MI: Eerdmans, 2000), and Darrell Guder and Lois Barrett, eds., *Missional Church: A Vision for the Sending of the Church in North America* (Grand Rapids, MI: Eerdmans, 1998). I am a latecomer to this conversation, which is heavily indebted to Karl Barth; my own views on missional ecclesiology are informed by the thinking of John Wesley, who did not use the term "mission" but fused personal and social holiness to such an extent that no other purpose besides worship and witness in the contexts where we serve justifies Christian communities' existence.

22. Outreach Red Bank is featured on the DVD "Soul Searching," which traces the stories of many of the young people interviewed as part of the National Study of Youth and Religion. To see a trailer or to purchase, see www.youthandreligion.org or visit amazon.com.

23. The congregation as the primary instrument of God's mission has been an ecumenically shared assumption since Vatican II. Cf. World Council of Churches, *Mission and Evangelism: An Ecumenical Affirmation* (Geneva, 1982), par. 25.

24. Walls, *Missionary Movement*, 24.

25. Andrew F. Walls, "The Translation Principle in Christian History," in *Missionary Movement*, 27–29.

26. Sanneh, *Disciples of All Nations*, 25–26, 28.

27. Andrew Walls, personal conversation, April 23, 2006 (Princeton, NJ).

28. Andrew F. Walls, "The Gospel as Prisoner and Liberator of Culture," in *Missionary Movement*, 7.

29. "Along with the indigenizing principle which makes his faith a place to feel at home, the Christian inherits the pilgrim principle, which whispers to him that he has no abiding city and warns him that to be faithful to Christ will put him out of step with his society; for that society never existed, in East or West, ancient time or modern, which could absorb the word of Christ painlessly into its system." Ibid., 8.

30. Darrell Guder, "Mission in a Pluralistic Society-Why?" (presentation, Mission Conference, Nyborg Strand, Denmark, June 9, 2006). An online version of the presentation can be found at http://fkm.dk/icms/filer/presentation-1-guder.pdf (accessed June 8, 2009).

31. Reuven Kahane, *The Origins of Postmodern Youth: Informal Youth Movements in a Comparative Perspective* (Berlin: Walter de Gruyter, 1997), 31.

32. A number of excellent resources urge churches to help young people extract themselves from the dominant "consumer narratives" of American culture. Cf. Tom Beaudoin, *Consuming Faith: Integrating Who We Are with What We Buy* (Lanham, MD: Sheed and Ward, 2007); Brian Mahan, Michael Warren, and David White, *Awakening Youth Discipleship* (Eugene, OR: Wipf and Stock, 2007); Katharine Turpin, *Branded* (Cleveland, OH: Pilgrim, 2006); Dorothy Bass and Don Richter, eds., *Way to Live* (Nashville, TN: Upper Room, 2002). A number of summer youth programs focus on theological reflection to this end; cf. The Youth Theological Initiative (Candler School of Theology, Atlanta), http://www.candler.emory.edu/YTI. The necessity for critical reflection to be part of young people's missionary mindset will be taken up in chapter 8.

33. Reinhold Neibuhr, *The Nature and Destiny of Man: A Christian Interpretation* (Louisville, KY: Westminster/John Knox, 2002), 72.

34. David Thomas, "Impact of This Game on Players' Lives Can't Be Overstated," Dallas-Fort Worth Star-Telegram (November 7, 2009), www.star-telegram.com/300/story/1743813.html (accessed January 20, 2010). Thanks to Sandy Redd of Covenant United Methodist Church in Arlington, Texas for sending me this article.

35. Walls, "The Gospel as Prisoner and Liberator of Culture," 4–6 (italics added).

Part 3, Chapter 6

The epigraphs in this chapter are drawn from:

Lamin O. Sanneh, *Disciples of All Nations: Pillars of World Christianity* (New York: Oxford University Press, 2008), 287.

Christian Smith with Melinda Denton, *Soul-Searching: The Religious and Spiritual Lives of American Teenagers* (New York: Oxford University Press, 2005), 191.

Walter Brueggemann, *Interpretation and Obedience: From Faithful Reading to Faithful Living* (Minneapolis: Augsburg Press, 1991).

1. Story condensed from "Eve Gets Naked in Church," December 23, 2005, www.spiegel.de/international/0,1518,392005,00.html (accessed September 10, 2007); also "Youths Reveal Racy Bible Calendar," BBC News, December 3, 2005, http://news.bbc.co.uk/2/hi/asia-pacific/4494938.stm (accessed September 10, 2007).

2. Martin Luther, preface to *The Small Catechism* (1529), translation by the Lutheran Church-Missouri Synod; http://www.lcms.org/graphics/assets/media/LCMS/smallcatechism.pdf (accessed August 16, 2007).

3. Cited in Martin Albrecht, "The Effects of Luther's Catechisms on the Church of the Sixteenth Century" (lecture, Dr. Martin Luther College and Wisconsin Lutheran Seminary, 1979), http://www.wlsessays.net/authors/A/AlbrechtEffects/AlbrechtEffects.PDF (accessed August 14, 2007).

4. Christian Smith with Patricia Snell, *Souls in Transition: The Religious and Spiritual Lives of Emerging Adults* (New York: Oxford University Press, 2009).

5. One notable exception is Jeffrey Arnett, *Emerging Adulthood: the Winding Road from the Late Teens through the Twenties* (New York: Oxford University Press, 2004), 174. Arnett's data stands in such stark contrast to the preponderance of research (and common sense) that even Arnett expresses surprise.

6. Smith, *Souls in Transition*; Smith's research reinforces earlier studies such as Peter Benson et al., *Effective Christian Education* (Minneapolis, MN: Search Institute, 1990).

7. Nancy Tatom Ammerman, Arthur Emery Farnsley et al., *Congregation and Community* (New Brunswick, NJ: Rutgers University Press, 1997), 360.

8. Ibid., 359.

9. Ibid.

10. John Smith, "The Language of Faith: Inside and Outside the Walls," *Conversations* 3 (Parkville, VIC: Centre for Theology and Ministry, n.d.,), 2; available at ucaconversations@ctm.uca.edu.au.

11. Ammerman, 360 (emphasis added).

12. Brueggemann, *Interpretation and Obedience*, 64.

13. Cf. Jacques Derrida, "Des Tours de Babel," trans. Joseph Graham, *Acts of Religion*, ed. Gil Anidjar (London: Routledge, 1985), 104–33.

14. Many books on translation theory trace the ebb and flow of this debate throughout history, starting with the ancient Greeks through theorists like Jacques Derrida; cf. Lawrence Venuti, ed., *The Translation Studies Reader* (London: Routledge, 2000), and Rainier Schulte and John Biguenet, *Theories of Translation* (Chicago: University of Chicago Press, 1992). The weight of the current debate follows Derrida, in which the interpreter holds the power to develop a "relevant" translation (Jacques Derrida, "What Is a 'Relevant' Translation?" trans. Lawrence Venuti, in Schulte and Beiguenet, 423–46). Hans Erich Nossack makes the point vividly: "A translated book that is merely grammatically correct is hardly more than a mannequin draped in the colors of a foreign country. There is no breath of life" (Schulte and Beiguenet, 230).

15. Lamin O. Sanneh, *Disciples of All Nations: Pillars of World Christianity* (New York: Oxford University Press, 2008), 25.

16. Andrew F. Walls, *The Missionary Movement in Christian History: Studies in the Transmission of Faith* (Maryknoll, NY: Orbis, 1996), 38.

17. Walls calls Protestantism "essentially Northern vernacular Christianity" because it first took hold in provinces where Roman rule was tentative. Ibid., 40.

18. Brueggemann, *Interpretation and Obedience* (Minneapolis, MN: Fortress Press, 1991), 30.

19. See Werner Jaeger, *Paedeia* (New York: Oxford University Press, 1943–44).

20. A summary and photograph of the event is available at the National Museum of the Performing Arts' website, www.peopleplayuk.org.uk/guided_tours/circus_tour/circus_performers/blondin.php.

21. Smith and Denton, *Soul-Searching*, 60.

22. Ted Smith, "Is Anyone (Even the Devil) Irreconcilable?" (lecture, 2008 Princeton Lectures on Youth, Church, and Culture, Princeton Theological Seminary, Nashville, TN, January 7, 2008).

23. See Edward Fenton, "Blind Idiot: The Problems of Translation," in *Crosscurrents of Criticism: Horn Book Essays 1968–1977*, ed. Paul Heins (Boston: Horn Book, 1977), 290–305.

24. Walls, *Missionary Movement in Christian History*, 43.

25. Andy Freeman and Pete Greig, *Punk Monk: The New Monasticism and the Ancient Art of Breathing* (Ventura, CA: Regal Books, 2007).

26. A 2005 Pew Internet and American Life study found over one-half of all American teens—and 57% of teens who use the Internet—could be considered media creators. (For the purpose of the study, a media creator is someone who created a blog or webpage, posted original artwork, photography, stories or videos online or remixed online content into their own new creations.) Most have done two or more of these activities. One-third of teens share what they create online with others, 22% have their own websites, 19% blog, and 19% remix online content. Contrary to popular stereotypes, these activities are not restricted to white suburban males. In fact, urban youth (40%) are somewhat more likely than their suburban (28%) or rural (38%) counterparts to be media creators. Girls aged fifteen to seventeen (27%) are more likely than boys their age (17%) to be involved with blogging or other social activities online. The Pew researchers found no significant differences in participation by race-ethnicity. Henry Jenkins et al., "Confronting the Challenges of a Participatory Culture" (paper, MacArthur Foundation, Chicago, IL, 2006, 11).

27. Jenkins, "Confronting the Challenges," 3.

28. Ibid., 7–8.

29. Ibid., 4.

30. Brueggemann, *Interpretation and Obedience*, 64.

31. Sarah Arthur, *The God-Hungry Imagination: The Art of Storytelling for Postmodern Youth Ministry* (Nashville, TN: Upper Room, 2007), 27 (emphasis original).

32. Ibid., 148.

32. Aristotle, *Poetics*, 22:I549A.

34. Edward de Bono, *Lateral Thinking: Creativity Step by Step* (San Francisco: Harper Colophon, 1973). See also Fred Balzac, "Exploring the Brain's Role in Creativity," *Neuropsychiatry Reviews* 7 (May 2006), www.neuropsychiatryreviews.com/may06/einstein.html (accessed October 1, 2008).

35. Pete Ward, "The Fluidity of Faithfulness," *Journal of Student Ministries*, www.thejournalofstudentministries.com/articles/20/1/The-Fluidity-of-Faithfulness/Page1.html (accessed October 1, 2008).

36. Talcott Parsons, *The Social System* (Glencoe, IL: Free Press, 1951), 208.

37. Cf. Lamin O. Sanneh, *Translating the Message: The Missionary Impact on Culture* (Maryknoll, NY: Orbis Books, 1989).

38. Anna Carter Florence, *Preaching as Testimony* (Louisville, KY: Westminster John Knox, 2007), 124.

39. Florence, *Preaching*, 125.

40. See Walls, *Missionary Movement in Christian History*, 8. Walls notes: "It is hardly possible to exaggerate the importance of this early controversy and its outcome;

it is a pivot on which Christian history turns" for it "built the principle of cultural diversity into Christianity in perpetuity" ("Old Athens and New Jerusalem: Some Signposts for Christian Scholarship in the Early History of Mission Studies," *International Bulletin of Missionary Research* 21 [4, 1997], 148). As Walls tells it, "the leaders of the Jerusalem community (swayed, in the Acts account, not by Paul's torrid eloquence but by the measured judgments of the seniors who had known Paul the best, Peter and James the Just) accepted the essentials of Paul's argument. Though circumcised, Torah-keeping Jews themselves, they recognized that Gentile believers in the Messiah could enter Israel without becoming Jews. They were converts not proselytes" (147).

Chapter 7

The epigraphs in this chapter are drawn from:

Christian Smith with Melinda Denton, *Soul-Searching: The Religious and Spiritual Lives of American Teenagers* (New York: Oxford University Press, 2005), 131.

Jim Forest, "Dorothy Day," in *The Encyclopedia of American Catholic History,* ed. Michael Glazier and Thomas J. Shelley (Collegeville, MN: Liturgical Press, 1991), 414.

1. Lynna Williams, "Personal Testimony," *Texas Bound: 19 Texas Stories* (Dallas: Southern Methodist University, 1994), 193, 197. I am grateful for Amanda Drury's helpful critique of this chapter.

2. The quote is from a student interviewed for Drury's research on testimony in high school juniors and seniors in evangelical congregations where testimony is explicitly encouraged. Amanda Hontz Drury, "Empowering Testimonies: A Grounded Theory Project in the Role and Function of Testimonies in Adolescent Spiritual Development" (unpublished paper, Princeton Theological Seminary, August 15, 2009).

3. *Jesus Camp*, directed by Heidi Ewing and Rachel Grady (A&E IndieFilms, 2006).

4. Smith and Denton, *Soul-Searching,* 171.

5. Christian Smith with Patricia Snell, *Souls in Transition: The Religious and Spiritual Lives of Emerging Adults* (New York: Oxford University Press, 2009), 290.

6. See William James, *The Varieties of Religious Experience* (New York: Simon and Schuster), 1997.

7. Ibid., 55. 23% of mainline Protestant, 24% of Catholic, and 9% of Jewish families "talk about God, the scriptures, prayer, or other religious or spiritual things together" every day or a few times a week.

8. Ibid., 46, 59, 46. 88% of LDS teenagers say they openly express their faith at school "some" or "a lot" compared to 56% of conservative Protestants, 56% of black Protestants, 43% of mainline Protestants, and 36% of Catholic and Jewish youth. There are nonverbal expressions of faith as well; nearly half of conservative (49%) and mainline Protestants (48%) wore jewelry or clothing expressing religious meaning, compared to only about two out of five youth from other religious traditions.

9. For a summary of these debates, see George Lindbeck, *The Nature of Doctrine: Religion and Theology in a Postliberal Age* (Louisville, KY: Westminster/John Knox Press), 1984.

10. On the limitations of interview method in sociological research, cf. Bennett Berger, *An Essay on Culture: Symbolic Structure and Social Structure* (Berkeley: University of California Press, 1995), 110–12; Jeffrey Stout, "Liberal Society and the Language of Morals," *Soundings* 69 (Spring/Summer 1986): 32–59; Ann Swidler, *Talk of Love: How Culture Matters* (Chicago: University of Chicago Press, 2001), 44–46. The National Study for Youth and Religion utilized standard research practices, adapted for teenagers, when employing its interview method (e.g., using same-culture interviewers, establishing relational rapport, finding multiple ways to ask the same question, etc.). While these practices lessen the risks associated with accurate self-reporting, they do not eliminate all risks.

11. Most teenagers experienced the interviews themselves as profound acts of care and empowerment. The presence of an interested adult willing to listen to them talk about themselves for two to three hours proved irresistible to most of the youth we interviewed, who frequently thanked us afterward.

12. Thomas G. Long, *Testimony: Talking Ourselves into Being Christian* (San Francisco: Jossey-Bass, 2004), 22.

13. See Richard T. Hughes, *Myths America Lives By* (Urbana, IL: University of Illinois Press, 2004). Only 2–3% of Christian teenagers in the National Study of Youth and Religion developed their own religious beliefs by putting together parts of more than one religion. Smith and Denton, *Soul-Searching,* 82.

14. Also see Jean Baudrillard, *Simulacra and Simulation* (Ann Arbor: University of Michigan Press, 1994), 2.

15. Peter L. Berger and Thomas Luckmann, *The Social Construction of Reality* (New York: Anchor/Doubleday, 1967), 152–54. While acknowledging the importance of nonverbal communication surrounding speech, the authors point out that speech retains a privileged position in conversation, by which they mean "that people speak with one another."

16. Ibid., 153. Emphasis added.

17. Smith and Denton, *Soul-Searching,* 267.

18. Steven Pinker, an outspoken advocate of the "critical period" in speech development, believes there is reason to question social and motivational explanations for language acquisition. Pinker believes that the reason children of deaf or pidgin English-speakers become fluent in English, even without "proper" grammatical modeling, is because of an innate human ability to discern pattern similarities that may be generalized to other circumstances (417). See Steven Pinker, *The Language Instinct: How the Mind Creates Language* (New York: HarperPerennial, 1995).

19. See Northrup Frye, *The Educated Imagination* (Bloomington: Indiana University Press, 1964).

20. Long, *Testimony,* 6.

21. Rosina Lippi-Green, *English with an Accent* (New York: Routledge, 1997), 31.

22. Ibid., 63.

23. Augustine, trans. Henry Chadwick, *Confessions* 6, 3 (Oxford: Oxford University Press, 1998), 92.

24. In ancient Greece, the word "rhetoric" had none of the negative connotations associated with today's popular use of the term. Insincere utterances were often ascribed to the Sophists—a school that used rhetoric to train speakers-for-hire capable of arguing any side in a given legal case.

25. As will become apparent, I am borrowing this definition of testimony from Anna Carter Florence's description of the classical definition of testimony. Florence, *Preaching as Testimony* (Louisville, KY: Westminster John Knox, 2007), xiii.

26. The following summer, the language game ran the other direction; when we picked her up from camp, we learned that she had instigated a heated debate over gender-inclusive language for God.

27. J. Lave and Etienne Wenger, *Situated Learning: Legitimate Peripheral Participation* (New York: Cambridge University Press, 1991). Lave and Wenger share many of the *paideia*'s assumptions, including apprenticeship learning models that involve significant relationships between the "master/student."

28. "The path to full participation includes learning how to talk, and be silent, in the manner of full participants" (Lave and Wenger, *Situated Learning*, 105). Lave and Wenger view communities as polycentric, with the "centers" of communities in flux, so they do not view the trajectory of "peripheral" participation as moving toward a community's center; rather, they view the trajectory as moving from partial to full participation.

29. I am tempted to encourage you to stop reading here and read instead Anna Carter Florence, *Preaching as Testimony* (Louisville, KY: Westminster John Knox), 2007.

30. Long, *Testimony*, 99.

31. Florence, *Preaching*, 68–69.

32. Paul Ricoeur, *Essays on Biblical Interpretation* (Minneapolis: Fortress Press, 1980), 119–20. Chapter 3, "The Hermeneutics of Testimony," is available online at www.religion-online.org/showchapter.asp?title=1941&;C=1773 (accessed August 24, 2009).

33. Florence, paraphrasing Walter Brueggemann, *Preaching*, 79.

34. Leif Enger, *Peace Like a River* (New York: Grove/Atlantic, 2001), 311.

35. Florence, *Preaching*, 64. Florence's research traces women's use of testimony as a form of "preaching from the margins." Mary Elizabeth Moore's fieldwork led her to observe the common practice of youth testimony in predominantly African-American congregations. Mary Elizabeth Moore, *Children, Youth and Spirituality in a Troubling World* (Atlanta, GA: Chalice Press, 2008), 273.

36. Stanley Hauerwas, "Carving Stone: Learning to Speak Christian" (lecture, 2007 Princeton Lectures on Youth, Church, and Culture, Princeton Theological Seminary, Princeton, NJ, April 30, 2007).

37. In the words of Vincent Palumbo, master carver at the Washington National Cathedral in Washington, DC: "The sculptor is the creator. He creates on clay. And

then when they cast on plaster is the death. And the carving is the resurrection. That's the motto of our branch of the stone business." Cited in Marjorie Hunt, *The Stone Carvers: Master Craftsmen of the Washington National Cathedral* (Washington/New York: Smithsonian Books, 1999), 77. Hauerwas relies on Hunt's portrayal of the craft of stone carving at the cathedral as the metaphorical foundation for his lecture, "Carving Stone."

38. Hauerwas, "Carving Stone."

39. Seamus Murphy, *Stone Mad* (Wilton, Cork: Collins Press, 2005), 19.

40. Among the Eastern church fathers, "'innovation' and 'blasphemy' were almost synonymous," but Eastern church history—while never calling doctrinal development "innovation"—evolved nonetheless. Jaroslav Pelikan, *The Spirit of Eastern Christendom (600–1700)* (Chicago: University of Chicago Press, 1977), 16, 282–85.

41. According to the 1999 wave of the National Longitudinal Survey of Youth (1997), while most teenagers consistently report that they "think highly of" or "want to be like" their mother or father, it should be noted that about 40% of teenagers surveyed did *not* have high opinions of their parents, and one in twenty "strongly disagree" with the statements above. These attitudes are most likely in adolescents who live apart from a parent or who live with a parent who is not their biological mother or father. (The research notes that a substantial proportion of teenagers still hold very positive feelings toward nonresidential parents and stepparents.) Kristin A. Moore et al., "Parent-Teen Relationships and Interactions: Far More Positive than Not," *Child Trends Research Brief* #2004–25 (Washington, DC: Child Trends, 2004), 3, 6.

42. Smith and Denton, *Soul-Searching*, 60, 226. Mormon teenagers list significantly more supportive, available adults in their lives than other teenagers—20% can name ten or more adults they can turn to for support and advice, not including parents, compared to the national average of 8%. Highly devoted teenagers reported more than twice as many supportive adults available to their parents (7.3, versus 3.4) and a third more adults available to them personally (8.4, versus 5.0) than religiously disengaged teenagers.

43. David Ford, *The Shape of Living* (Grand Rapids, MI: Baker Books, 1998), 46. Ford's thesis offers a theological corollary to the developmental theory of Robert Kegan, who argues that human development proceeds by successive experiences of finding ourselves "in over our heads." Robert Kegan, *In Over Our Heads* (Cambridge, MA: Harvard University Press, 1994).

44. Ford, 49. For a more extended discussion of the relationship between the "immersed" life and youth ministry, see Kenda Creasy Dean et al., *Generation OMG: A Postmodern Youth Ministry Handbook* (Nashville, TN: Abingdon, 2010).

45. Roughly half of Jewish young people have attended a religious camp at least once. Smith and Denton, *Soul-Searching*, 53. For research on religious camps and Jewish identity in college students, cf. Ariela Keysar and Barry Kosmin, "Research Findings on the Impact of Camp Ramah: A Companion Study to the 2004 'Eight Up' Report on the Attitudes and Practices of Conservative Jewish College Students" (National Ramah Commission, Inc. of the Jewish Theological Seminary, New York)

www.campramah.org/news/keysar_kosmin_summary.pdf (accessed July 17, 2007).
The report includes a review of several other studies that reach similar conclusions.

46. 53% of mainline Protestant young people have attended a religious camp at
least once, compared to 24% of Catholics (24%) and 33% of black Protestants. Smith
and Denton, *Soul-Searching,* 53.

Chapter 8

The epigraphs in this chapter are drawn from:
Christian Smith with Melinda Denton, *Soul-Searching: The Religious and Spiritual
Lives of American Teenagers* (New York: Oxford University Press, 2005), 242.

Dorothee Söelle. *The Silent Cry: Mysticism and Resistance* (Minneapolis, MN:
Fortress Press, 2001), 90.

1. Used with permission.

2. G. Jeffrey MacDonald, "Rise of Sunshine Samaritans: On a Mission or a
Holiday?" *Christian Science Monitor,* May 25, 2006, www.csmonitor.com/2006/0525/
p01s01-ussc.html (accessed July 27, 2007). More than 55 million Americans have
taken vacations involving volunteer service, and at least twice that many say they are
considering such a vacation for themselves in the future. See Margaret Jaworski,
"Volunteer Vacations Gain Popularity," *Transitions Abroad Magazine,* September/
October 2006, www.transitionsabroad.com/publications/magazine/0609/volunteer_
vacations_gain_popularity.shtml (accessed September 7, 2007). Short-term mission
trips, lasting two weeks or less, drew 1.6 million Americans to foreign mission projects
in 2006 (Robert Wuthnow, cited in MacDonald, "Rise of Sunshine Samaritans").

3. Robert J. Priest et al., "Researching the Short-Term Mission Movement,"
Missiology 24 (October 2006): 432. Priest and his colleagues extrapolate these numbers
from estimates and data collected by Robert Wuthnow. Thanks to Karla Koll for
pointing me to this research.

4. Karla Ann Koll, "Taking Wolves among Lambs: Some Initial Thoughts on
Training for Short-term Mission Facilitation" (paper, Richmond Forum on Mission
and Missiology, Richmond, VA, February 25, 2008), 6. Cited with permission. For a
discussion of issues raised by mission trips for youth ministry, see Don Richter,
Mission Trips That Matter: Embodied Faith for the Sake of the World (Nashville, TN:
Upper Room), 2008.

5. I have critiqued the unreflective, "parachuting" nature of many short-term
mission trips in youth ministry in chapter 7 of Dean, *Practicing Passion: Youth and the
Quest for a Passionate Church* (Grand Rapids, MI: Eerdmans, 2004), 192.

6. In the interest of full disclosure, I served on the staff of one such project, a
branch of Appalachian Service Project in Cadiz, Ohio, as a college student in 1980,
and have regularly accompanied young people on so-called mission trips within the
United States involving disaster relief, hurricane cleanup, home construction and/or
home repair in my own ministry as a pastor, campus minister, and (today) as a
volunteer.

7. Cf. Jean Pierre de le Caussade, *Abandonment to Divine Providence,* trans. Algar Thorold (Rockford, IL: TAN Books and Publishers, Inc., 1993); Charlotte C. Radler, "Living from the Divine Ground: Meister Eckhart's Praxis of Detachment," *Spiritus* 6 (Spring 2006): 26–47. In his treatise *On Detachment,* Eckhart writes: "Detachment is nothing else but a mind that stands unmoved by all accidents of joy or sorrow, honour, shame or disgrace." In Sermon 43 he says, "The less we turn our aims or attention to anything other than God, and in so far as we look to nothing outward, so we are transformed in the Son, and so far the Son is born in us and we are born in the Son and become the one Son." See Halcyon Backhouse, ed., *The Best of Meister Eckhart* (New York: Crossroad, 1993).

8. C. S. Lewis, *The Screwtape Letters* (New York: Macmillan, 1961), 106–7.

9. Ibid., 20.

10. See Robert Kegan, *In Over Our Heads: The Mental Demands of Modern Life* (Cambridge, MA: Harvard University Press, 1994).

11. Tim Clydesdale, "Abandoned, Pursued, or Safely Stowed?" (paper, Social Science Research Council, 2006; published February 6, 2007), 5. Available at http://religion.ssrc.org/reforum/Clydesdale.pdf (accessed May 29, 2009). For a more extended discussion, see Tim Clydesdale, *The First Year Out: Understanding American Teens after High School* (Chicago: University of Chicago Press, 2007).

12. Clydesdale, *First Year Out,* 5–6.

13. Fritjof Capra, *The Web of Life* (New York: Anchor, 1996), 29, 37.

14. Donald A. Schon, *Educating the Reflective Practitioner: Toward a New Design for Teaching and Learning in the Professions* (San Francisco: Jossey-Bass, 1987), 158–59.

15. Paulo Coehlo, *The Alchemist* (San Francisco: HarperOne, 2006), 93.

16. The definition of "religious experience" is contested; see David Yamane, "Narrative and Religious Experience," *Sociology of Religion* 61:2 (2000): 171–89, http://findarticles.com/p/articles/ml_m0SOR/is_2_61/al_63912433/print (accessed August 29, 2007). Yamane accepts Sir Alister Hardy's definition: "Religious experience . . . refers to all of the individual's subjective involvement with the sacred: the sense of peace and awe, mysticism and conversion, the presence of God, absorbing ritual experience, and on and on." I find this a more satisfying definition than the operationalized definitions used in the National Study of Youth and Religion; it captures what I mean by the "liminal principle" of the gospel that insists that revelation includes a personal or communal sense of God's presence and grace. See Alister Hardy, *The Spiritual Nature of Man: A Study of Contemporary Religious Experience* (Oxford: Clarendon Press, 1979).

17. Smith and Denton, *Soul-Searching,* 44–45.

18. Numerous studies point to a correlation between religious experience and accelerated religious interest and positive attitudes toward Christianity. A Gallup survey reported that a "remarkable and consistent one-third of Americans report a profound spiritual experience, either sudden or gradual, which has been life-changing," and notes that these occurrences often become "the focal point in faith development." George Gallup Jr., "Religion in America: Will the Vitality of Churches

Be the Surprise of the Next Century?" in *The Public Perspective* (Stamford, CT: Roper Center for Public Opinion Research, 1995, repr. in *U.S. Society and Values, USIA Electronic Journal* 2 [March 1997], http://usinfo.state.gov/journals/itsv/0397/ijse/gallup.htm [accessed September 30, 2008]). Also, see Leslie J. Francis et al., "Attitude toward Christianity and Religious Experience: Replication among 16–18-year-old Adolescents in Northern Ireland," *Research in Education* (November 2006), http://findarticles.com/p/articles/mi_qa3765/is_200611/ai_n17194296/print (accessed August 26, 2007). Francis replicated earlier studies conducted over a twenty-year period and confirmed their finding that students' acknowledgement of personal religious experience is associated with the promotion of a more positive attitude toward Christianity among young people in Northern Ireland. The stability of this research during a period when "the religious climate of Northern Ireland was changing and eroding" suggests to Francis that this correlation has a psychological as well as a cultural basis. He concludes his article with advice to churches: "Churches concerned with the promotion of a positive attitude toward Christianity among their young members may well wish to consider strategies for enabling their members to reflect on and to apply the religious interpretation of life experiences."

19. Those most likely to consider God a "personal being involved in the lives of people today" were conservative Protestant (77%), LDS (76%), and black Protestant youth (74%)—though only Jewish and nonreligious teens were generally unlikely to view God this way (44% and 30%, respectively). Smith and Denton, *Soul-Searching*, 41.

20. Ibid., 41–42.

21. This triadic view of the self is at the heart of H. Richard Niebuhr's theological anthropology; see H. Richard Niebuhr, *The Meaning of Revelation: An Essay on Christian Moral Philosophy* (Louisville, KY: Westminster John Knox, 1999), 77ff.

22. Carl Jung believed an integrated self requires us to make peace with the "shadow" self, composed of all the aspects of the self we want to disown. Cf. C. G. Jung, *Psychology and Religion: West and East*, in *Collected Works*, 2nd ed., vol. 11, ed. H. Read and G. Adler, trans. R. F. C. Hull (Princeton, NJ: Princeton University Press, 1975), 76 (par. 131).

23. James E. Loder, *Logic of the Spirit* (San Francisco: Jossey Bass, 1998), 105.

24. Thin places might be natural wonders or humanly constructed monuments like the passage tombs in Ireland, constructed five thousand years ago (before Stonehenge or the pyramids), designed to mark the soul's passage through the afterlife based on various astronomical phenomena.

25. Marcus Borg, *The Heart of Christianity: Rediscovering a Life of Faith* (San Francisco: HarperSanFrancisco, 2003), 156.

26. Baptism and the Eucharist dramatize, with special clarity, the realities to which they point, increasing their importance as identity-shaping practices.

27. Mark William Radecke, "Service-Learning and Faith Formation," *Journal of College and Character* 8 (July 2007): 7.

28. Karla Ann Koll, "Taking Wolves among Lambs," 14.

29. "What is it about religion that might produce positive outcomes in the lives of teenagers? . . . The nine specific factors that exert the religious influences are moral directives, spiritual experiences, role models, community and leadership skills, coping skills, cultural capital, social capital, network closure, and extracommunity links." Smith and Denton, *Soul-Searching*, 240.

30. The NSYR assessed the presence of religious experience, not its significance—a move that would have required a different research strategy, as Smith and Denton point out: "Beneath our survey measures of factors such as religious service attendance, religious devotion, spiritual seeking, and the like, lay multiple layers of complicated religious and spiritual meanings, perceptions, experiences, assumptions, and feelings that require different research methods to adequately access and interpret." Smith and Denton, *Soul-Searching*, 117. The limits of quantitative and qualitative research methods for interpreting religious experience are summarized in David Yamane, "Narrative and Religious Experience," *Sociology of Religion* 61:2 (2000): 171–89, http://findarticles.com/p/articles/ml_m0SOR/is_2_61/al_63912433/print (accessed August 29, 2007).

31. For Turner, people who lived in permanent liminality included shamans, mediums, priests, those in monastic seclusion, hippies, and hoboes, among others. Permanent liminality (marginalization) is not always a self-chosen state; the experience of racial marginalization, in which skin color or accent always places one "betwixt and between," with no potential for reassimilation into a given culture, has also been described as a liminal state. Victor Witter Turner, *Dramas, Fields, and Metaphors: Symbolic Action in Human Society* (Ithaca, NY: Cornell University Press, 1974), 233. Turner considers some practices of Christianity (like pilgrimage) to be liminoid experiences, while Christian life itself—in which participants stand, in some ways, outside the culture until death reincorporates us into the communion of saints—is liminal. Victor Witter Turner and Edith L. B. Turner, *Image and Pilgrimage in Christian Culture: Anthropological Perspectives* (New York: Columbia University Press, 1978), 253.

32. "Like certain other genres of symbolic action elaborated in the leisure time of modern society, pilgrimage has become an implicit critique of the life-style character-istic of the encompassing social structure. Its emphasis on the transcendental, rather than mundane, ends and means; its generation of *communitas*; its search for the roots of ancient, almost vanishing virtues as the underpinning of social life, even in its structured expressions—all have contributed to the dramatic resurgence of pilgrim-age." Ibid., 38; also, see Turner, "Pilgrimage as Social Process," in *Dramas*, 166–230.

33. Matt. 17:1–9, Mark 9:1–8, Luke 9:28–36.

34. Mark Yaconelli, *Contemplative Youth Ministry* (London: Society for Promoting Christian Knowledge, 2006), 51.

35. Ibid., 52.

36. Speaking about visitors to San Salvadore, Dean Brackley notes how interaction with the poor reveals the God's power and grace: "If we allow [the poor] to share their suffering with us, they communicate some of their hope to us as well. The smile that

seems to have no foundation in the facts is not phony; the spirit of fiesta is not an escape but a recognition that something else is going on in the world besides injustice and destruction. The poor smile because they suspect that this something is more powerful than injustice. When they insist on sharing their tortilla with a visiting gringo, we recognize that there is something going on in the world that is more wonderful than we dared to imagine." Dean Brackley, S.J., "Meeting the Victims, Falling in Love," *Salvanet,* January/February 2000, www.crispaz.org/news/ snet/2000/0100.pdf (accessed September 8, 2007). Thanks to Mark Radecke for alerting me to this remarkable essay.

37. Ibid.

38. Sang Hyun Lee, "Marginality as Coerced Liminality: Toward an Understanding of the Context of Asian American Theology," in *Realizing the America of Our Hearts: Theological Voices of Asian Americans,* ed. Fumita Matsuoka and Eleazar Fernandez (St. Louis, MO: Chalice Press, 2003), 11–28.

39. See Yongming Tang and Charles Joiner, *Synergistic Inquiry: A Collaborative Action Methodology* (Thousand Oaks, CA: SAGE Publications, 2006).

40. Yongming Tang, "Synergic Inquiry (SI): An Alternative Framework for Transformative Learning" (paper, Adult Education Research Conference, Stillwater, OK, 1997), www.edst.educ.ubc.ca/aerc/1997/97tang.html (accessed July 31, 2006), 1.

41. Jack Mezirow, the recognized pioneer of transformative learning, breaks these stages into ten nonsequential steps: (1) a disorienting dilemma; (2) self-examination with feelings of fear, anger, guilt, or shame; (3) a critical assessment of assumptions; (4) recognition that one's discontent and the process of transformation are shared; (5) exploration of options for new roles, relationships, and actions; (6) planning a course of action; (7) acquiring knowledge and skills for implementing it; (8) provisional trying on of new roles; (9) building competence and self-confidence in new roles and relationships; (10) a reintegration into one's life on basis of conditions dictated by one's new perspective. See Jack Mezirow et al., *Learning as Transformation* (San Francisco: Jossey-Bass, 2000), 22.

42. Mezirow's view is that transformational learning means "learning to think like an adult." See ibid., 3–34.

43. Erik H. Erikson was among the first to attribute a heightened desire "to be moved" to developmental factors, noting the adolescent need for "locomotion," both physically and existentially (e.g., teenagers' love of fast cars and movies, as well as rapt conversations and a desire to participate in the social movements of the day). See Erikson, *Identity, Youth, and Crisis* (New York: W. W. Norton, 1968), 115–16.

44. Learning transference—unfortunately named, since it inevitably connotes the psychoanalytic use of the term "transference—is the process of taking what is learned in one situation and applying it to other situations. Wilderness education programs, in particular, have focused on learning transference as a measurable outcome. Cf. "Point 18: Teaching, Processing, and Transference," Wilderness Education Association, http://www.weainfo.org/en/cms/146 (accessed June 9, 2009).

45. Mezirow, *Learning as Transformation,* 22.

46. This picture and story can be found in several places online; cf. "Jesus in the Snow," http://easyweb.easynet.co.uk/~philipdnoble/snow.html (accessed January 12, 2010).

47. Some versions of the story add that he was praying on the way home, "Lord, if I could only see your face, I would believe." Instantly a voice spoke to his heart: "Take a picture. Take a picture." He could see only unattractive patches of melting snow, but he took the picture, developed the film, saw Christ gazing at him in the photograph filled with tenderness and love, which caused the photographer to convert to Christianity. "Jesus in the Snow," http://easyweb.easynet.co.uk/~philipdnoble/snow.html (accessed January 12, 2010).

48. Adapted picture from "Jest Kidding," http://www.jestkidding.com/kids-corner/jesus-in-the-snow-help (accessed June 8, 2009).

49. John Calvin, *Institutes of the Christian Religion, The Library of Christian Classics*, vols. 20–21 (Philadelphia: Westminster Press, 1960), vol. 1, 1.1. Calvin's corollary, of course, is that without knowledge of God there is no knowledge of self, either.

50. A much-beloved introduction to the Ignatian prayer of examen is Dennis Linn et al., *Sleeping with Bread: Holding What Gives You Life* (Mahwah, NJ: Paulist Press, 1995).

51. Ignatius of Loyola, and George E. Ganss, *Ignatius of Loyola: The Spiritual Exercises and Selected Works* (New York: Paulist Press, 1991).

52. Ibid., 257.

53. Conflating the symbol with the deep meanings it represents is characteristic of people who exhibit what James Fowler calls "synthetic-conventional" faith, a cognitive outlook and approach to meaning-making that is characteristic of many adolescents. Cf. James Fowler, *Stages of Faith* (San Francisco: Harper and Row, 1981), 163.

54. Jack Mezirow, *Transformative Dimensions of Adult Learning* (San Francisco: Jossey-Bass, 1991), 26.

55. Plausibility structures are especially important when an individual "switches worlds," as Peter Berger and Thomas Luckmann call a shift in worldview—or conversion, as it is generally known in the church. The new worldview must be legitimized by the plausibility structure every step of the way, repudiating one's old reality is experienced as a "biographical rupture," so the new reality must be consistently legitimated by one's new community of belonging. Christian theology complicates Berger and Luckmann's theory; the Holy Spirit alters the process of internalizing social structures by making it possible to live in an asymmetrical tension between subjective reality (God) and objective reality (culture). For Christians, "switching worlds" is made possible by grace, not socialization. See Peter L. Berger and Thomas Luckmann, *The Social Construction of Reality: A Treatise in the Sociology of Knowledge* (Garden City, NY: Anchor/Doubleday, 1967), 157–67.

56. Among the ordinary means of grace (i.e., ordinary channels of God's grace) are the Lord's Supper, baptism, prayer, searching the Scriptures, fasting, Christian conferencing, and works of mercy to our neighbor. While God can and does act graciously in extraordinary ways (and, as Wesley points out, God needs no means at

all to give us grace; (cf. John Wesley, "The Nature of Enthusiasm" [Sermon 37], http://
gbgm-umc.org/UMHistory/Wesley/sermons/serm-037.stm [accessed August 24,
2006]), we are called to regularly meet God in the ordinary practices that God has ordained
(in fact, "regular" was not enough for Wesley; he advocated "constant communion," that
is, to receive it as often as we can. "The Duty of Constant Communion" [Sermon 101],
http://new.gbgm-umc.org/umhistory/wesley/sermons/101/ [accessed January 21, 2010]).
Wesley also left room for extraordinary means of grace—for example, healing,
discernment, languages, miraculous experience—but cautioned against letting the search
for these divert us from the responsibility of receiving "ordinary" means of grace on a
regular basis.

Chapter 9

The epigraphs in this chapter are drawn from:
David Bosch, *Believing in the Future* (New York: Continuum International
Publishing Group/Trinity Press, 1995), 15.
G. K. Chesterton, *The Collected Works of G. K. Chesterton*. San Francisco: Ignatius
Press, 1986), 382.
1. The word "hope" comes from an Old English word that means "to expect" or
"look forward to something."
2. Cf. Jeffrey Stout, *Democracy and Tradition* (Princeton, NJ: Princeton University
Press, 2004), 300.
3. Tom Beaudoin, a critic of the study, posed this problem for me to consider in
interpreting the results of the National Study of Youth and Religion. Telephone
conversation, May 9, 2007.
4. The NSYR notes a pervasive preoccupation by adults with significant problems
that distract them from raising teenagers, as well as the "structural disconnect"
contemporary society creates between adults and teenagers in our increasingly
age-stratified society (Christian Smith with Melinda Denton, *Soul-Searching: The
Religious and Spiritual Lives of American Teenagers* [New York: Oxford University
Press, 2005], 182–89). Adult abandonment of teenagers is also a pervasive theme of
much anecdotal and ethnographic literature describing contemporary adolescence. Cf.
David L. Marcus, *What It Takes to Get Me Through* (New York: Houghton Mifflin,
2005; Chap Clark, *Hurt* (Grand Rapids, MI: Baker Academic, 2004); Patricia Hersch, *A
Tribe Apart* (New York: Ballantine, 1998). A more insidious form of abandonment
comes as the result of consumer society itself, which makes purchasing power—not
maturity—the key to full participation. With maturity increasingly optional in
contemporary American culture, adults are less apt to take on adult roles in teenagers'
lives, while media encourage adults to extend aspects of their own adolescence well
into their parenting years.
5. Cited by L. Gregory Jones, "Think Big," *Christian Century* (August 23, 2005),
29. Burnham designed the 1893 Chicago World's Fair, Manhattan's Flatiron Building,
and Union Station in Washington, DC.

6. Smith with Denton, *Soul-Searching*, 117.

7. Howard Gardner, *Intelligence Reframed: Multiple Intelligences for the 21st Century.* (New York: Basic Books, 1999), 60–66.

Appendix B

1. Christian Smith with Melinda Denton, *Soul-Searching: The Religious and Spiritual Lives of American Teenagers* (New York: Oxford University Press, 2005), 31, 37, 50, 68. To test whether these numbers reflected parents forcing their children to attend services, students were asked if they would attend religious services if it were totally up to them. The study found youth said they would be even *more* likely to attend, if it were up to them, than they currently do (38). In terms of youth group participation, 69% of respondents either participate currently, or have previously participated, in a religious youth group. Unlike worship attendance, youth groups tend to be regular-or-nothing commitments; few youth attending youth groups reported infrequent attendance.

2. Ibid., 45.

3. Ibid., 40.

4. Ibid., 127.

5. Ibid., 124–26.

6. NSYR data on Jewish youth is drawn from such a statistically small sample that it is quite difficult to generalize and are therefore omitted here. Furthermore, many Jewish youth consider Jewishness to be a cultural rather than a "religious" identity. See Smith and Denton, *Soul-Searching*, 297–98.

7. Ibid., 261.

8. Ibid., 262.

9. Ibid., 131 (emphasis original).

10. Ibid., 131–32.

11. Ibid., 133.

12. Ibid., 262.

13. Ibid.

14. It is worth quoting Smith and Denton *in toto* on this point: "Despite the fact that religion seems quite weak at the level of adolescent subjective consciousness, that most teens can hardly coherently articulate their own beliefs, that religion seems to operate mostly as an unfocused, invisible dynamic operating in the background of teenagers lives, and that many social and cultural forces exert effects that tend to undermine serious religious faith and practice, we nevertheless observe sizable and significant differences in a variety of important life outcomes between more and less religious teenagers in the United States. Highly religious teenagers appear to be doing much better in life than less religious teenagers."

15. See Patricia Hersch, *A Tribe Apart* (New York: Ballantine, 1999).

16. Smith with Denton, 264.

17. Ibid., 264.

Index

abandonment, 242n7, 247n4
adolescence, 8–9, 18, 31, 93, 160, 216,
    218, 228, 245; barometer of culture,
    9, 21, 25, 29, 134, 204; ego
    development in, 8, 49, 79, 81, 161,
    173; moratorium, 8, 230n36
African American church. *See* black
    Protestants
Almost Christian, The, vi, 4, 5, 15
American Civil Religion, 30
Ammerman, Nancy, 113, 217, 233
anamnesis, 96, 99
Anderson, Emily, 87
Andrews, Christian, 94–95
Anglican Church, 92
anxiety versus love, 168–69
Apostles' Creed, 39, 215
Aristotle, 127
Arnett, Jeffrey, 8, 18, 235n5
Arthur, Sarah, 127
articulacy, 19, 131, 136–37, 142, 204;
    faith vocabulary, 16, 19, 28, 36, 67,
    114, 124, 132–35, 138, 140–42, 149,
    154–55, 168; theological language,
    18, 23, 28, 67, 69, 98, 127, 132, 138,
    142–56
Augustine, 143
authoritative communities, 72–73, 79

Baker, Jonny, 85
baptism, 56–59, 80, 88, 119–20, 149, 153,
    166, 183
Baptists: 28, 74, 144; black, 29, 71;
    Hispanic, 66; Southern, 56
Barkowski, John, 51

Barth, Karl, 90, 94–95, 218n11, 233n21
belonging, 7–8, 10, 22, 29, 38, 40, 42,
    48–50, 54–56, 72–74, 95, 114, 145,
    214, 221, 227, 244
Benedict, 119
benign whatever-ism, 17, 22–24, 28,
    37–39, 42, 45, 202
Berger, Peter, 140, 246n55
Berrigan, Daniel, 88
Bonhoeffer, Dietrich, 89, 218n11
Borg, Marcus, 165
Bosch, David, 185
Bible. *See* faith practices
black Protestants, 20, 42, 47, 71–72, 74,
    76, 78, 135–39, 194, 203, 207–9
boundaries, 31, 33, 37, 58, 64–65, 72,
    97–98, 103, 156, 173–74
Bourdieu, Pierre, 48
Brackley, Dean, 171, 244–45n36
Brigham Young University, ix, 46
Brueggemann, Walter, 61, 109, 112–13,
    117, 126, 237
Brunner, Emil, 64

call, 6–7, 10, 22, 33–34, 37–39, 42, 48–49,
    53–56, 60, 63–65, 79–81, 84, 89,
    94, 98, 100–103, 113, 139, 143, 179,
    186–88, 193–97, 246–47n56
Calvin, John, 179
camps and conferences, 100, 123, 131–33,
    144, 154–55, 182, 186, 196, 209, 225
Capra, Fritjof, 162
catechesis (Christian formation), 7, 15,
    17, 23, 35, 50, 62, 90, 98, 100, 111,
    115–25, 143–48, 173, 183;

catechesis (*continued*)
   behind-the-wall conversation, 100,
      109, 113–17, 126, 130, 154; on-the-
      wall conversation, 100, 113–17,
      125–27, 130
Catherine of Siena, 72, 229n19
Catholics, 19–20, 27, 29, 45, 47, 56,
   75–78, 81, 132–36, 163, 199, 202–4,
   207–9
chairos time, 166
Chaucer, Geoffrey, 34
Chesterton, G. K., 34, 185
Christendom, 91–92
Christian education, 5, 17, 28, 115, 122,
   137
Christian doctrine. *See* Christian teaching
Christian formation. *See* catechesis
Christian maturity, 4, 22–23, 42, 50, 53,
   62–63, 78–82, 95, 120, 135, 151, 153,
   161, 179, 211, 229
Christian teaching, 11–12, 16, 27–28, 33,
   68, 98, 111–12, 117, 172, 183, 190,
   203, 219n (unnumbered)
Christianity: conversational, 137–39,
   144, 146, 149; degeneration of, 3;
   particularity of, 32–33, 135, 139,
   156, 193, 196
chronos time, 166
church as Body of Christ, 5–6, 11, 139,
   145–46
Church of Jesus Christ of Latter-day
   Saints. *See* Mormons
Clydesdale, Tim, 6, 47, 161, 216, 221,
   240
cognitive schema, 178
communion, 27, 38, 166, 242, 245; Lord's
   Supper, 244. *See also* Eucharist;
   sacraments
community, 7, 15, 23, 38, 46–60, 72–75,
   94–96, 109–13, 143–55, 194–97
congregations, importance of, 6, 17, 55,
   72–74, 79, 83, 106, 211
connectedness, 27, 55, 72–75, 79, 93, 125,
   142, 157, 162, 227
consumerism, 5, 14, 34, 59, 104, 175,
   189–90, 197, 205, 223n5, 234n32,
   247n4

conservative Protestants, 14, 20, 45, 51,
   66–69, 73, 76, 132–38, 154, 163, 194,
   203–204
conversion, 52, 68, 181–183, 228n13,
   242n16, 246n47; ongoing nature of,
   79, 181–82; paradigm shift, 166, 176,
   179; "switching worlds," 246n55
Council of Jerusalem, 129
creed, 7, 22, 29, 39, 42, 48–50, 54, 60, 70,
   84, 90, 111, 133, 139, 143–44, 196,
   215, 221n6
cultural interpretation, 115–18, 121
cultural literacy, 100, 126
cultural toolkit, 22–23, 47–50, 60, 68–69,
   95, 98, 143, 150, 175, 196, 223n15
cultural tools, 22, 26, 42, 45–50, 53,
   59–63, 70, 78, 80, 106, 114, 118, 127,
   133, 138, 148, 160–61, 172, 175, 193,
   194, 196, 223n15

Day, Dorothy, 131
Declaration of Independence, 39
Denton, Melinda, ix, 3, 13–14, 17–19, 21,
   25, 28–30, 45, 47, 61, 75, 77, 85, 109,
   131–34, 142, 157, 163, 167, 194, 199
Derrida, Jacques, 115, 235n14
detachment, 100, 103, 106, 157, 159–60,
   165–69, 171, 175, 182–83, 194–95
decentering practices. *See* detachment
Didache, 144
discipleship, 6, 15, 33, 63–64, 76, 79, 81,
   83, 96, 100, 105, 144, 151–55, 161,
   193, 211
discouragement, 189, 190, 191
disorienting dilemma, 173–83, 245n41
doubt, 7, 53–53, 103, 140, 142,
   161, 182, 185, 188, 208, 224n23
Dr. Seuss, 34
Drury, Amanda, 235

ecclesiology, 37, 89, 95, 96, 233n21
emerging adulthood, 9, 16, 112, 216
Emerson, Ralph Waldo, 1
empire, 114, 125
Enger, Leif, 147
Erikson, Erik, 68, 223n14, 230n36,
   245n43

eschatology, 58–59, 77–78, 91
ethic of giving, 81, 89, 194
Eucharist, 27, 31, 96, 111, 134, 166, 183
evangelicals, 51, 132–34
Exemplary Youth Ministry Study, 79, 83,
    193, 211, 219n21

faith: assets, 79, 80, 211, 213; attributes of,
    79, 80, 207; bilingual, 112, 123–24;
    consequential, 5, 7, 11, 22–24, 38, 45,
    50, 59, 62, 83–84, 95, 106–7, 110–16,
    118, 126, 193–96; generative, 22, 23,
    61; immersions, 100, 144, 153–55;
    inarticulate, 18–19, 131, 134, 137,
    142, 204; life outcomes, 21, 205,
    220n36, 248n15; maturity of, 20, 22,
    23, 50, 53, 62, 78–82, 120, 135, 151,
    211; Protestant principle of, 218n11
Faith Christian School, 85, 105
faith practices, 8, 16, 18, 23, 51, 54, 70,
    96, 133, 137, 148, 153, 166, 190, 214;
    Bible reading, 41, 55, 61, 80, 83, 128,
    129, 134–35, 162, 214; contempla-
    tion, 149, 168–69, 174, 183, 221n6;
    definition of, 70; hospitality, 23, 33,
    80, 89, 100, 212, 221n6; pilgrimage,
    100, 166, 168, 183, 244n31; prayer,
    23, 41, 61, 80, 83, 100, 103, 134–35,
    143, 153, 162–63, 168, 179–80, 183,
    211–14, 221n6, 225n32, 231n39,
    237n7; singing, 136, 143, 153;
    talking about faith, 19, 27, 35–36,
    51, 56–57, 77, 131–47, 151, 153, 204,
    225n32, 230n29, 237n7; teaching,
    100, 112, 116, 120, 121, 136, 148,
    172, 183, 188, 190; worship, 1, 80,
    96, 130, 142, 145, 147, 148, 153,
    162–63, 166, 208, 211, 212, 221n6
families, 11, 27, 39, 42, 49, 51–56, 59,
    67–69, 97, 111–13, 119, 135–38,
    146, 152, 155–56, 161, 182, 190, 205,
    209, 214
Florence, Anna Carter, 128–29, 146–47,
    149, 239n25
Ford, David, 153, 238
Fowler, James, 53, 244
Francis, Leslie, 241

Francis of Assisi, 155
fruits of the Spirit, 81
Frye, Northrup, 142, 238n19
Fulghum, Robert, 83–84

Gainesville State Tornados, 85, 87, 88, 105
god-image, 54, 71–72, 81, 114, 177, 221n6
Guder, Darrell, ix, 101, 233n21

Hall, Douglas John, 3, 7, 63–64, 217n
    (unnumbered), 218nn10–12
Hamas, 49
Hauerwas, Stanley, 150–52
Hersch, Patricia, 205, 245
Hirsch, Alan, 90
Hispanic youth, 33, 66, 227n42
Hitler Youth, 49
Hogan, Kris, 86–87, 105
holiness, 38, 134, 233n21
hope: attitude of, 22, 83–84, 133, 194,
    196–97; etymology, 189; future, 47,
    49, 51, 53, 63, 79, 80, 90, 114; to
    hold onto, 42, 76, 77, 78, 191;
    importance of, 58; in youth
    ministry, 185–88, 192

identity: Christian identity, 5, 6, 27–28,
    63–66, 69, 80, 139, 146, 179, 195;
    diffused identity, 195, 224n24,
    230n36; foreclosed identity, 53, 79,
    195, 224n24, 230n36, sacramental
    identity, 182–84; triadic self, 164,
    243n21
identity lockbox, 161
Ignatian examination of consciousness,
    179–80, 246n50
imitation of Christ, 27, 40, 50, 66, 70, 93,
    96, 112, 130, 150–51, 226n41
Incarnation, 22–23, 27, 64, 66, 89, 91, 93,
    97, 99, 101, 105, 112, 124, 141, 183
indigenizing principle, 22, 99, 100, 117,
    118, 139, 149, 231

James, William, 134
Jehovah's Witness, 199
Jenkins, Henry, 125, 232n13, 236n26
Jesus Camp, 132–33

Jesus in the Snow, 176–78, 246n47
Johnson, Benton, 51
Jones, Gregory L., 192
Judaism, 14, 21, 141, 204; Jewish youth
    and, 20, 29, 119, 135, 154, 163, 199,
    203, 221n8, 230n35, 237n8, 240n45,
    243n19, 248n6
Jung, Carl, 164

Kegan, Robert, 160, 230n35, 240n43,
    242n10

Language. *See* articulacy
language communities, 149
lateral thinking, 127
Latter-day Saints. *See* Mormons
Lee, Sang Hyun, 171
legitimate peripheral participation,
    144–146
Lewis, C. S., 25, 43, 160
liminal principle, 22, 100–103, 160, 165,
    182, 242n16
liminality, 102, 168, 171, 174, 244n31
liminoid experiences, 168, 244n31
Loder, James, 165, 171
Long, Thomas, 138, 142, 143
Luckmann, Thomas, 140, 238n15, 246n55
Luther, Martin, 91, 110–12, 116

MacArthur Foundation Report on
    Digital Learning and Media, 125
MacDonald, George, 82
mainline Protestant, 14, 17, 19, 20, 27,
    29, 45, 47, 53, 75–78, 132, 136, 163,
    192, 204, 207–9
Marcia, James, 224n24, 230n36
means of grace, 5, 60, 166
martyr. *See* witness
media, 36, 96, 114, 125–26, 138, 140,
    168, 202, 205
mentors, 11, 18, 100, 120–21, 125, 151,
    153, 196, 203, 212–13
Methodist, 17, 121, 196
Mezirow, Jack, 245nn41–42
Metanoia. See repentance
missio dei (mission of God), 15, 37, 64,
    89, 104, 124, 141

mission: incarnational view of, 93, 97–99,
    105, 124, 141; as translation, 91, 97,
    105–6
The Mission-Shaped Church, 92
mission trips, 57, 59, 76, 154–59, 166,
    170, 175, 179, 181–83, 185, 209,
    241n5, 241n6
missional: church, 65, 88, 89, 91, 94–96,
    106, 130; faith, 23, 165; imagination,
    22, 63–65, 84–87, 97, 99, 104–5,
    115–17, 130, 138, 141, 148, 156–58,
    183, 190, 193–95; language, 93;
    leadership, 93; nature of
    Christianity, 39; practices, 100, 115,
    theology, 90
missionary God, 37, 93, 195
Moralistic Therapeutic Deism: beliefs,
    14, 29, 39; colonization of American
    churches, 3, 14, 22, 82, 104,
    194; common creed, 29;
    Golden Rule Christianity, 219n17;
    homogenizing, 30
morally significant universe, 75, 76, 79
moratorium, 224n24
Mormons: articulacy of faith, 136;
    Book of Mormon, 45, 226n36;
    community, 54–56; cultural tools,
    48–50; Donnie and Marie Osmond,
    46; doubts, 52–53; family, 52, 55, 59,
    225nn32–33; health, 203, 223n16;
    highly devoted youth, 20, 42, 47, 51,
    53, 57, 136, 139; meaning of life, 58;
    music, 137; relation to culture, 59;
    religious camps, 154; seminary, 45
Mormon practices: abstinence, 45, 56, 59,
    224n18; baptism, 222n2, 226n36;
    dating, 59; evangelism, 52, 57;
    family home nights, 52, 56;
    leadership, 55, 57; marriage, 52,
    57–58; missionary service, 46, 52,
    56–58; modesty of dress, 59;
    worship, 163
Murphy, Seamus, 150
music, 6, 46, 59, 122, 136–37, 143, 153

Napoleon Dynamite, 46
National Study of Youth and Religion

(NSYR): longitudinal study, 16, 111, 134, 154, 218n7, 220n27; religious affiliations of U.S. adolescents, 76, 199; *Soul Searching*, 199, 209, 233n22; *Souls in Transition*, 218n7, 220n27, 234n4, 235n6, 237n5; summary of findings, 201, 205

Newbigin, Lesslie, 90–91

niceness, 10, 12–15, 25, 28, 32–33, 38–40, 134, 156

Niebuhr, Reinhold, 104, 218n11

Niebuhr, H. Richard, 243n21

nonreligious youth, 17, 29, 73, 163, 167, 202–3

oral tradition, 141–44, 150, 155

Orthodox, 134, 199, 222n (unnumbered), 240n40

Ostler, Blake, 54

Otherness: divine, 159, 166, 183; human 30, 31, 33, 161

Outreach Red Bank (ORB), 93, 233n22

paideia, 144, 172–73, 239n27

Papaderos, Alexander, 83–84

parasitology, 12–13

parents: religiosity of, 16, 59, 193, 203, 207; religious influence of 24, 39, 47, 52, 54, 81, 109, 111, 194, 201

Parsons, Talcott, 128

participatory culture, 125–26, 168, 236n26

passion, 4, 38, 94, 129, 133, 143, 148, 192–93

peers: importance of, 60

Piaget, Jean, 178

pilgrim principle, 22, 99–101, 139, 149, 153, 156, 233n29

Pinker, Steven, 238n18

Placher, William, 70

plausibility structures, 182, 245n55

pluralism, 30, 35, 85, 91, 92, 202

postmodern, 35, 93, 98, 102, 114, 168, 191

practices. *See* practices of faith

Presbyterian, 27, 87, 94, 226–27n41

psychosocial identity theory, 224n24

puberty, 9

purpose. *See* call

Quakers, 132, 134

Radecke, Mark, 166, 214, 245n36

reflexivity, 23, 52, 69, 159, 160–74, 179–83, 196

Reilly, Rick, 86–87

religious bigotry, 189–90

religious experience: answered prayer, 163, 208; closeness to God, 19, 41, 46, 164, 207, 228n13; commitment, 35, 192, 201; miracles, 163; in worship, 28, 80, 145, 148, 153, 162, 166, 212

religious services. *See* faith practices: worship

repentance, 164, 168, 181

retreats, 38, 80, 100, 133, 154–55, 166, 209, 227n44

Ricoeur, Paul, 53, 147

Roman Empire, 91–92, 116, 142, 232n11

sacraments, 111, 134, 165, 168, 219, 182

Saint Ignatius, 179, 181

Saint Patrick, 116

salvation, 11, 40, 54, 56, 97, 113–14, 132, 139, 141, 160, 189, 197

sacrificial love. *See* self-giving love

Sanneh, Lamin, 92, 97–98, 107, 115, 128

Schon, Donald A., 162

sectarian hermeneutic, 114

self-giving love, 5–6, 11–12, 15, 37–40, 64–66, 81, 88–89, 99, 104–5, 117, 130, 145, 155, 183, 194–96

service-learning, 159

situated learning, 100, 144, 149, 230n27

Small Catechism (Luther), 110–11

Smith, Christian, ix, 3, 13–14, 17–19, 21, 25, 28–30, 35, 45, 47, 61, 75, 77, 85, 109, 131, 134, 143, 157, 163, 167, 194, 201–5, 215, 226nn38–39, 235n6, 248n1

Smith, James K. A., 5

Smith, Joseph, 45, 48, 53

Smith, Ted, 122
Soelle, Dorothy, 157
Spiderman, 12–13, 30
spiritual apprenticeship, 100, 149, 152–53
spiritual seeking, 18, 202, 242
Stark, Rodney, 71–72, 221n9, 229n16
stone carvers, 150–52, 239–40n37
suffering love. *See* self-giving love
subcultural identity theory, 154,
    226nn38–39
Sunday School, 35, 39, 67, 136, 209
Swidler, Ann, 22, 48, 223n13, 223n15,
    238n10
Symbiote, 12–13, 15, 34, 40, 189

Taylor, Charles, 142
Tertullian, 91
testimony, 23, 53, 56–57, 100, 106, 114,
    131–32, 144–49, 153, 155, 194–95;
    definition of, 239n25
thin places, 165–68, 182, 243n24
Thomas, David, 105
transformation: 15, 50, 52, 72, 76, 100,
    103, 134, 158, 159–60, 167–79; holy
    encounters, 161–62; morphosis, 172
transformative imagination, 114, 126–27
transformative learning theory, 100, 170,
    172, 173, 176, 179
translation: as metaphor for mission,
    91–93, 96–105; incarnational nature,
    22, 97, 112, 117, 123–24;
    translatability of the gospel, 99,
    115–18, 121–29
Trilling, Lionel, 70
Turner, Victor, 168, 244n31

Vernacular, 124–25, 139
vocation, 46, 50, 57, 59, 60, 68–69, 75–76,
    83, 139, 194, 197, 228

void, 165–66, 171

Walls, Andrew, 22, 84, 92, 97–99, 105–6,
    123, 127, 159
Ward, Pete, 127–128
Wesley, John, vi, 4–5, 217n (epigraph),
    218n4, 233n21, 246–47n56
White Castle, 120
Whitefield, George, vi, 4, 217n
    (epigraph), 218n4
Williams, Lynna, 131
Williams, Mark, 86–87
witness, 34, 37, 59, 75, 87–90, 96, 98,
    101, 110, 114, 117, 132–34, 140–41,
    144–48, 171
Wulfila, 116
Wuthnow, Robert, 4, 218n13, 229n20,
    241n2

Yaconelli, Mark, 168–69
Yoder, John Howard, 87
youth: attitude toward religion, 27,
    242–43n18; church attendance
    of, 72, 207, 244n30, 246n1;
    conventional faith of, 18, 29, 201;
    god-images of, 48, 53–54, 71–72;
    highly devoted, 19–22, 40, 42,
    45–50, 53–54, 60, 66, 68, 70–79,
    82, 132–35, 154, 186, 193, 205,
    220n36, 224n23, 227n43, 228n9,
    240n42, 248n14; ideal religious
    types of, 40–42; theological
    language of, 18
youth groups, 11, 19–20, 35, 41, 46, 57,
    59, 93, 117, 123, 145, 194, 201,
    203, 208
youth ministers, 11, 18, 23, 83, 93,
    98, 116, 127, 166–68, 173,
    203, 213